"[A] consistently compelling, thought-provoking book. . . . A must-read for anyone who cares about educational—and societal—reform."

—*Kirkus Reviews* (starred review)

"A comprehensive and elegantly written overview of higher education in the U.S. since World War II, this book is a must-read for anyone trying to understand how we got to our current political crisis. Bunch expertly weaves the human story of the American dream in the twentieth century with the political story of attacks on higher education to explain how a country that once prided itself on knowledge has fallen into the grip of those who proudly reject science. This book is simply terrific."

—Heather Cox Richardson, publisher of the
"Letters from an American" Substack

"Really interesting. . . . There's a ton of terrible sh*t which is rightly exposed in this book. . . . Tie[s] together this college issue with the really significant social movements that have come out of it."

—Dax Shepard, *Armchair Expert* podcast

"With masterful storytelling and deep reporting, Will Bunch traces the history of how American higher education evolved from a public good into a massive industry that has saddled a generation with huge debt but without the return on the investment of previous college graduates. But it's much more than that: Bunch gives a blueprint for how we should rethink college and work for young adults. This indispensable book should be read by politicians, higher ed leaders, parents, students, and anyone else who cares about the future of our country in a rapidly changing world."

—Jeffrey Selingo, *New York Times* bestselling author of
Who Gets In and Why and *There Is Life After College*

"A wrenching analysis of a nation fractured along stark educational lines. . . . Sparkles with fascinating sidenotes and insights. . . . Bunch does a masterful job of explaining how college gradually became a center of contention in the culture wars. . . . Striking."

—Inside Higher Ed

"No other country except the United States makes people go $30,000 or $40,000—or more—into debt to get an education or certain job skills. In *After the Ivory Tower Falls*, Will Bunch does a masterful job explaining exactly how we got into the mess, and offers some good ideas for getting us out of it. A must-read for anyone who cares about fixing our ruptured politics and making higher education a public good once again."

—Ro Khanna, member of Congress and author of *Dignity in a Digital Age: Making Tech Work for All of Us*

"A thought-provoking portrayal of the role that higher education plays in fueling the nation's stark political divisions. . . . Written with the verve and historical details one expects from an expert reporter like Bunch, the book offers a well-informed . . . take on the 'college problem' and how to fix it."

—*Forbes*

"For regular readers of Will Bunch's insightful columns in the Philadelphia Inquirer, it will come as no shock that his book about American politics and the state of college education is both perceptive and provocative. Bunch traces the bitter divide between voters who went to college and those who didn't, and skillfully explores the consequences of college being affordable only for the select few, with so many others either shut out or forever mired in student debt. Bunch's reporting skills are on full display in After the Ivory Tower Falls, and so are his talents for seeing broad patterns and for original thinking. This is an important and necessary book."

—Margaret Sullivan, media columnist, *Washington Post*

"Punchy. . . . Bunch convincingly drills into the betrayal felt by people who took on debt to pay for 'beer and circuses' at state universities but failed to land solid middle-class jobs."

—*Financial Times*

"Provocative."

—*Politics War Room with James Carville & Al Hunt*

AFTER THE IVORY TOWER FALLS

How College Broke the American Dream and Blew Up Our Politics—and How to Fix It

WILL BUNCH

WILLIAM MORROW
An Imprint of HarperCollins*Publishers*

For the trailblazers,
including Fred Boccella and the late Arline Hammond Bunch,
and the rest of my wonderful family
who all believed in the power of education

AFTER THE IVORY TOWER FALLS. Copyright © 2022 by Will Bunch.
All rights reserved. Printed in the United States of America. No part of
this book may be used or reproduced in any manner whatsoever without written
permission except in the case of brief quotations embodied in critical articles
and reviews. For information, address HarperCollins Publishers,
195 Broadway, New York, NY 10007.

HarperCollins books may be purchased for educational, business, or sales
promotional use. For information, please email the Special Markets
Department at SPsales@harpercollins.com.

A hardcover edition of this book was published in 2022 by William Morrow,
an imprint of HarperCollins Publishers.

FIRST WILLIAM MORROW PAPERBACK EDITION PUBLISHED 2023.

Library of Congress Cataloging-in-Publication Data has been applied for.

ISBN 978-0-06-307700-3

23 24 25 26 27 LBC 5 4 3 2 1

CONTENTS

CONTENTS

COLLEGE LIKE MY GRANDMA USED TO MAKE

My grandmother never got a chance to go to college.

Yet she started one.

That's a slight oversimplification—she actually took over a small, struggling secretarial school and turned it into an accredited college awarding bachelor degrees to the middle class of Middle America—but still, her unlikely story tells us a lot about what college became during our bold twentieth century. And what it no longer is today.

By the time Arline Hammond Bunch passed away in 1987, at eighty years and one week of age, she'd handed out thousands of diplomas from Midstate College in Peoria. To Central Illinois farm girls dreaming of taking flight in the heyday of Pan Am. To Caterpillar assembly-line refugees seeking a pathway to the American Dream inside the ledger book of accounting, and to the tempest-tossed victims of 1980s layoffs yearning to learn computers. The degrees she conferred on others had once been an impossible dream for a farmer's stubborn daughter like her.

ARLINE WAS BORN IN LOWRY CITY, MISSOURI, POPULATION ROUGHLY 460, almost dead-center U.S.A. The year was 1907, and a booming industrial nation was finding its confidence that each generation should, and would, do better than the one before it. Lowry City is located in St. Clair County, a place where the Ozark Mountains surrender to endless American flatlands, where the options for even the smartest girls were few, or maybe none—even if your late-life father had been the most prosperous cattle farmer in town.

I can only imagine Arline Hammond, eighteen-year-old high school grad in 1925, as a younger version of the Grandma Arline I got to know decades later—a big-boned, cattle-calling-loud, determined woman, with maybe a dollop of the entitlement that came as a Brahman living among the cows of west-central Missouri. After high school, she taught in the local one-room schoolhouse—the only possible job for a bright young woman—until the first pangs of wanderlust sent her to an out-of-town secretarial school. There, one day, she had her lightbulb moment while working the keys on her manual typewriter. She could teach this stuff so much better than her instructors, she thought. It was the beginning of an odyssey that took her all the way to California and back, where the vision would become reality as Midstate College.

Like any good yarn, there are many places where this saga could have run off the rails. In 1929, after her brother-in-law had a bizarre run-in with lawmen in Lowry City who accused him of selling the same cows to two different men, he'd fled to California. So Arline, her sister Thelma, Thelma's two young kids, and the sisters' mom all piled into a Ford Model T and headed West, *Beverly Hillbillies*-style. Arline thought the Golden State could be a golden opportunity for a secretarial school. She hadn't anticipated the sizzling hot day when the Ford overheated on the first dusty iteration of Route 66 in the desert of the American Southwest, and she had to ask a band of local Native Americans on horseback to lead them to a mechanic. Or what happened when they finally reached the Pacific coast on October 29, 1929—the exact day of the great Wall Street Crash. Or that the young man that Arline married out west—a "pump jockey" from the newfangled gas station named Russell French—would learn his stomach pains on their honeymoon were in fact terminal cancer. Eventually, there'd be small secretarial schools in Anaheim and St. Louis and Peoria and points in between that came and went. Her early business partners also came and went, including one who took the money and ran off to Mexico. And yet through the decades of raising her three kids and nursing my occasionally ill grandfather, A. B. Bunch, along with everything else, the dream of Midstate College persisted until finally it happened. There was a momentum in mid-twentieth-century America, always pointing skyward.

Arline and A.B. finally bought that small, struggling business school in Peoria in 1966, and renamed it Midstate College. She was dean of students, and she didn't correct people who understandably assumed that she herself must certainly have a bachelor's degree. After all, postwar America had changed so quickly from Arline's youth that now anybody with a little gumption could go to college—a point that Arline and A.B. hammered home as they sat in the living rooms of Illinois farmers and pleaded with them to send their daughters to Peoria, despite its (well-deserved) reputation as a rum-soaked "Sin City." Grandma Arline recruited new college students with an almost evangelical fervor, earning commissions that got her and her three kids through some lean years when A.B. was sick, and filling Brown's Business School with so many upwardly mobile girls that it started to look like a good future investment.

After America helped win World War II, it seemed like any farmer's daughter or son of the assembly line at East Peoria's massive Caterpillar tractor plant had a shot at doing even better, of working with their brains instead of their hands, of becoming not just smarter folks but more civic-minded ones. College had once been a narrow pathway to success for the pampered elites—handing out bachelor's degrees to just one of every twenty U.S. young people—but in this new age of mass higher education, college had transubstantiated to become the living embodiment of the American Dream, and Arline and A.B. sold that notion to the rural gentry and their wide-eyed daughters with the zeal that less scrupulous hustlers used to sell encyclopedias.

It's no surprise, then, that Arline drummed it into her children—especially her oldest, Bryan, a brainy proto-beatnik who was listening to his Charlie Parker records when the other kids at Peoria's Central High School's Class of 1953 were at football practice or the drive-in—that they would be the first Bunch or Hammond offspring to actually go to college.

So when Bryan Hammond Bunch jumped the ladder a couple of rungs and won a full scholarship to go east and attend a small, elite private institution—Trinity College in Hartford, Connecticut—an idea became firmly cemented in my family, never to fade away. College—and what college could do for you—was indeed the American holy grail. Bryan went back to Peoria long enough to literally marry the girl next door, then zigzagged back to New York, where he worked in publishing while the oldest of his three children—me—was born in 1959. At some point very early in my childhood consciousness—even before any inkling of sex or death and all that existential jazz—came an almost instinctual awareness that success, as a human being, would hinge on where I went to college.

More than a half century after the baby booms and economic booms and the atomic booms of the 1950s and '60s, we are still clinging to the fast-melting permafrost of a now no-longer-new idea that college is the American Dream. So much so that we are refusing to admit that somewhere in the middle of a long and stormy postindustrial night, the dream has morphed into a nightmare. That a ladder greased with a snake oil called meritocracy has changed from joyous kids climbing higher than their parents to a panicked desperation to hang on to the slippery middle rungs. And that even at the polluted top, neither bewildered parents nor stressed-out graduates are quite sure what they've just bought for all that cash (or, increasingly, a mountain of debt).

That's why I've been thinking so much lately about the journey from my Grandma Arline and Midstate College all the way through my own kids, and how and why higher education came to mean so much to my family—and quite likely yours—over the course of an American century. Because I sensed that understanding this slippery ladder would be one small step toward getting my arms around an even bigger story I'd been pondering for years. That one only starts with looking at how the American way of college went off the rails. All those modern ailments—the unfathomable tuition bills, the massive student debt that collectively has risen to $1.7 trillion (or more than the nation owes on all its credit cards), the elite schools with the single-digit admission rates that today resemble luxury spa hotels more than academies of learning, the growing number of middle-middle-class kids forced to eat from food pantries or even experience homelessness in a desperate paper chase for college credentials—have had profound consequences extending far off campus.

Our current conversation about "the college problem" in America doesn't cover the half of it. Even if the revolution actually comes in the 2020s and we adopt a far-left, Bernie Sanders–style vision of free public universities that also wipes away most or even all of that mountain of student debt, those fixes will only work for the roughly half of Americans attending—or at least trying to attend—college. Why aren't we talking more about what happens to the folks who never left Lowry City like my Grandma Arline did, or people in a place like Peoria who thought they were following the footsteps of men like my

Grandpa A.B., by signing on with Caterpillar—only to become one of the company's twenty thousand union workers in central Illinois whose jobs have vanished since the 1990s? Our leaders give patronizing lectures to America's youth that college is their only way to survive in a twenty-first-century "knowledge economy"—and yet that system is effectively walled off from half the public.

ME? IT TOOK AWHILE FOR ME TO RECONCILE THE BIG ISSUES I WAS writing about as a journalist for the *Philadelphia Daily News* and as a part-time author with the stuff I was increasingly doing to make ends meet. I had to overcome some self-inflicted personal setbacks at the turn at the millennium that made me wonder how on earth I would ever send my own two kids away to a good school, especially the two years they'd be in college at the same time, as tuition and board at private universities raced past $50,000 a year. My only "hobby" in mid-adulthood was spending my weekend on drudgery freelance writing projects for OK-but-not-great pay—a history of a local bank, endless profiles of small-time CEOs—to ward off the moral failure of not being able to afford the right college. But even though this Hail Mary strategy kind of worked out in the end, and my offspring did go to very good private institutions, the experience still felt totally different from how I'd imagined. The excitement that my high school friends and I shared in the 1970s when we snuck into bars and spent hours nursing a beer and talking about which college we thought we were going to get into had become the twenty-first century's existential dread of whether higher ed was even worth it.

My son was a college senior in the fall of 2016 as that year's intense presidential election unfolded. The previous year, I'd become obsessed with the upstart bid of Vermont senator Bernie Sanders, who clearly inherited the mantle of Occupy Wall Street, and who made eliminating that $1.7 trillion college debt a core promise of his campaign. His message didn't resonate with my generation of baby boomers thrilled to see a woman whacking on the White House glass ceiling in Hillary Clinton—and who didn't think twice when she called Republicans rallying to the reality-TV demagoguery of Donald Trump "a basket of deplorables." Trump seemed to know just one thing about politics, which was how to stoke voters' resentment against look-down-their-noses elites. At a rally in Nevada, Trump blurted out, "I love the poorly educated!"

And they loved him back . . . all the way to the White House.

Trump's stunning upset victory on November 8, 2016, launched a cottage industry of trying to figure out what the hell just happened. News organizations like the *New York Times* kept sending reporters to run-down diners in southern Ohio or West Virginia again and again and again, determined to find the magic answer. Was it "economic anxiety," or racism, or something else? Their antennas picked up the resentment, but no one dug deeper into who resented whom, or why. As a now-veteran political journalist, I saw everyone still dancing around the problem. No one wanted to contemplate the collateral damage from a rigged system where college now locked in America's gross inequality—meaning a gilded adulthood for a select few and back-breaking debt for millions more, while everybody else locked out of this "knowledge economy" were told they must be a sucker or a loser.

I wanted to tell this story because its root cause demands to be no longer ignored. While the nation's political journalists remain largely locked into the tropes of the twentieth century, a few academics were doing yeoman's work about "the college problem" of the twenty-first century, but missing the connection to America's political breakdown. I wanted to start back in those heady, optimistic years after World

War II to tell the entire history of how college became the American Dream . . . only to instead crush it. And I wanted to see what was happening on today's campuses with my own eyes. The United States needs a better, different conversation about fixing all the pathways into adulthood, and understanding how we got here is the first step. And there was that one other thing. Thanks to my Grandma Arline, I thought the story of college was in my DNA.

WHEN ARLINE AND A.B. BOUGHT BROWN'S BUSINESS COLLEGE, AND renamed it Midstate, their timing seemed terrible. As the New Deal became LBJ's Great Society, government was expanding its support for public education, including a wave of new community colleges that would offer a similar curriculum but at little or no cost, thanks to taxpayer subsidies. What eventually became Illinois Central College opened in East Peoria, near the biggest Caterpillar plant, in 1967. During that era, a lot of so-called business colleges shut down. But Midstate grew. Arline pushed for Midstate to gain a higher accreditation, to offer four-year bachelor's degrees, and—after she died, under the leadership of my Uncle Dale (Arline's other son)—to move from its downtown quarters to a roomier campus on the edge of the city.

How'd they succeed? Partly, I think, because Arline and Midstate clung to the notion—then popular, now quaint—that education was a tool of self-betterment and not just rote career training. Students training to become executive assistants didn't just learn typing and shorthand but were required to take general education, even a course on how to comport one's self in the world of business. "There was always a feeling," recalled my dad (who eventually served on Midstate's board), "that you had to have skills but also had to have a general education, and learn how to be a better employee."

But Midstate also rode the changing zeitgeist of what college in America meant. When community college and expanded public universities gave those farm girls coming out of high school more, cheaper options, Midstate changed its recruitment and its schedules to attract more midlife adult students. By the late twentieth century, a college diploma was less an academic trophy and more an admission ticket to an increasingly dog-eat-dog workforce, and grown-ups who hadn't gotten the memo at age eighteen now needed to get back in the game. But the game kept slipping away from them.

When faith in the American way of college began to wane after years of runaway tuition, Wall Street smelled blood in the water. The growing pressure on the nation's working classes for a credential to earn a living wage created a huge opportunity for grift. It was filled by an avaricious new breed of for-profit college chains, backed by big-time financial equity. In the 2000s, these sharks competed for students, and when Washington tried to impose new rules to crack down on the abuses (which had left hordes of young people deep in debt, for often worthless diplomas), the good guys like Midstate suffered every bit as much as the bad guys.

On July 22, 2019, Meredith Bunch—my first cousin, and the school's then-president—announced the inevitable: Midstate was closing for good, in a matter of days. Its values forged in the optimism that burned brightly after the New Deal and World War II were crushed by the cold realities of the twenty-first century. The campus would be sold off to a blood-disorder clinic.

In the end, it wasn't crazy for Arline Bunch with her high-school diploma and her Route 66 dreams to start a college, though maybe it was a little insane to think it could last forever. But what about her vision, and her seemingly ancient notions about the power of higher education, and the unexpected doorways it could open, and not just for country-club heirs? If the American Dream isn't college anymore, can we start working on a better one? And could that Next New Thing arrive before political rage and resentment trigger a new civil war? In the spirit of a dusty, nearly forgotten 1929 road trip, this is my expedition into the world of college. I like to think Grandma Arline would be proud.

CHAPTER 1

LIFE DURING WARTIME IN KNOX COUNTY, OHIO

The bobbing hills of central Ohio's Allegheny Plateau take a motorist driving east on Gambier Street past bland nursing homes and freshly painted ranch houses. The occasional yard sign—JUST SAY NO TO SOCIALISM—does more than hint at the political leanings of most residents of this small town in Ohio. There is little clue that Kenyon College, a place where parents from the real canyons of the Hollywood Hills or the artificial ones of the Upper West Side spend upward of $300,000 over four years to send their children, will be quickly coming up on your left.

One last downhill plunge into the late-winter fallow farmland of the Kokosing River takes a driver past a picture-perfect farmhouse adjacent to a barn, a small grain silo, and a defiant blue TRUMP/PENCE 2020 yard sign. Maybe that's a metaphorical middle finger to the airport buses that come from Columbus, an hour away, bringing America's future progressive elites to the sloping hillside just behind it. Even this close, the only hint of Kenyon's presence is a massive construction crane that looms far above the thickets of white swamp oaks. Such a crane is a familiar site in the skylines of big cities, or universities with research medical centers that never stop growing. But it looks so out of place on this two-lane road in the dead middle of Ohio that, at least to a city slicker, feels very much the middle of nowhere.

The giant crane exists in Gambier, Ohio (pop. 2,391) because an anonymous donor in 2017 gave Kenyon a whopping $75 million so that the liberal arts college could build a new West Quad, including a sleek modern library with a long glass atrium and a new admissions office. The updated academic luxury will help the elite school impress kids and their parents, and entice them to pay up to $75,000 a year—without which Kenyon would be unable to service the bonds that cover the rest of the $150 million project. The heavy construction equipment now turning an anonymous billionaire's dream into reality arrived on campus right around the same time the German corporate giant Siemens announced it was shutting down one of the last remaining sources of good blue-collar jobs in nearby Mount Vernon, the flag-draped county seat where Gambier Street originates. Gone were the final 134 jobs at a factory campus that had employed 2,400 two generations ago.

In pondering what I came to think of as America's "college problem," I should make clear that Kenyon College is not typical—nor would the leaders of this 198-year-old citadel of higher learning ever want you to think that. The school's writer-in-residence, in the quote that gets the biggest type on Kenyon's website, calls it "The kind of place that can feel like the heart of the universe . . . when you picture a college, you see a place like Kenyon." But does that mean when you picture higher learning in America in the 2020s, you must picture a place where—according to the *New York Times*, in 2017—one of every five students strolling across the campus green in ripped jeans hails from the top 1 percent of the wealthiest families, and where 60 percent of students are from the top 20 percent of income? Or, to look at the other side of the coin, must the heart of America's college universe also rank in the bottom five of all U.S. colleges and universities in the percentage of its students accepting government Pell Grants, which go to middle-class and disadvantaged families making less than $60,000 a year?

I had come to Knox County, the home of Kenyon since its founding in 1824, exactly because the place is so atypical. And because it rises from the throbbing Heartland of a nation where political division—increasingly pitting college-educated liberal elites, like the four hundred or so who graduate in Gambier every spring, against the undiplomaed classes who live in places like Mount Vernon just down the road—has America wondering whether we stand on the brink of another civil war.

So for nearly a week in March 2021, when the promise of warmer days and new vaccines was finally drawing Kenyon and its neighbors out from a yearlong coronavirus cocoon, I embedded myself in Gambier.

THIS COMMUNITY IS AN UNUSUAL COUNTERPOINT TO THE SO-called Big Sort that placed college degree holders, with their ambitious careers in a new "knowledge economy," in big cities and their suburbs. That left an increasingly aggrieved middle class to survive in rural areas or smaller towns, with little real interaction between these rival groups. There are relatively few places in twenty-first-century America where the two groups coexist—or fail to—like they do in Knox County, Ohio.

You don't need a pricey Kenyon degree in math to add up the difference when it comes to pure politics. When Gambier—mostly a cloistered community of Kenyon professors, staff, and hangers-on, as well as students who registered here to vote instead of their hometowns—went to the polls on November 3, 2020, some 89.4 percent cast ballots for Democrat Joe Biden and only 9.4 percent for the GOP incumbent president, Donald Trump. But in the rest of Knox County, the numbers were reversed, with Trump getting 72.8 percent (about 5 points better than he'd performed there in 2016) while Biden only received 25.5 percent. Trump crushed it in Knox County even as his Democratic foe was winning the national popular vote by about 7 million ballots and capturing the presidency with the help of states like New York and California, the states from which many Kenyon students hail and will return after their four years in "the heart of the universe," when it's time to cash in on that $300,000 investment with the kind of well-paying job you simply won't find in Mount Vernon.

Sean Decatur, Kenyon's president, is one of the few Black men in Knox County, and certainly the most prominent. In 2018, he wrote a thoughtful essay about his own life as the African American leader of a liberal arts college in the heart of Trump country, and his real discomfort over seeing Confederate flags on front porches or in the cab of pickup trucks when he picks up his kids at the movies. But he said he also understood how campus arrivals from the affluent East and West Coasts can seem "elite, aloof, and unwelcoming" to the locals, adding that Trump's election victory reminded him of the Thestrals, creatures in the Harry Potter books who only appear during the trauma of death. "Similarly, race, class, and culture divisions in Knox County and elsewhere existed before the election of 2016; these divides were not created on Election Day," he wrote, "but rather like the Thestrals became visible, and the appearance was shocking and disorienting."

On November 8, 2016, Kenyon students were so shocked by Trump's victory that some professors canceled class the next day. About two hundred students and faculty attended a hastily called meeting—under what the *Kenyon Collegian* student newspaper called an "impromptu stage, a table framed by a purple, white, and green genderqueer flag and an LGBTQ+ flag"—where students invoked the Reverend Martin Luther King Jr. on "the arc of the moral universe" as many choked back tears. A stunned freshman stood up and said, "We need to go out into the community and ask them what their story was." Knox County politics had come to look like a map of Germany in the mid-twentieth century, with Gambier as a kind of a West Berlin, a tiny walled-off enclave surrounded by the armies of a radically different ideology on all four sides.

Yet actual encounters between the red and the blue of central Ohio are sporadic, unexpected, and culturally jarring, like the stars and bars of Confederate flags that shock students on the bus ride over from the airport, or the sheriff's deputies with an uncanny knack for pulling over Kenyon's Black and Brown students. Then there are the expeditions—when the Christian fundamentalists protest LGBTQ+-friendly books at kids' story time in Gambier, or Saturdays on Mount Vernon's main square when the county's liberals, anchored by some of Kenyon's professors and staff, hold up protest signs against the radical right—while their bête noire circle around them ominously in pickup trucks with massive Trump flags.

Sure, a key part of the divide is the ridiculous collegiate price tag—not just the sticker shock of Kenyon's $76,620 list price for 2021–22, but the way inflation filters down to Ohio State and even to Central Ohio Technical College in Mount Vernon—and how it all contributes to America's total $1.7 trillion student debt. But that is literally only the half of it. Something broke in this country, somewhere after the 1960s—when our leaders, amid a moral panic that kids today were maybe learning just a little too much about democratic values, convinced their voters that college isn't really a public good, and that universal higher education would no longer be a national goal. Instead, they created a privatized regime with a diploma as a golden ticket for just over a third of America's young people, and they called this arguably rigged system "a meritocracy"—thus telling the other two-thirds, who dropped out when they eyeballed the bill, or who simply weren't cut out to start their twenties inside a classroom, that obviously they lacked merit. And those decision-makers shrugged at the consequences—how the anger over America's brutal sorting hat would breed resentment and even hatred, and how it would change not only who people voted for, but how they treated their neighbors.

By the dawn of the 2020s, you had one encampment rallying under the bright rainbow of an LGBTQ+ flag, while the other side was kneeling in front of church pews waiting for the Lord to smite America over gay marriage. In Knox County, people spent a lot of time talking past each other, or maybe about each other—but precious little time talking *to* each other. On one gray and windy March afternoon, I heard both sides of the modern American story—five miles of Gambier Street and a million light-years apart.

THE KID YELLING INTO THE BULLHORN IS GRAHAM BALL, A TWENTY-two-year-old Kenyon senior from Cleveland Heights. His home zip code is not the richest in Ohio, but it might be the most cosmopolitan. Ball probably never pictured a day like this back in 2017 when he enrolled in Kenyon expecting to change the world—but by majoring in physics, not by chanting angry slogans at college administrators. It was high noon, and about fifty other students marched behind in not-quite-lockstep underneath Kenyon's stately, two-hundred-year-old oaks, some lagging behind as they glanced impulsively at their iPhones.

"Hey hey, ho ho! Where'd that hundred million go?!!" Graham chanted.

"Shut 'em down!" he shouted next. "Gambier is a union town!"

"Stop the hypocrisy! Labor democracy!"

The thin line of young men and women in torn jeans and worn, walkable sneakers, peering out over their mandatory masks after one full year of the COVID-19 crisis, followed Ball's lead, if sometimes awkwardly and out of rhythm. Clearly, they'd never done this kind of thing before. In a sense, no one ever had.

This was believed to be the first time in American labor history that undergraduate student workers—library aides, lifeguards, workers who manned Kenyon's large farm down the hill—had formed a union and gone on strike, even if it was just for one day. The Kenyon Student Worker Organizing Committee, or K-SWOC, had first seemed a natural outgrowth of the labor affinities of a growing number of students drawn to democratic socialism—the political movement that had ballooned with the popularity of Vermont senator Bernie Sanders. But then came the seeming academic apocalypse of the pandemic, including Kenyon's sudden drop in revenue. In short order, the school cut work hours for kids who increasingly needed those dollars, either to keep up with their wealthiest friends or just to make college work, financially.

Kenyon had acted one way toward the young people of K-SWOC when they were upscale consumers, pitched on coming to this quiet, thousand-foot-high hill of knowledge where they could debate social injustice or tackle climate change while never deviating from the path toward a rewarding, lucrative career, while the literary echoes of past alums like Robert Lowell or E. L. Doctorow whistled through the leaves. But when the virus hit, these undergrads said they learned a lesson they weren't expecting at their picture-perfect American college, in this era of privatization: how the academy treated them when they were no longer consumers, but instead merely the help.

"I think it's important to see how student workers really run this campus, and we have to be honest and say that Kenyon is a business, and we for so long have been taking that for granted," Sigal Felber, a senior from Verona, Wisconsin, a leader of the K-SWOC strike who normally works in the library, had told me a couple days earlier. Fittingly, Felber and other strike leaders were talking to me on the sleekly curved, Victorian-style porch of the sociology building named Palme House for the 1948 Kenyon graduate Olof Palme, the future Swedish prime minister who was inspired to become a socialist during his American studies, after writing his thesis on the United Auto Workers.

Nearly seventy-five years later, Felber told me it was her student job, and not the classroom, that had taught her about unfair labor practices. Now, their conflict with the college "exists in the space where you're critical of the institution that raised you." She grasped to find the right words to express her frustration with her time at Kenyon, surely compounded by one full year of COVID-19. "The strike is not an overnight sensation. It's these compounded disappointments you see with this institution."

Ball, the young man with the bullhorn, had also seen his time on the elite, cloistered campus push him in unexpected directions. He'd arrived in 2017 planning a career path aligned with his major in physics, but steadily felt the gravity of politics instead. It was an unusual orbit, though, starting with a faraway interest in the Middle East that centered on his affection for the Kurdish people in their struggles with Iraq, Syria, and Turkey, among others. "When Trump pulled out of Syria and abandoned the Kurds," he said, "that was a radicalizing event for me."

That's when Ball realized the rest of Kenyon wasn't as radical, or as active, as he believed they should be. He and some friends formed a group called Active Students Helping the Earth Survive: ASHES. They took classmates to the jail in nearby Morrow County, Ohio, where they protested that county's contract with U.S. Immigration and Customs Enforcement, or ICE. During the tumultuous summer of 2020, Ball dodged tear gas canisters with his allies in Black Lives Matter in the streets of downtown Cleveland. But when the senior—who told me that he'd been first drawn to Kenyon as "a place where I could really be involved in the community"—was finally allowed to move back on campus in January 2021 after the long COVID-19 interruption, his radicalized gaze turned inward, to the college itself. It was arguably a form of what the counterterrorism experts like to call "blowback."

The summer and fall of 2020 was something of a bloodbath for all higher education. Schools refunded students millions of dollars of room and board money after they were forced to move off campus during the pandemic. Then came the drop in enrollment, or pressure for rebates, from families who didn't see the value in paying full freight for Zoom classes, without the glam campus lifestyle that had been so aggressively marketed. The sudden drop in revenue due to the coronavirus led to an array of budget cuts, including faculty and staff layoffs—as well as an awareness that maybe the arms race of fancy gyms and gourmet food courts to attract the children of the 1 Percent had created a shaky economic Jenga, one that could topple when just a single piece was yanked away.

Kenyon's posturing as the quaint dictionary-page image of the American college didn't spare it from the carnage. In June 2020, the institution—which had seen its debt load triple since the dawn of the millennium, to $270 million, as it strived to match alumni donations for its building spree—announced $19.3 million in budget cuts, including a proposed one-time reduction in pension-plan contributions. Members of K-SWOC joined with the main blue-collar staff union at Kenyon, UE Local 72, to successfully protest and beat back the plan—giving the activist student workers a sweet taste of solidarity. But when the student workers lost hours, and thus money, during several campus lockdowns to contain the coronavirus, K-SWOC members grew increasingly angry over the college's straight-up refusal to recognize their first-of-its-kind union. The March 16, 2021, strike didn't win them recognition, but it gave the undergrads a chance to vent that money had corrupted everything about the modern American way of college, from the priorities of the campus administrations to the financial pressures on youth that interfered with their liberal education.

"For many of us, the money we make from our Kenyon jobs is how we pay for textbooks, food, medicine, and essential items," senior Dani Martinez wrote on behalf of the strike in a testimonial. "Losing two weeks of pay is unacceptable, and we deserve better from an administration which recently received a donation of $100 million"—a reference to Kenyon's newest huge anonymous gift from a rich donor, allowing the college to tear down two well-maintained but older dorms to build posh new ones.

The strike was the talk of the campus in March, even if it wasn't exactly clear what the one-day walk-off would actually accomplish in the short run, other than serve as an outlet for frustration. The college and its board of trustees remained adamant in not recognizing K-SWOC, and the reality was that at least initially the strikers weren't even a full majority of Kenyon's student workforce. Graham Ball seemed to acknowledge that—but at age twenty-two he also seemed to understand the bigger picture, that he and his liberal-arts college peers were playing the long game. When I asked him about the strike and about why Kenyon students didn't push for social change in the surrounding Knox County community, his savvy answer suggested to me that he'd learned a lot when he switched his major from physics to poli-sci.

He said young campus activists didn't cross that invisible line much because everyday Ohioans see them as "uppity," that there's "a stigma" against them. "They think that we're pretentious and we think we know better than them . . . and they're right." He was basically arguing that if activists like the young democratic socialists of Kenyon really want to change the world, they should change the minds of their classmates before they leave Gambier and move back to the great power centers like New York City or Silicon Valley, where they will shape society.

But what of the people in the valley, the left behind?

For about-to-graduate Graham Ball, facing the prairie wind in a stylish olive jacket and marching boots, his higher power was soon at hand, but as he scanned the other marchers, he voiced a more immediate concern. "What happened to my bullhorn?"

PASTOR BILL DUNFEE DIDN'T NEED A BULLHORN, OR ANY OTHER kind of amplification beyond the fire and brimstone of the wrathful Old Testament God that he seemed to prefer over the more loving gospels of Jesus Christ. It probably helped that his audience was small—just a dozen folks, most of them middle-aged like him and attired casually in faded blue jeans and sneakers, as they sat in a circle of folding chairs. His occasionally booming voice was also amplified by echoes in this utterly unorthodox setting for a Tuesday night prayer service: the corrugated garage of J.C.'s Autos, a tiny used-car dealership near the banks of the Kokosing on the faded fringe of downtown Mount Vernon.

I reflexively scootched my metal folding chair back an inch or two from the pulpit, anxious about the fact that I was the only person inside the fetid air of the garage who was wearing a mask—or what one of the attendees, a burly, heavily tattooed man named Luis Trasvina, called "a ritualistic shame muzzle." This even as cases of COVID-19 were spiking across the Upper Midwest for the fourth time. He insisted to me that "the manufacturers themselves tell you that they don't stop anything. You're just virtue signaling."

Dunfee never announced a title for the night's sermon, but to an out-of-town visitor who was generously invited to listen, the overall message came through loud and clear: America in the twenty-first century is weighed down by sin, and that a judgmental God, brimming with wrath, has us in His sights now that Donald Trump is no longer in the White House to protect them.

"If we don't know the God of the Old Testament, we get a dis-torted vision," Dunfee preached. A few of the faithful—ringing the long pit where the mechanics at J.C.'s Autos dumped out oil or other fluids working on old cars during the day—nodded their heads and grunted in assent. Everyone seemed to get Dunfee's shorthand—that God can't be endlessly forgiving and endlessly loving, no matter what the pro-tolerance, pro-sodomy crowd up the hill in places like Gam-bier or out there in New York or California wants to believe. God can get angry, and so could Pastor Bill Dunfee—at times conversational but then suddenly shouting, his words bouncing off the metal shelves, the rows of toolboxes and cans of motor oil and, of course, a deep blue TRUMP/PENCE sign, right next to the banner for Doc Fixit's Honda on South Main. The volume especially spiked when this informal, fifty-something preacher—in a checked work shirt and dusty pants, with bright silver hair busting out of a trucker cap—veered from the Bible to a Fox News buffet of national politics, as he did every minute or two.

Dunfee was trying to preach the cautionary tale of Achan, a Bibli-cal figure from the Book of Joshua who'd disobeyed the Lord's com-mand not to loot the treasures of a fallen Jericho—thus incurring the Old Testament God's wrath to the point where Israelites stoned to death not only Achan, but his children. But the minister kept getting pulled back to the heavy rocks that awaited the sinful United States of America.

"God said to Joshua what he still says to every man—which is, get up, stop crying, shake yourself off, and fix the problem! What was the problem? Sin!" Then, a sudden 90-degree right turn from Pastor Dun-fee. "We want to lay around and cry, "Oh Biden's in the presidency," right? I just heard today that the Biden administration has weapon-ized, has fully funded the Internal Revenue Service for the purpose of coming after us!"—meaning the righteous people of the American Heartland.

A woman in a folding chair audibly gasped at this. That quickly, Dunfee had transitioned from Jericho to a more recent battle, one that had just occurred on January 6.

"And all those patriots that were on Capitol Hill! All those patriots that dare post things on the internet and social media! All those patriots that dare express their concerns for the well-being of the United States of America . . . it only takes one Internal Revenue Service agent to GET YOUR NAME!! What is the purpose? What is it all about? How did he get there to begin with?" Trying to follow, I wasn't sure if "He" was now Achan or God or Joe Biden—or if it mattered much. "It was a stolen election!! 'You aren't on that train, are you?'"—in a liberal-mocking voice. "I ain't gittin' off that train! Amen." He paused, but for less than a second. "So they go to war, and the next thing Ai defeats the Israelites . . ."

I'd been invited to attend the service by the owner of J.C.'s Autos, who is not Jesus Christ—despite the Calvary-style cross that replaces the "T" in the word "Auto" in the dealership's logo—but Jeff Cline. Cline, a genial-talking but insistent man, has lived in Knox County all his life. He accepted Donald Trump into his life a couple of decades after doing the same to Jesus Christ, initially in order to ward off the bottle. Cline lives right on the outskirts of Gambier, on the banks of the Kokosing. Looking up the hill, he can see the Kenyon campus, but it's the blue-collar life of the valley that's in his blood.

"Continental Can, Cooper-Bessemer, Chattanooga Glass, Pittsburgh Plate," Cline rattled off quickly when I asked him about all the factories that had closed in Mount Vernon. Cline grew up in the heyday of the baby boom in the 1960s and '70s. His father had been a cog in that industrial workforce, but what he mainly remembers of him was the drinking. "My dad was a full-blown alcoholic," he told me. "That's all I seen when I was a kid—my grandparents, aunts and uncles, they were all alcoholics. You'd get together for the holidays and they'd end up in a fight on the front porch . . . rednecks. You grow up that way, and think that's life." Cline's commentary called to mind the bestselling *Hillbilly Elegy*—about that rugged and hard-drinking Appalachian lifestyle, and the politics it produced—which sprung from life in a small Ohio town about 150 miles down the road.

Certainly, the factory shutdowns took both an economic and psychic toll on Mount Vernon. Closing the Pittsburgh Plate and Glass campus—just a stone's throw from Cline's dealership—in 1976 cast adrift the Belgian glassmakers who'd emigrated here during the twentieth century, foreshadowing the coming Cooper-Bessemer layoffs. The director of the Knox County Historical Society has said that around the 1960s Cooper had become more international and thus "tended to hire people with a Harvard Business School degree and not people who graduated from Mount Vernon High School." Today, the town's stability comes somewhat from Kenyon, Mount Vernon Nazarene College, and the local medical center, but mainly from folks commuting more than an hour to the fairly prosperous, cosmopolitan city of Columbus.

The decline in blue-collar job opportunities in Knox County had dovetailed with what local officials conceded was an alarming spike in local drug abuse—first with opioids and later with meth, which was tied in 2019 to 89 percent of cases in its criminal courts. Yet to Cline, the area's real problems are moral, and not in any way economic. "Back in the day, my dad had two jobs—we can't blame it on jobs," he said dismissively. He was sitting in the smallish office of his car dealership, cluttered with baseball pictures of his beloved Cincinnati Reds broken up by political or spiritual bumper stickers that were a mash-up of the 10 Commandments and the 2nd Amendment. Barack Obama's controversial words about people in the Heartland clinging to their guns and their religion seemed embedded in Cline's walls. "We've got to blame it on where the problem lies," he tells me. "If we get back to our Judeo-Christian values, God will bless this country. Right now, this nation is being judged."

Cline was well down the same road his dad traveled—drinking, using drugs—when he had a "come-to-Jesus moment" in his thirties, after a serious accident and some stern words from his future wife. "The two books I believe in are the Constitution and the Bible," he said. "At one point in my life, all I believed in was the barstool." He found a spiritual home in Dunfee's nondenominational, fundamentalist New Beginnings Ministries Church in nearby Warsaw. For years, Cline joined Dunfee in a long-running war against a strip club on U.S. 36 called The Foxhole—during which church members stood outside with signs like "Protect Children Not Strippers." At one protest, Dunfee was arrested for trespassing. Female employees of the club responded one Sunday by showing up at his church, topless, which is apparently legal in Ohio.

The strip club follies were just a warm-up for Cline's inevitable embrace of Donald Trump as the earthly embodiment of the moral spanking that America needed. "He's successful, he's bold, and he stands on principles," Cline said. When some friends told Cline in 2016 that Trump was a bully, Cline countered that the government was a bully. "So we need a bully to bully the bullies"—to stand up to what he'd later call "the Deep State." He added that when government loses its way, the people must follow God's law, not the government. "They followed Hitler right into the cattle cars, and we're headed into the same thing about Marxism and socialism in our country." When I asked what specific policies he was talking about, he said, "We've got so much molesting of little kids—all this child trafficking and the government does nothing." It sounded very much like the bat-guano-crazy QAnon conspiracy theory, but Cline insisted to me that he wasn't a follower of that.

Cline did have some odd, through-the-looking-glass views of what really goes on up the hill at Kenyon, home of what he calls "the God haters" who "hammered me" when Cline ran unsuccessfully for the Mount Vernon school board and the county commission. His particular foil was the mayor of Gambier, Leeman Kessler, a 2004 Kenyon grad and an actor who moved back to the village with his pastor wife and was elected to the post in 2020. Cline squared off with Kessler over a kids' story-time event in Gambier where Cline claims children were read pro-LBGTQ+ books, and he added he was shocked to learn "a homosexual" babysits Kessler's two kids. But what really threw Cline for a loop was a series of YouTube videos where Kessler portrays the early-twentieth-century horror writer H. P. Lovecraft. "He is evil," Cline claimed of the mayor. "Just pull up his website and look at some of his multiple personalities!"

Mount Vernon's leading Trumpist was equally dismissive of the Kenyon professor who led the posse of Knox County's progressive minority with whom he and his allies had squared off with on most Saturdays in the Mount Vernon town square throughout 2020. The leader of the local anti-Trump resistance is also a leading American microbiologist, with a Ph.D. in molecular biophysics and biochemistry from Yale, as well as an award-winning science fiction writer, but Cline waved her off as what he called "an evolution professor . . . Joan somebody."

JOAN SLONCZEWSKI WAS ACTUALLY THE VERY FIRST PERSON I MET IN Knox County. I'd read about her nearly five-year involvement in a weekly left-leaning protest in Mount Vernon's Public Square called Signs on the Square—where anywhere from a dozen to fifty people, some from the Kenyon community, had gathered every Saturday at noon to voice opposition to Trump or call for action on issues like climate change. Occasionally, they'd drawn pro-Trump counterprotesters—some of them armed.

So we met, six feet apart, on a bench in the Public Square. Midway through our interview—noon on Sunday, when the square and downtown Mount Vernon were largely deserted—a massive Ford F-150–style pickup truck made the slow, one-way loop around the square, with one of those massive, deep-blue TRUMP/PENCE 2020 flags flying from the back. It was the kind of rig that looks just like those of the Taliban patrolling some dusty town in southern Afghanistan, on the prowl for women without face coverings or some other violation of sharia law—but on this early Sunday afternoon the driver just kept on rolling through.

Slonczewski grew up not far from me in Westchester County, New York—the offspring of so-called Rockefeller Republicans when "a Republican meant balancing the budget and maintaining services"—but has been teaching biology at Kenyon and living in Knox County since the 1980s. In addition to the weekly protests, she said she's knocked on thousands of doors in the Republican stronghold as a volunteer trying to elect Democrats. Like many other liberal, educated baby boomers, Slonczewski is convinced the problem with America today is as simple as too much bad information.

"The people are brainwashed," she said flatly, blaming the end of the Federal Communication Commission's Fairness Doctrine near the close of the Ronald Reagan administration, which created the right-wing talk radio that folks in Knox County listen to all day. "You can hypnotize people to believe total falsehoods. That's what led to the Capitol mob, which I refuse to call an insurrection, because that's an insult to true revolutions!"

Both Slonczewski and a Kenyon colleague who was also a founder of the Signs on the Square protest—Jeanne Griggs, who runs the writing center at the college—have great faith in the power of higher education. They challenged me on any suggestion that the American way of college has been a negative influence—or that administrators are paid too much. Griggs told me when I met her outside the Kenyon bookstore in Gambier that "people vote the way that they do because they haven't been able to get the education they need to do critical thinking."

She arguably wasn't wrong, and it didn't help when, just three months before the 2020 election, the eighty-year-old *Mount Vernon News* local newspaper was bought out by a secretive corporation accused of running "pay-to-play" websites promoting Republican causes. But the explanations for Knox County's divisions offered by Slonczewski and Griggs also feel like waving a red flag in front of the folks who say they are angry, resentful, and tired of college know-it-alls who look down their noses at them even as they beg them not to pull the lever for Donald Trump—or the next guy who might be worse.

Mount Vernon's Public Square is the civic center of Knox County, and embodies all the many contradictions of more than two and a half centuries of American democracy. Its focal point is the towering granite Soldier's Monument, a tall, fluted granite column, atop which stands the figure of a Union soldier, looking pensively south toward the site of an earlier rebellion against the authority of the federal government. The story of the Civil War and the great victory for the troops in blue who ended slavery is a story that, in various ways, both Knox County and Kenyon College tell themselves in order to live. But the real history of how central Ohio has viewed race, class, and what it means to be an American is much, much more complicated.

YOU COULD START WITH THE TANGLED SAGA OF THE AFRICAN AMERICAN Snowden Family Band, who performed and farmed the land just north of Mount Vernon throughout the nineteenth century and who may—yes, quite ironically—have written the South's battle anthem "Dixie," even though a white man with close ties to Knox County named Dan Emmett claimed credit for the tune (and its valuable royalties).

In 1863, just before the tide of the conflict turned at Gettysburg, a local Democratic congressman named Clement Laird Vallandigham—leader of a faction called the Peace Democrats, popularly known as the "Copperheads"—drew a massive crowd of ten thousand people at the Mount Vernon Public Square for a speech pleading for Abraham Lincoln to end the war and to leave the South, and thus slavery, alone. (He was soon arrested for treason.) In the 1920s, the site of Knox County's fairgrounds was purchased for a time by the Hiawatha Park Association—which turned out to be a front for the Ohio Ku Klux Klan, which held rallies there.

Downriver, Kenyon College was always intended as a cloistered retreat from the chaos of nineteenth-century America. The school was founded in the 1820s by the first Episcopal bishop on what was then the Ohio frontier, Philander Chase. He used his connections back in England—most notably, the baron George Kenyon and Lord Gambier—to purchase the eight-thousand-acre property overlooking the Kokosing in 1825, declaring famously after hiking to the top of the hill, "Well, this will do."

The Episcopal clerics who came down from Gambier Hill are mostly forgotten by history, but other high priests of the American arts and sciences would flourish on the isolated, idyllic campus. Mirroring the contradictions of Knox County around it, Kenyon College would educate both the winning strategist of the Civil War—Lincoln's Secretary of War Edwin Stanton—and the U.S. president, Rutherford B. Hayes, who would undo its gains by ending Reconstruction in 1877.

In the twentieth century, tiny Gambier became a major amplifier as America made its big move in world literature, with the launch of the influential *Kenyon Review* in 1937, not long before the 1940 graduation of the poet laureate Robert Lowell. In the G.I. Bill years immediately following World War II, Kenyon—like so many overflowing U.S. campuses—exploded as a kind of a supernova for an American Century, producing progressive world changers like Sweden's Palme, the Ohio-born actor Paul Newman, the inventive comedian Jonathan Winters, and writers like E. L. Doctorow, William H. Gass, and James Wright.

Visiting the campus today is to be overcome with a sense of ghosts—a thought I jotted down in my notebook even before I learned about the "ghost tours of Kenyon," or the frequent sightings by undergrads of otherworldly presences. It doesn't help that an actual cemetery occupies prominent real estate on the main campus green. There, Kenyon luminaries like its Civil War president Lorin Andrews, who volunteered to fight even before Fort Sumter and died months later of typhus contracted in the Virginia campaign, are spending eternity. The faded headstones—a few simple crosses or rounded markers, blackened by the ancient soot of the Industrial Revolution or just old age and today hard to read—are surrounded by winter's dead, brown leaves that seem to be everywhere, their stomping the only sound made by socially distanced stray students in masks, hauling backpacks or the occasional guitar. Every fifteen minutes, as students trek past the Gothic spires of Old Kenyon or under the sculpted crows that look down from this stone fortress, Westminster chimes ring out from the Church of the Holy Spirit, its 1879 tune all but screaming "Tradition!" Tradition, of course, cannot be built from scratch, and in today's frantic market for an elite diploma, it's arguably worth hundreds of millions of dollars.

The students I met in Gambier said money is never mentioned at Kenyon—maybe because it looms over everything. Like many elite private schools, Kenyon aims to offer middle- and lower-income families as much scholarship money, in lieu of debt, as possible—but, similar to other top-tier schools, there's still a gap. According to the Department of Education, families in the middle-class income bracket of $48,001 to $75,000 paid an average of $14,182 to send a child to Kenyon for a year. It was largely these middle-class kids, whose parents were tapped out and who needed the cash from their student jobs to buy books, or do laundry, or to tag along when their upscale pals decided to splurge for late-night pizza, who suffered when COVID-19 wreaked havoc with their hours, and who walked the picket line for K-SWOC.

The idyllic campus that Philander Chase created to forge Episcopal preachers for Ohio became instead a secular mecca for families from the Upper West Side, the Westside of L.A., or overseas elites willing and eager to pay the full $76,000 a year for the cachet of an American diploma. That escalating class divide heightened the otherness of the Gothic, cloistered community on Gambier Hill, but so, perhaps, did the irony that Kenyon's admission officers strived for more diverse faces even as the student body also became more affluent. The concept of strained "town-gown relations" is something of a cliché, but—coincidentally, or not—around the time that more Black and Brown kids came to Gambier and the foreign owners of Mount Vernon's factories moved more jobs to places like Mexico, those relations took on a harsher edge.

In the fall of 2017, during the first year of Donald Trump's fraught presidency, Sofía Alpízar Román arrived from her native Costa Rica at Kenyon, where she now majored in political science and Latinx studies and has helped launch a Spanish-language newspaper. During her orientation week for international students, she found herself kayaking in the middle of the Kokosing River with a fellow freshman who was Chinese, and who said he wanted to learn Spanish. So Alpízar Román was trying to teach him a few phrases, loudly over the gentle river current, when she was shocked by a stranger's abrupt voice from the banks.

"Who cares!" the woman shouted. "You're in America! Speak American!" Nearly four years later, Alpízar Román's retelling of the incident still conveys her sense of shock. "No one had ever talked to me like that before!" But other Kenyon students had similar experiences arriving in Knox County.

Alexia Aimsworth, who was a junior when I interviewed her on the lawn at the busy Wiggin Street Coffee that faces Kenyon's main gate, said she was still stunned over what happened when she arrived from Northern California ahead of her freshman year for a summer writing program, and went with two new friends—both people of color—to shop at a discount store in Mount Vernon. "It was the first time I heard somebody shout a racial slur."

This new age of tension was foreshadowed one night in January 2001, about a week after George W. Bush's inauguration. That evening, there was a snowball fight—a big one, outside one of the Kenyon dorms. Campus security officers, believing that it had gotten out of hand, inexplicably called in outside police, including Knox County sheriff's deputies. Things escalated, with officers pelted and taunted, but still nothing that seemed especially serious. Until one Kenyon student was arrested for disorderly conduct and handcuffed, which is when a sheriff's deputy named David Shaffer started randomly pepper-spraying kids. "The person who maced the students was Officer Shaffer and he didn't warn anyone," one student told the *Kenyon Collegian* in 2001. "He arbitrarily maced a bunch of students."

Officer Shaffer wasn't disciplined for escalating the melee. To the contrary, in 2012 he was elected Knox County sheriff, running on the Republican line. During his time in office, Kenyon students complained about the sheriff's deputies assigned to Gambier, but particularly around the issue of racial profiling of the college's Black and Brown students. The controversy boiled over in September 2019 when a Black Kenyon sophomore named Mo Kamara was driving a golf cart with three older alumni attending a celebration of the fiftieth anniversary of the college's Black Student Union—when suddenly she saw the blue flashing lights of a sheriff deputy's cruiser.

The bizarre traffic stop—the deputy told the *Kenyon Collegian* that Kamara was driving illegally on the sidewalk, while Kamara insisted her group was profiled for driving while Black—triggered days of controversy over what exactly is Ohio law about driving golf carts and, understandably, the role of race. Kamara said it was her fourth negative interaction with this particular deputy, including a 2017 writers' conference in which she and two other Black teens were accosted for merely walking shoulder to shoulder in the road. She told the *Collegian* that when the golf cart stop happened "I was not myself, 'cause in my head I was thinking, 'No one on this campus can help me . . .'" The matter became an issue in 2020's Gambier mayoral race, and the victor, Leeman Kessler, eventually worked to reduce the number of deputies in the village from two to just one.

"The sheriff's role on campus—it's almost explicitly punitive in that if someone drinks too much and has to go to the hospital, the sheriff will follow and arrest them," Djibril Branche, a sophomore from Pittsburgh who is president of the Black Student Union at Kenyon and also active in K-SWOC, told me. The sheriff controversies fed right into anxieties around the 2020 presidential election. The grief many students felt on November 9, 2016, had morphed into paranoia ahead of the 2020 vote. "If violence breaks out in Ohio," Branche recalls thinking, "we might be the center." He was picturing riots in tiny, Victorian Gambier, with its church bells and lily-white clapboard siding.

But the Kenyon community had already watched political tensions escalate five miles down the road in Mount Vernon—at that exact same spot where that rogue congressman had urged an insurrection against Abe Lincoln and an early end to the Civil War a century and a half earlier. This time, the verbal combatants in the town's Public Square were opposing the 45th president, Donald Trump—and their words came not from fiery speeches but were posted on cardboard for Signs on the Square. They started coming at noon on Saturdays right after Trump was elected in November 2016, with signs like one carried by the Kenyon microbiologist Slonczewski—one of the initial organizers—that read OUR PLANET MATTERS—WE CAN'T BREATHE.

Others were also from the Kenyon community, but many were older professional folks or retirees from all over Knox County. They were baby boomers who cared about the boomer issues—the environment, reproductive rights, partisan disgust at Trump. The protests only occasionally drew Kenyon students, whose politics tended to be more—to invoke the most loaded word of the 2020s—"woke," such as a flap over whether Kenyon's sports teams should still be called the Lords and the Ladies, or the original campus play that was canceled in 2018 when students rejected its portrayal of a Mexican immigrant. To its leaders like Slonczewski, Signs on the Square was a silent yet loud message to the other 66 percent of Knox County who'd voted for Trump in 2016. We are right here, in your community.

The protests fluctuated from fifty people to a hearty dozen on some Saturdays, but they came week after week. At some point in 2020, it was all too much for Jeff Cline and the people who'd honed their mischief-making in protesting the nearby strip club. That spring, after the police killing of George Floyd in Minneapolis triggered a racial reckoning all across America, local conservatives and arguably even the organizers were a little floored when seven hundred people—some faculty and staff from the Kenyon community, but many of them local high school kids, their teachers, or other professionals—showed up for a Black Lives Matter march through Mount Vernon.

Luis Trasvina, who'd called my COVID-19 mask "a ritualistic shame muzzle," was watching on Fox News the vandalism and looting that had occurred in other cities, and so he showed up near the Public Square with a man he described as "my friend Marv, who's Black"— and with his open-carry firearm. "Black Lives Matter has destroyed communities," Trasvina told me. He said he told marchers who confronted him that night, "We're just here to protect property and life and make sure nothing gets burned down." Needless to say, nothing did—but as summer and then the contentious fall election arrived, people like Jeff Cline and some of his friends started showing up to counterprotest Signs on the Square.

One Trump supporter named Alan Hoyle even drove up from North Carolina with a large truck that was plastered with wackadoodle signs about the pandemic that said things like VACCINES GIVES (SIC) YOU THE VIRUS or MASK HIDES IDENTITY/ENCOURAGES RIOTING/COPS DIE. Other Trumpists stood in front of the bank across the street from the Public Square, at times openly carrying their weapons.

While I was reporting in Knox County, a local photographer named Graham Stokes sent me hundreds of photos that he'd taken in 2020 and 2021 in and around the Public Square. Scrolling through them was like meeting the bastard offspring of Norman Rockwell and Leni Riefenstahl—a mix of American (and Trump) flag-waving partisans holding their cute grade-schooler kids aloft in front of Main Street store windows would be interspersed with a shot of a man's collection of nine or ten pistols and long guns splayed across the massive front hood of his steroid-pumped pickup truck.

The conflict between the Copperheads of the twenty-first century and the sign-waving Unionists in a place literally called the Public Square made for a great story, and several news sites from down the road in Columbus covered it during the tense run-up to the 2020 election. At the same time, the bigger things that were driving Knox County—and America—apart weren't so photogenic, or even visible.

JEFF CLINE MAY HAVE BEEN THE LOUDEST DONALD TRUMP SUP-porter in town, but he was far from the most important. That would be Karen Buchwald Wright, the heir to Mount Vernon's last remaining large industrial employer, Ariel Corp., a leading maker of gas compressors. Wright has been CEO of the firm and its 1,200 workers since 2001. There is more than one way to look at this somewhat reclusive boomer—now in her late sixties, with a full head of blond curly hair and given to driving around the hometown where she attended high school in a silver Bentley. The *Columbus Dispatch*, in a 2013 profile, went with "quiet philanthropist."

And without a doubt, Wright, whose late father is said to have founded Ariel in his garage, is a key reason why Mount Vernon seems in a kind of holding pattern—not a stereotype of Rust Belt decay like Youngstown to the northeast, but with its flag-draped front porches freshly painted and well-kept. Not only is her firm a source of OK-not-great-paying blue-collar jobs, but the Ariel CEO has stepped in with cash contributions every time downtown Mount Vernon showed signs of strain. She partnered with the local colleges—including Kenyon (where she was a trustee and two of her sons are alumni)—to fill empty buildings with new projects like the $6 million Wright Center, a former food warehouse that now houses a film center for Kenyon and a science play area for local school kids.

Still, some locals were a little surprised in 2019 by the revelation of another large beneficiary of Wright's financial largess: Donald Trump. During the Ukraine scandal that led to the 45th president's first of two impeachments, a key figure in the scandal made public a video of a small private dinner the then-president attended at the Trump D.C. hotel in which two of the prominent guests were Wright and her husband, Thomas Rastin, an Ariel executive. They were there because the power couple from little Mount Vernon had donated a whopping $1 million to Trump's political action committee, or PAC, called America First Action. The donation was a small slice of the nearly $10 million they had donated to Republican and conservative causes during Wright's tenure as CEO. The video showed how Rastin used his exclusive access to the president of the United States to personally lobby for America to manufacture more compressed natural gas vehicles, which would be a huge boon to Ariel.

Indeed, Wright's story seemed a parable for America in the Trump and now–post Trump era. Her acts of philanthropy—however generous and worthwhile—were made possible by the nation's low taxes on the wealthy in a time of skyrocketing CEO compensation. In fact, her beneficiary Trump had further lowered tax rates on her, Rastin, and corporations like Ariel in signing his 2017 tax bill. Meanwhile, the firm's business prospects centered on burning more fossil fuels in a time of climate change—including Ariel's support for the exploitive Keystone XL pipeline, which Trump had sought to ram through—and also by keeping labor unions out of her nondescript factory on the south side of Mount Vernon. When the neighboring Siemens facility closed, local leaders told Kenyon's *Collegian Magazine* the workers were unlikely to land jobs at Ariel because they'd be considered "pro-union." "Their culture is very right wing," an anonymous machinist wrote on the job-review site Indeed. "Nothing wrong with that, but [I'm] more left and it makes it very uncomfortable to speak freely." A former engineer concurred, writing, "get ready for the propaganda to make you nuts."

Of course, the $1 million that Wright and her husband donated to back Trump—who'd lowered their taxes while cheerleading for fossil fuels—was probably to spend to buy Facebook or cable-TV ads that riled up middle-class voters over unrelated "culture war" issues in order to keep pro-business Republicans in power. This scheme worked great for multimillionaires, and it thrilled anti-strip-club, anti-abortion warriors like Cline or the Reverend Dunfee—but what hope was there for the true middle class?

SOME OF THE WORST PROBLEMS IN KNOX COUNTY ARE THE ONES happening behind closed doors—especially the drug-abuse crisis that began in the 2010s with opioid abuse and had devolved by 2019 into a methamphetamine emergency. Nationally, the average age of meth users was twenty-three, which rang true for experts who attended a 2019 Knox County summit meeting on drug use. Author Javier Sanchez told the gathering that young people in the county facing a rough environment around college and jobs were under enormous pressure to be perfect. "This is that pivotal moment in their life where they are figuring out, you know, who they are, what they care about, what they value and how to live that out in their daily life," Sanchez said. The drug crises were just one reason that local young men and women with diminished prospects seemed left out of the debate over their future.

What I saw during my time in Knox County hardened my belief that a half century of bad decisions and generational change had sliced America into fourths, like a lazy pizza cutter. Despite mostly coming from a position of more wealth than their peers, the Kenyon democratic-socialist vanguard of K-SWOC and its leaders like Graham Ball were characteristic of what I called the Left Broke—young people and their families for whom the enlightenment of college education was weighed down by worries around money and an unequal society. On the other side of Gambier Street were their peers coming out of high school. This second quadrant, using drugs or video games to cope with the tedium of fast-food McJobs or warehouse work were increasingly Left Out. Their parents like Jeff Cline or the Reverend Bill Dunfee—clinging to rituals as the middle-class culture they were born into crumbled before their eyes—were Left Behind. And yet the people like Joan Slonczewski or Jeanne Griggs on the Kenyon faculty—who'd gone to college when tuition was low and American optimism was high—struggled to understand why today's students weren't interested in the same issues, or why the Trumpers in the rest of Knox County drowned in their own ignorance. Their own struggles to come to terms with the rapid changes in American politics made these well-educated types the Left Perplexed.

These four groups didn't just have different worldviews but literally waved different flags, on a spectrum from the purple, white, and green genderqueer flag on the Kenyon campus to the Trump/Pence banners on Ford F-150s circling the streets of Mount Vernon. They spoke different languages in parallel worlds where an honored microbiologist becomes a figure out of the Scopes monkey trial, or an American cable TV channel is seen as Nazi-caliber propaganda—where H. P. Lovecraft is either a literary icon or some form of devil worship, or where Bible study borders on hate speech. The rusty edge of this pizza cutter hacking at American society was college, in a time when the only thing worse than the struggle of paying for a diploma were the struggles facing those who'd never have one.

And yet underneath the crazy discord was an odd yearning. These Americans who'd been tested and sorted and scrambled into warring tribes occasionally seemed desperate both to understand the other side—in the spirit of that baffled Kenyon kid who said "we need to go out in the community" the morning after Trump won—and also filled with a vague hope that somebody on that other side was listening.

Some of this was formal and organized. Kenyon's president, Decatur, in addition to writing essays about his experiences as a Black man in Knox County, actively pushed for more programs that would get students out of Gambier and into the local community. One faculty member who answered the call was Slonczewski, who teaches a seminar in which Kenyon biology students get course credit for helping in Knox County's main emergency rooms, sometimes an up-close look at the opioid crisis. "They learn what the community is really like," she said. "They learn about impoverished people."

Even Jeff Cline, the pro-Trump spewer of vitriol toward LGBTQ+ people, college professors and Democrats in general, had this yearning to be listened to, and understood. As the Tuesday night prayer service wound down and the other worshippers headed for home, I was out in the J.C.'s Autos lot. Amid the van with the speaking platform from 2020's Trump rallies with the D.C. SWAMP—DRAIN BABY DRAIN! bumper sticker and the big ICE SCREAM 4 JESUS truck, Cline, surprisingly, ran after me. The questions I'd asked him about Kenyon, the college that looked down on him from the hillside, had stayed with him. "It's our job to go to these Kenyon people and say it doesn't matter what's in our heart, that we care about your souls, we care about your lives," he told me. "We need to start that movement that prays for an arrival—no, prays for an awakening!"

Remember Sofía Alpízar Román, the Kenyon student from Costa Rica who was heckled over speaking Spanish during her first week in Knox County? During that same freshman year, she actually lived with a family as part of a program where local residents host international scholars. The head of the household was an Evangelical minister who had an interest in Costa Rica because he had studied there as a young man—and was also a passionate supporter of Donald Trump.

Because she frequently visited a boyfriend at another Midwestern college, the minister would gladly drive Alpízar Román to the bus terminal in Columbus—while he'd complain about Black Lives Matter or tell her that "building the wall" on the Southern border was humane, because migrants would have to come legally instead of making a dangerous desert trek. But she also recalled that "he had a conversation with my Mom in Spanish; that anything she needs, he will be there." Relating his politics to his Evangelical beliefs, Alpízar Román said, "he helped me to humanize Trump voters."

It wasn't until after that Sunday evening on the wraparound porch at Kenyon's Palme House that I would read up on Kenyon alum Olof Palme and how his work among the blue-collar auto workers of the Upper Midwest drew him toward the egalitarian worldview of socialism, and had inspired him to lead his native Sweden. This casual 1940s solidarity between Ohio's working class and those kids who were often the first in their family to attend college seemed no longer possible in the 2020s, when the university-bound and those left behind in a declining middle class were trapped in deep silos. The ghosts that truly haunted me after my days in Knox County weren't the Civil War vets buried under Gambier's oaks but the more recent generation that included Palme's socialism and the philanthropy of Paul Newman, when giving a kid a shot at higher education inspired them to give something back. That sprang from a recent yet very different time when college in America was widely seen as a uniter, not a divider. To understand how to get that back, I'd have to start at the beginning.

The beginning was 1944.

CHAPTER 2

WHEN COLLEGE IN AMERICA ALMOST BECAME A PUBLIC GOOD

In 1943, a super-smart kid from Washington, D.C., named Donald Balfour—future member of Mensa, the society of high-IQ geniuses—cheated on a vision test and, unknowingly, tricked his way onto the front lines of American history.

It was the middle of World War II. Balfour, the son of Jewish immigrants, who for a couple of years had been working toward a college diploma through night classes while he struggled to pay for it, was eager to join the fight against Adolf Hitler. There was just one problem: his congenitally bad eyesight. Now, as he sat in the hallway of the Selective Service office, Balfour realized he could hear the doctor administering the eye test to the young man just ahead of him. He listened carefully, and put that Mensa-caliber memory to work.

Balfour aced the test, and was soon riding cross-country to his basic training at a U.S. Army base in Oregon—but his trick could only travel so far. Before he could be shipped overseas, Balfour was told to take a second eye exam—and this doctor knew enough to keep his door shut while the G.I. waited outside. By the end of 1943, Balfour was back in the nation's capital, honorably discharged from the Army and free to pursue his college degree at George Washington University.

The young Balfour was energetic, seemingly restless. He didn't just take classes in international relations but also joined the glee club and the drama club and quickly became editor of GW's student newspaper, *The Hatchet*. In June 1944—just days after G.I.s with better eyesight had stormed the beaches of Normandy on D-Day—Balfour had an idea for a story. He'd seen that President Franklin D. Roosevelt had just signed a law called the Servicemen's Adjustment Act of 1944, which offered full college tuition and other benefits to returning troops. You might have gotten the idea by now that Don Balfour was the kind of person his own people might call a mensch.

He quickly arranged an interview with the Veterans Administration bureaucrat who was running the new program—already popularly dubbed the G.I. Bill—just a few blocks away in downtown Washington. And when Balfour arrived at the VA for the meeting, he had a trick up his sleeve. He brought his Army discharge papers with him. After a few questions about how the G.I. Bill would work for current or prospective college students, he pulled the documents from his pocket and asked the man: Could he enroll in this new program, which promised not just full college tuition but a living stipend? As in, right now?

One can only imagine Balfour's pleasure when the official, John M. MacCammon, took the letter, called in his secretary, and dictated a letter on the spot approving Balfour's application. It wasn't just that Balfour—who would earn his bachelor's degree in 1945, thanks to the government aid—was OK'd for the G.I. Bill benefits. He was the very first veteran ever approved—the first of a cohort that would eventually produce more than 2.2 million college grads and radically change how Americans perceived higher education. The story that America tells itself about Don Balfour and the G.I. Bill is emblematic of an invented national narrative that has grown more and more powerful with the passage of time. Crystallized by an eponymous book by TV anchorman Tom Brokaw, people with the midcentury pluck and ambition of a Balfour became America's "Greatest Generation"—those who built a great society from the rubble of wars and a Great Depression that would have crushed a weaker cohort.

At first glance, the plucky and irrepressible Don Balfour fits the Greatest Generation storyline all too well. Growing up in the Great Depression as the son of a Jewish native of Syria who came to America to avoid fighting for the Ottomans in World War I and a mother who, after a divorce when Don was just twelve, moved him from Brooklyn to Richmond and then D.C. and sold jewelry to support the family, Balfour learned to work hard and pounce at any opportunity. But his pathway to the affluent middle-class of postwar America wasn't merely the product of his own personal spunk. It was laid out before him, by a society and its government willing and able to offer its citizens a helping hand, inspiring its beneficiaries to give something back.

Don Balfour was the first American to benefit from this specific piece of legislation. But he rode the cresting wave of a much bigger and bolder idea: that higher education belonged in the growing basket of government programs broadly hailed as "the public good." The success of the unlikely experiment that was the G.I. Bill sold the nation on the even bolder concept that college both could and should be broadly accessible—not just for veterans but for anyone with ambitions for a better life. In stark contrast, the collapse of this utopian vision would become the secret sauce behind our modern political gridlock, the revolts of the Tea Party and Occupy Wall Street, the resentment-fueled rise of Donald Trump, and finally a deadly insurrection on Capitol Hill.

So what exactly was the 1944 G.I. Bill? Politically, and perhaps psychologically as well, it was a bridge between the federal intervention of the New Deal, which beat back the worst of the Great Depression, and the last hurrah of the American welfare state that would be Lyndon Johnson's Great Society. Its enactment was very much in step with the dominant political worldview of the United States at the mid-twentieth century—that a benevolent government and technocratic know-how could both prevent the problems caused by unfettered capitalism and also stem ideologies like communism and fascism. And yet at the same time, the powerful reach of 1944's G.I. Bill—especially the all-important college benefit—was also something of a fluke. To say the bill's impact on the next seventy-five or so years of American life was unanticipated even by its architects would be a monumental under-statement.

The starting point was less a vision of a rosy future than the memory of a recent nightmare: the botched reintegration of America's return-ing veterans from World War I. With the backing of the newly formed American Legion, returning soldiers from that war complained of un-grateful treatment and lobbied Washington for five years for a bonus check. When it was finally approved in 1924, the federal government scheduled it for a date more than two decades in the future, 1945. In mid-1932, however, the worsening Depression caused a so-called Bo-nus Army of veterans to march on the nation's capital and establish a large protest encampment, demanding the money right away. Active U.S. troops ultimately clashed with the "Bonus Army," resulting in two deaths, and burned down their camp, an incident that arguably sealed the defeat of Herbert Hoover that fall.

With 1944's successful D-Day invasion and the end of World War II on the horizon, no one wanted a repeat of that. Also, 1944 was a pres-idential election year. Roosevelt had smashed through a longstanding political norm when he'd won a third term in 1940; four years later, America's progress in the war became his rationale for a fourth, even as Roosevelt's health was fading fast. In making his case for reelection a third time, Roosevelt also sought to rekindle the fading spirit of his New Deal for the American working class, against the cross-currents that Congress was now a lot more conservative, and the momentum for domestic change had ebbed. "Freedom from want" was a cornerstone of FDR's famous "Four Freedoms" State of the Union address that January, but most of the 32nd president's progressive agenda on the home front—higher taxes on the rich to pay for housing, health care, and other social programs—was politically dead on arrival. Benefits for returning veterans, however, had a chance.

The G.I. Bill happened in a sweet spot where a liberal package of taxpayer-funded perks won the backing of normally conservative, pro-veteran allies including the American Legion, who wanted returning troops to get the kind of "bonus" that had been so problematic after World War I. This time, however, the veterans lobby was willing to consider a more complex plan that involved aid for housing and education, or unemployment benefits, instead of cash. Ironically, the bill's champion on Capitol Hill was a segregationist, anti-Semitic, and virulently anti-Communist Mississippi World War I vet, Representative John Rankin. In his sweeping history of the G.I. Bill, *Over Here*, author Edward Humes makes the case that the cagey Roosevelt understood something the lawmakers and lobbyists did not—that a strong government boost for veterans would make the case for bigger aid programs to offer "freedom from want" for all Americans. Unfortunately, he wouldn't live to see his hunch confirmed.

While today the G.I. Bill is synonymous with the rocket launch of the modern American university, in 1944 its college benefits were an afterthought, and emerged from the Capitol Hill negotiations only as somewhat of an accident. To understand why the monumental notion of essentially free college for millions of veterans was largely shrugged off seventy-five years ago, it's important to take a step back and remember that higher education just wasn't part of the conversation for the typical young American then.

True, by the 1940s, college attendance had been growing steadily for the better part of a century, since the end of the Civil War and the creation of so-called land-grant universities at the state level. In the first half of the twentieth century, the success of the Industrial Revolution and the need for elite managers and professionals had caused enrollment to grow exponentially—but "exponentially" from a base of mostly moneyed East Coast elite families that started at close to zero. The bottom line is that by World War II, just 5 percent of U.S. adults had earned a bachelor's degree—a tiny fraction of today's figure of 37 percent.

Thus, many members of Congress didn't sweat the higher-ed details of the G.I. Bill, focusing more on the blue-collar-friendly provisions of the proposal, such as housing aid and unemployment benefits. After all, fewer than half of the troops who served during World War II had even graduated high school. Initial projections were that a relatively small number of G.I.s would have any interest in redeeming the higher-ed benefits—maybe 1 million, tops, or fewer than one in ten. But the argument that a college option would relieve pressure on what would be a crowded job market—with so many vets reentering it at the same time—made it easier for one of FDR's New Deal allies, Representative Elbert Thomas of Utah, to sweeten the pot.

The final measure that Roosevelt signed on June 22, 1944—just sixteen days after the D-Day invasion—promised to cover not just four years of college, but even a book allowance and a healthy living stipend for those who'd served at least nine months active duty. Still, conservatives counted this a victory; they'd whittled down FDR's vast 1944 ambition for an expanded welfare state to one lonely program for veterans.

A lot of America didn't think that the farm boys and sons of coal miners and immigrant laborers who'd fought on Iwo Jima or in the Battle of the Bulge were really college material, to be shamefully honest. That was especially true of the men who ran the country's best-known and longest-standing universities, who saw the G.I. Bill not as an opportunity but as a threat to their hegemony. These college gatekeepers clung to their beliefs that it wasn't because of inherited wealth and elite privilege that they only educated the top sliver of Americans, but rather because the other 95 percent didn't have the brain matter, or "merit," to cut it.

"Hobo jungles" was the alarming and offensive prediction from University of Chicago president and G.I. Bill opponent Robert Hutchins, who believed that campuses would be overrun by unqualified, uninterested young grunts who were only there to collect the monthly stipend. Hutchins, who'd notoriously dropped his school's wildly successful varsity football team in the 1930s, thinking it a distraction from academics, now predicted rival colleges would take these "hobos" and their government tuition checks because "educational institutions, as the big-time football racket shows, cannot resist money." Then-president of Harvard, James B. Conant, concurred—the G.I. Bill failed "to distinguish between those who can profit most from advanced education and those who cannot." So too did many other administrators. Some—in contrast to Hutchins—worried about a culture clash between older, often married vets and the "Boola Boola" campus life of mixers and, yes, football, while others warned of platoons of angry warriors who would reject classroom authority and discipline.

What happened instead changed America—and changed the perception of what ordinary Americans were capable of. The trickle of eligible veterans like Don Balfour who redeemed the educational benefit in the early weeks of the program—just 8,200 returning troops in that first year—became a flood when millions came home after 1945's victories over Germany and Japan, and as word of what the G.I. Bill could offer spread quickly. By late 1946, veterans comprised nearly half of America's two million college undergrads, a number that had been unthinkable before the war. Many venerable institutions watched their enrollment double, or more; the student population at New Jersey's Rutgers University, for example, went from 7,000 pre–World War II to 16,000 within a short time after the end of the conflict.

With the end of the global conflict, surplus Quonset huts began popping up on America's overstuffed campuses, filled with vets already used to cramped, temporary living conditions. Some schools, like Rensselaer Polytechnic Institute in upstate New York, raced to erect scores of prefab housing units, while other former troops bunked, sometimes with their wives and the first babies of the baby boom, in narrow off-campus walk-ups. This era marked the start of evening classes, to accommodate this flood, as well as a frantic scramble to employ professors' wives, or anyone else they could rouse up, as teaching assistants. True, some of the predicted "culture clashes" did occur—at Colgate, vets put a quick end to the ridiculous practice of freshmen wearing beanies. But the new students also infiltrated college football rather than rejecting it, exemplified by Navy vet Johnny Lujack winning the 1947 Heisman Trophy for Notre Dame. Yet where the millions of new students really overperformed was not so much on the gridiron but in the classroom.

The G.I. Bill students weren't "hoboes" looking to freeload on a federal stipend, but instead rose to this unexpected opportunity with the same level of determination their comrades had shown in liberating France, outpacing the formerly beanie-wearing teens that the G.I. Bill beneficiaries now called "civilians." "The civilian kids consider most of us doddering imbeciles," said one Lehigh professor, as quoted years later by Michael D. Haydock in *American History* magazine. "But the veterans seem to be impressed with our knowledge. They are old enough to realize that they know very little." Administrators from coast to coast were shocked at how few of the G.I. Bill students flunked out or dropped out. Even the once-dubious Harvard president Conant had to admit he'd been wrong, that veterans proved to be the best students the Ivy League bastion had ever had for their "seriousness, perceptiveness, [and] steadiness."

The first G.I. Bill ran until 1956—like any surprise, runaway hit, there'd be a series of sequels—and its impact was revolutionary. There are the statistics—the staggering 450,000 engineers and 91,000 scientists, filling job categories that had been barely a blip in the U.S. economy prior to the war, not to mention 238,000 teachers to handle all the boom-babies now in the pipeline. But most histories are anchored by personal narratives of human pluck, showing how the sons (because they were overwhelmingly sons) of unschooled factory workers and farmers became innovators and inventors in one generation, with that adrenaline shot from the American taxpayer.

A remarkable fourteen winners of the Nobel Prize in scientific categories as well as three future presidents—Nixon, Ford, and Bush 41—received G.I. Bill benefits, but just as notable are the everyday people who never would have gone to college without the subsidies and who—diploma in hand—became pillars of their communities. Luke LaPorta, who fathered the Little League baseball movement in upstate New York, was typical in describing the G.I. Bill as "a hell of a gift, an opportunity, and I've never thought of it any other way." If you're a baby boomer like me, you probably grew up around family members or mentors who had similar stories to tell. My own father-in-law, Fred Boccella—who guarded the bomb-pockmarked streets of Berlin as part of the Allied occupation in late 1945 (and is still going strong at age ninety-five as I write this)—came home to Philadelphia and was shunted into night classes overflowing with other vets eager to use their federal benefits, en route to La Salle

University and a lifetime of mentoring city schoolkids as a guidance counselor.

The fact that my father-in-law's story is so unremarkably common is a tribute to the enduring power of the G.I. Bill and what we can now see—unfortunately—as a unique moment in American history, when the political and social planets, as it were, lined up in exactly the right way to show us our nation's better angels. The promise of this United States—delivered imperfectly, as has always been the way since 1776—was one of equal opportunity, regardless of one's social class at birth, allowing for upward mobility. What happened to regular folks like Don Balfour and Fred Boccella shows how a college diploma became the shining symbol of a nation's promise—the American Dream.

But that American Dream came with a massive asterisk. With 2020s hindsight, it's more easily understood that the American prosperity of post–World War II America that peaked in the 1950s and early '60s—encapsulated by *Father Knows Best* reruns of a white suburban dad in a gray flannel suit and a stay-at-home mom—accrued heavily to the benefit of white men. And the G.I. Bill was no different. It practically goes without saying that a bill offering aid to returning troops would be stacked against women; of the nearly 2.3 million Americans who benefited from the law, less than 3 percent—64,728, to be exact—were female, and research suggests that the late-1940s surge of male vets actually crowded out civilian college applicants who were women.

The impact of the G.I. Bill on African Americans—even male Black vets—was only slightly better, for reasons that are more complicated. As noted by Mississippi State University historian Joseph Thompson, Mississippi's Rankin—the segregationist who sponsored the G.I. Bill—included a provision that gave regional Veterans Administration bureaucrats power over administering the law, so in the South those officials often steered Black applicants toward vocational training over college. And historically Black colleges and universities—HBCUs—

didn't have access to the surging tax revenues of the booming postwar years that made it easier for predominantly white public state universities to hire more professors and build new dorms as they rapidly expanded.

Despite these roadblocks, enrollment at HBCUs as an overall share of the college population roughly tripled during the 1940s, according to one study, while Black enrollment at integrated white public universities in the North also rose sharply during this period. This small and largely-ignored-at-the-time bump in college enrollment would lay the groundwork for the lunch-counter sit-ins of 1960 that shifted the civil rights movement into higher gear.

Likewise, women may not have benefited much directly from the G.I. Bill, but the virtuous upward cycle of college expansion that continued beyond the returning vets would bring more female undergrads by the 1950s—and graduate them into a society that didn't yet know what to do with educated women. What writer Betty Friedan famously called in 1957 "the problem that has no name" was the kindling for the women's movement that lay ahead. In other words, the G.I. Bill was the rare proverbial rising tide that—although unevenly—would eventually offer some lift to all boats, even with all the flotsam and jetsam in the way.

FDR didn't live to see it—he died on April 12, 1945, less than ten months after signing the Serviceman's Readjustment Act—but the new president, Harry Truman, and some of his key aides saw the Quonset huts and the packed classrooms around the country and debated whether the federal government should assume a greater role in supporting them. Even as it dealt with Europe in ruins, the early days of the Cold War, and a wave of labor unrest here at home, the Truman administration rolled out its Commission on Higher Education on July 13, 1946. The president himself would later cite the problem of campus overcrowding and teacher shortages, adding that "we are challenged by the need to insure that higher education shall take its proper place in our national effort to strengthen democracy at home and to improve our understanding of our friends and neighbors everywhere in the world."

Truman's words—and the yearlong deliberations of his blue-ribbon panel—capture the zeitgeist of the era, and help explain why mass college education was suddenly seen as a new national priority and a public good, and not just for World War II vets.

Nicholas Strohl, a Wisconsin-based education historian who has studied and written about the Truman Commission and the early debate over federal funding for higher education, said the commission members—an array of leading academic and religious leaders—felt a strong sense of moral duty. Most had grown up during World War I, and then as adults watched the planet helplessly spiral downward into World War II. Many were moved, in particular, by the fallout from the United States dropping two atomic bombs on Japan to end the war, and the new fear that either the brewing Cold War or some other conflict could result in a nuclear World War III that might destroy the planet.

"In a real sense the future of our civilization depends on the direction education takes, not just in the distant future, but in the days immediately ahead," the panel's final report would say in 1947. As Strohl observed, the authors believed that universities could be the anchor of a global future based around rational thought and dialogue between cultures that would foster mutual understanding. "Disaster is not inevitable," the Truman commission report stated, addressing the fifteen-kiloton elephant in the room. "Man can choose the path he will have." Promoting knowledge would not just better humanity, in other words. It might actually save it from doom.

The commission's report placed less emphasis on more down-to-earth workforce development and instead stressed lofty ideals of "general education," which, it argued, would be "the means to a more abundant personal life and a stronger, freer social order." The Truman Commission even envisioned a kind of classless America, where "through education society should come to recognize the equal dignity of all kinds of work, and so erase distinctions based on occupational classes." Some campus contemporaries thought the Truman panel's idealized vision for this new post–high school "general education" as a little, well, out there. Yet many top schools, from Harvard on down, did begin to emphasize the notion of a "liberal education," rooted in the study of Western civilization and the ideas that had nurtured modern democracy. General education, as related by the education historian Roger L. Geiger, held "an aversion to specialization and vocationalism," which had held sway in the 1920s and '30s—a pendulum that would swing back, of course, in future decades.

Indeed, some of the idealistic postwar rhetoric sounds a little *woo-woo*-ish today, like the dawning of an Age of Aquarius. The reality, though, is a little more complicated. America's leaders wanted to avoid World War III—but they also wanted to make sure that if it came, their side was equipped to win it. Strohl's research shows that a key motivator of the Truman administration's education push was military research conducted at the height of the just-concluded war. It showed that college graduates performed better on an array of tasks than soldiers lacking higher education. In hindsight, that finding might seem like a no-brainer, but for leaders in the mid-1940s it was something of an eye-opener. Remember, the prevailing conventional wisdom was still the elite college model, where just one in twenty earned diplomas and college was a waste of time for everyone else. Now Pentagon planners started to envision winning the world's next great war in the classrooms of the University of Michigan or Berkeley.

World War II is clearly a pivot point about how humankind, and Americans in particular, came to view the role of knowledge—especially science and technology—in economic and social progress but also in military advantage. The top line item was clearly the atomic bomb, and the clouds of radiation had barely lifted over Hiroshima and Nagasaki before a national mission launched to harness the atom for peaceful uses. In part, this sprung from a real need for cheaper sources of electrical power, but also to justify the moral stain of mass civilian death unleashed in Japan. The race to win World War II, backed by massive government spending, had also sped up advances in rocket science, radar technology featuring microwaves, the first large-scale computers (ENIAC, completed in early 1946), and rapid progress in medicine highlighted by the commercial development of penicillin.

With the war's end, America's growing network of colleges and universities were suddenly viewed by Washington as an underutilized resource that—through both basic and applied science and research—could be both the nation's secret weapon in winning the Cold War as well as a driver of peacetime prosperity. One of the key agenda items for the Truman Commission as it met in 1946 was whether Washington—still swollen from the growth of the federal bureaucracy during World War II—should create a central authority to oversee and direct this critical research at the university level. While this era would lead to the creation of the National Science Foundation in 1950 as a government vehicle for advancing research, the federal government declined to take on a broader role in directly mandating or even overseeing research on campus. This happened for a variety of reasons—Truman's personal aversion to a heavy-handed federal role, concern among educators about maintaining the diversity of America's various colleges, and typically bureaucratic concerns about who would control research dollars. But the broader consequence was one of many blown opportunities to establish higher education as a public good.

Rather than the stick of centralized planning, Truman and subsequent administrations offered the carrot of federal dollars. The idea was crystallized in a report published in July 1945—one month before the dropping of the first atomic bomb on Hiroshima—written by Vannevar Bush, who'd overseen military R&D efforts during the war. It was titled simply *Science—The New Frontier,* and argued for an expansive federal role in scientific research during peacetime. What would become the NSF was the cornerstone of Bush's effort, but during the five years it took for the foundation to come into existence his ideas were also adopted by other agencies such as the National Institutes of Health, the newly formed Atomic Energy Commission, and growing defense agencies like the Office of Naval Research which saw their budgets—and their grants to university researchers—grow by as much as tenfold during these years.

Much like the debate over scientific funding, the Truman Commission envisioned both a vast expansion of higher education in America and a stronger federal role in making this happen. The reality was that such an expansion did come, but with little or no leadership from Washington. "The time has come," stated the Truman Commission's report, titled Higher Education for American Democracy, "to make education through the fourteenth grade available in the same way that high school education is now available."

The finding, which envisioned the national network of community colleges that would indeed arise in the decades after World War II, planted the seed for the idea of universal higher education in America, with a more learned America making better decisions about war and peace. But the Truman Commission findings led to no legislation in Congress and no pool of federal tax dollars to make the dream happen.

Part of the reason, as Strohl and other historians have documented, was infighting among the commissioners on the Truman panel over several issues which foreshadowed future problems for expanding college access. There was also resistance from Southern college presidents over the possibility that the report might explicitly condemn segregation, which remained the rule across their region.

An explicit commitment to make universal higher education a human right, backed both legally and financially by the federal government, might have rivaled other programs of the last century—such as Social Security, Medicare, or the Affordable Care Act—in rewriting the American social contract, to the benefit of millions. Had there been such legislation in the more optimistic era of the late 1940s, the pathologies of the twenty-first century—sky-high tuition, the student debt crisis, and the political divide between cosmopolitan college grads and those in struggling small towns lacking access to higher ed—might have been averted. But no such bill was passed.

Still, at the time, this did not seem especially concerning. Universities were growing rapidly at the end of the 1940s and into the '50s without any strong federal mandate. From the end of World War II through the tumultuous 1960s, the new American way of college would be invented and then enshrined in the public's mind by a remarkable and virtuous upward cycle. The rushed campus building boom made necessary by the flood of veterans under the G.I. Bill didn't go to waste because—aided by the surge in postwar prosperity, upward mobility, and white-collar workers now outnumbering the blue-collar working class for the first time in U.S. history—the next generation of young people was ready and eager to fill those new dorm rooms. The share of eighteen-to-twenty-one-year-old Americans attending college passed 25 percent by the early 1950s and didn't stop growing, hitting 31 percent by the end of the decade. Much of this spike was fueled by government-funded public universities with very low (or, in places like California or New York City, zero) tuition that over the 1950s not only expanded their existing campuses but created new ones. The traditional private bastions of academia like the Ivy League also grew during this generation, but at a much slower rate.

The first two stages of this rocket launch—the postwar veterans and ladder-climbing kids of the 1950s—would soon give way to a massive booster shot. The baby boom—a sharp spike in the birth rate triggered almost immediately by men returning from overseas when the war ended in 1945—greatly expanded the pool of potential students. While enrollment at the established private colleges and universities roughly doubled over the course of the 1950s and '60s as these so-called boomers started arriving on campus, the population at the emerging public campuses rose by a staggering fivefold, from about 1 million students in 1951 to more than 5 million by 1969. Geiger, writing in his *American Higher Education Since World War II*, states "the pace of change was almost breathtaking."

Again, the virtuous cycle went to work. Government funding—mostly at the state and local level—to build new laboratories, dorms, or urban campuses, hire tens of thousands of new professors, and fund basic research was quite politically popular, at a time when both the booming postwar economy and high rates of taxation—another legacy of World War II—meant that governors and state lawmakers had dollars to spend. Despite the undercurrent of anxiety about nuclear war in the heyday of classroom "duck and cover" drills, most Americans in the 1950s venerated both new technology and scientists and physicians such as Dr. Jonas Salk, whose success in the development of a polio vaccine made him arguably the most admired man in the nation. Public approval of scientific research spiked to 88 percent in the mid-1950s. It would never be that high again.

From 1956 to 1970 as "the Silent Generation" gave way to baby boomers, college enrollment in America tripled—yet spending on higher education rose sixfold. This massive public investment was supported across the board—not just by state governments but by private philanthropies, swollen by twentieth-century industrial fortunes, and also by the increasing interdependence between the Pentagon and universities in a new phenomenon that wouldn't be named until President Dwight Eisenhower's historic 1961 farewell address: the military-industrial complex.

America's growing obsession with the Cold War metastasized around the mid-1950s, with reports that the Soviet Union had exploded a hydrogen bomb. Then, on October 4, 1957, near the end of a scientific project of international exchanges and conferences known as the International Geophysical Year, or IGY, the Soviets surprised the world by becoming the first nation to successfully launch an artificial orbiting satellite, Sputnik. Although this major advance—months ahead of a similar program in the United States—wasn't initially viewed with great alarm, the public grew concerned at the notion that America's rival superpower seemed to be gaining a technological advantage. These fears were exploited for political gain on Capitol Hill by one of the shrewdest politicians ever to roam the corridors of the U.S. Senate—the Texan Lyndon Johnson, then the Senate majority leader—who complained that "soon they'll be dropping bombs on us the way schoolboys drop rocks from freeway overpasses." LBJ held congressional hearings and demanded that the nation retake the lead in what was soon dubbed "the space race."

Less than a year after Sputnik, Congress passed the National Defense Education Act of 1958, which not only further boosted funding for campus research (and science and math education in K-12, which primed the pump for future growth) but contained a new provision for student loans aimed at boosting college enrollment. There is a strong parallel to the G.I. Bill: Just as the end of World War II inspired a reluctant Congress to pay for veterans' higher education, the Sputnik crisis convinced balky lawmakers that America might lose a missile race to the Soviets without ensuring that more lower-income kids with skill in math or science attended college. But the decision to offer loans—to assuage House conservatives who called money for college education "socialism"—instead of grants would have profound impact to this day.

Ike also created a new panel, the President's Science Advisory Council, which advocated for increased research and, in a 1958 report, calling thriving American universities "inescapably a responsibility of the federal government." Between these new initiatives like the NDEA and the post-Sputnik creation of the National Aeronautics and Space Administration (NASA) and the Pentagon's Defense Advanced Research Projects Agency, or DARPA, as well as the already flourishing pipelines such as the AEC and NIH, the floodgates of aid cascading from Washington were wide open. Between 1958 and 1964, federal dollars for university research quadrupled, from $200 million to $800 million, as large research centers opened on the top-tier public campuses from coast to coast.

In hindsight, the late '50s and early '60s were the peak—the pinnacle of the post—World War II rocket launch that had changed college in the United States from a rite of passage for a narrow, wealthy elite to the American Dream for a middle class intoxicated by the possibilities of a better life. Every force you can think of—political, economic, social—was pushing this capsule to unthinkable heights, and in record time.

The success of the G.I. Bill and the discovery that millions more Americans were "college material" than anyone realized. The faith that higher education was a magical elixir that could preserve democracy and prevent World War III. The popularity of science and the obsession with technology, from housewives wanting a new dishwasher to generals craving new fighter jets. And the economic prosperity that sparked both a baby boom and suburb-soaked visions of upward mobility.

But one doesn't have to dig far beneath this lush, verdant surface to find the muddy roots of future discontent. For starters, any debate about either moving toward a truly universal higher education—at least through "the fourteenth grade," as desired by the Truman Commission—and toward a more expansive government role in paying for that, was heavily weighed down by the issue of segregation. Southern lawmakers who held seniority and power on Capitol Hill were determined to block any federal dollars that might compel their public universities to admit Black students. Meanwhile, in a decade marked by the "Red Scare" and the rise and fall of McCarthyism, conservatives pressed concern that rising campus enrollment would expose America's youth to indoctrination from leftist professors, including those who'd once been drawn to the Communist Party at the depths of the Great Depression. Indeed, a growing number of universities declined to take money from the 1958 NDEA law because of a provision that anyone receiving federal dollars through the act would have to sign a form of loyalty oath, disavowing any belief in overthrowing the U.S. government.

But it was hidden and wildly unexpected social currents that would bring the most powerful consequences. Simply put, the rapid expansion of young men and women on campuses—whether it was the ivy-covered traditional schools, the gleaming high rise of the new public universities, or even the new network of community colleges—was an epic disruption in the traditional rhythms of American life. For millions of youth in the sixteen-to-twenty-two age bracket, the new college pipelines meant an extended adolescence and a liberation from the harsh physical demands of either farming or industrial work. That would have profound, hard-to-predict political and social consequences. Undergrads with leisure time and the extra pocket change that trickled down from middle-class prosperity used this new freedom to create a "youth culture" that by the peak of the baby boom would become an even wilder "counterculture." None of the blue-ribbon panels like the Truman Commission could have predicted Elvis Presley, blue jeans, or reefer madness.

Unfortunately, we won't linger here on the nexus between rising college enrollment and sex, drugs or rock 'n' roll. But what does matter, greatly, for our story are the unintended consequences of the stated and lofty political goals of the Truman Commission or the sponsors of the G.I. Bill—that better educated young Americans would become the bulwark of democracy. The college experience in the generation that immediately followed World War II very much reflected this ambitious ideal, with a decline in careerism and rising enrollment in the humanities and social sciences. But this quickly became a collision course, because at the same time that Young America was immersed in philosophical ideas of moral good and human rights that define classical liberalism, the government that was promoting mass higher education was also betraying its democratic principles. The hypocrisy wasn't immediately apparent—the relative calm of the 1950s on America's campuses before the storm of the '60s and '70s is what prompted the nickname "the Silent Generation"—but over time the new college dorms would become breeding grounds for unrest over Jim Crow in the Deep South or U.S. support for overseas dictators in the name of winning the Cold War. It was increasingly hard not to notice that these universities meant to promote international understanding and prevent World War III were funded by the Pentagon so they could invent new ways of killing our enemies.

Another aspect of launching mass college education in America probably hadn't occurred to Washington higher-ups or even some campus leaders: opening up universities to the new middle-class also promoted other kinds of diversity. Most famously, Ivy League universities had a long and deeply regrettable history of discriminating against high-achieving Jewish applicants; for much of the early twentieth century, Harvard's widely respected president A. Lawrence Lowell worked aggressively to limit the number of incoming Jews he claimed would "ruin the college." After Lowell's proposed 15 percent Jewish quota didn't work, he engineered a change in admissions practices—evaluating factors beyond academic rank and giving a boost to the legacy children of alumni (factors that remain, controversially, in the twenty-first century). Only when the wider floodgates opened after the G.I. Bill did "the Jewish quota" at Harvard, and similar practices at other private universities, fade away.

The suddenly wide pipeline of brains and ambition that flowed from the then-thriving public high schools in New York and other big cities to the fast-growing universities of the 1950s and '60s changed America for good. Consider just the well-known celebrities and high achievers who emerged in the 1950s from a small circle of public high schools in just a few central Brooklyn zip codes and who mostly passed through college on their way to fame: Ruth Bader Ginsburg, Bernie Sanders, Carole King, Woody Allen, Chuck Schumer, Barbra Streisand, Neil Diamond, and a slew of future prominent top professors, scientists, and Nobel Prize winners. These young Jewish Americans, most of them the children or grandchildren of immigrants, diversified college campuses not only with their presence but their perspective. Famously, some were the offspring of union activists or political rebels from the Great Depression—the so-called red diaper babies who grew up with a decidedly leftist perspective. But many also lost beloved family members or were deeply moved by the tragic and painfully fresh stories of the Holocaust that decimated Europe. The experience created students who were highly receptive to the reports of racism coming from the Deep South, and drawn to the notion that higher ed could promote international understanding and world peace.

But that was just one intriguing offshoot of a much broader social revolution that was starting to stir. The sudden rise of college opportunities for the growing American middle class fed all sorts of viewpoints. Although still grossly underrepresented, the 1950s and '60s brought more Black students who nurtured radical new ideas on how to challenge white supremacy, and more educated women who chafed at their expected role in a deeply entrenched patriarchy. Like their Jewish neighbors from densely packed industrial cities, the offspring of Catholic immigrants grew up in the Church and would often arrive as freshmen with ideas about morality, peace, or U.S. meddling in Latin America at odds with the prevailing establishment culture.

WITH HINDSIGHT, THE MOST FASCINATING ASPECT OF THE NEW American university was not the bricks and mortar of the gleaming new campuses but the soul of this massive new machine. The idea that higher education could shape a new generation of citizens who'd be mindful and enthusiastic about democracy, with an international outlook and an aversion to military conflict, who'd embrace liberal arts over careerism was, in many ways, brought to life by these students who packed classrooms—even ahead of the advancing baby boom. But what young people absorbed was actually a pure distillation of democracy, not the corrupted version that America was selling with wads of dollar bills or the points of bayonets in Africa or Latin America or Southeast Asia. The kids, it turned out, were executing the blueprint of the Truman Commission and the postwar idealists. It was the grownups that were screwing it up.

The experience on the ground of undergraduates majoring in sociology, spending summers in poor Mexican villages or writing diatribes against racial segregation was largely missed by the university presidents flying high at 37,000 feet while their campuses bathed in money from the Pentagon or big-money foundations. In many ways, the zenith of American university power was embodied by one erudite, high-profile man for all seasons: Clark Kerr, the president of the University of California.

When Kerr was elevated in 1957 from chancellor at the Berkeley campus to chief of the statewide system, he inherited a long California legacy of leadership in the notion of higher ed as both a public good and an economic engine. The Golden State had embraced the broad, bipartisan Progressive movement and upped state spending to expand college opportunities at the turn of the twentieth century. Earl Warren, the state's Republican governor when the G.I. Bill was enacted in 1944, and later the chief justice of the most liberal Supreme Court in American history, spent generously on higher education which he saw as "a shock absorber" for the economic cycles that had buffeted California during the "Grapes of Wrath" years. Kerr wanted to shatter any lingering perceptions of college as merely a vehicle for privileged elites. "The campus is no longer on the hill with the aristocracy," he wrote, "but in the valley with the people."

A native Pennsylvanian who moved West after his undergraduate days at Swarthmore College, Kerr studied economics and industrial relations at the peak of New Deal collectivism and developed an ethos around the managed division of labor, and the art of compromise. "He was a Quaker—not a practitioner of the religion but a philosophical Quaker who believed in public service, humility, and equality," wrote the English academic Simon Marginson in his studies of Kerr and the California ideals. For the first twenty years of his rise through the ranks at Berkeley, Kerr displayed a remarkable ability to walk the high wire amid the competing winds of campus liberalism and the pressure from the political McCarthyism of "the Red Scare." Famously, he himself signed a McCarthy era loyalty oath while defending the right of colleagues to abstain.

Kerr—who died in 2003 at the age of ninety-two—is remembered for two landmark efforts that laid out both a detailed blueprint and a lofty vision for the role that a universal system of higher education could play in American life. The blueprint came in 1960, as Kerr spearheaded the drafting of a California Master Plan for Higher Education that would be adopted as a model across much of America. Sparked by awareness of the baby boom that was about to swamp the state's existing system, the California master plan was ambitious in offering every citizen access to higher education, without economic barriers—yet it also acknowledged differing abilities and interests among this surge of new students. Kerr's solution was a tiered system in which the elite research universities—the main Berkeley campus and the University of California–Los Angeles to the fast-growing south—would admit the top high school students, with a middle tier of California State Universities with new campuses in growing population centers like San Diego and Irvine, and community colleges that would be open to all and could feed their most ambitious graduates into the universities.

At the time of the plan's adoption in 1960, California was already a beacon of expanding opportunity; about 45 percent of its young people in the eighteen-to-twenty-two age bracket were attending college, compared to about 25 percent of the rest of the nation. While in-state students paid relatively minor fees for non-academic costs, the master plan "reaffirm[ed] the long established principle that state colleges and the University of California shall be free to all residents of the state."

This Era of Good Feeling in the otherwise fraught politics of higher education in America masked a foundational question that might have been seen as largely academic amid the optimistic New Frontier of incoming president John F. Kennedy but which would eventually drive a painful wedge into the heart of American politics. While the nation had universally accepted the idea of K-12 education for all, its views on college were more complicated—a hangover, perhaps, from the long-time opinion of Ivy League presidents that a rigorous and meaningful higher education was intended for the few.

This juggling act by Kerr and the other postwar gurus of college expansion aimed to provide equality of opportunity, or potential access, within a system where the best outcomes awaited students with the most merit. It's fitting that social critics invented a new word— "meritocracy"—in 1958, right as Kerr was drafting California's master plan. Surprisingly, the public intellectuals such as Hannah Arendt or the British sociologist and satirist Michael Dunlop Young who first coined the term also understood the negative context of a meritocracy that would become more widely accepted in the twenty-first century—as a system prone to elite manipulation, with serious social consequences for the left behind.

But the Clark Kerrs of the world embraced the notion of merit in higher education without irony or concern. The French economist Thomas Piketty, author of the income-inequality bible, *Capital in the Twenty-First Century*, argues that a fluke of history—the crushing of inherited wealth and the anti-rich sentiments of the Great Depression, compounded by World War II—led to this period in which success was seen not as inheritance but the payoff for hard work and study. Awash in prosperity, no one worried about a future in which the fantasy of merit-based success became entrenched, but the equality of opportunity needed for a real system of merit would disappear.

In April 1963, Kerr delivered a series of lectures at Harvard that before year's end were published as a book titled *The Uses of the University*. The lectures are noteworthy both as a vision for the future but also as a public acknowledgment of the frenetic changes that had occurred in the previous two decades. The modern campus was now a focal point for the new postwar America—both as a driver of upward mobility for its young people and the innovation that a booming economy and an unrivaled world superpower required. Although he didn't use the exact phrase, Kerr essentially laid out the connection between the best and the brightest who emerged from campuses such as Berkeley and a new and powerful feature of modern life: a knowledge economy. Wrote Kerr: "What the railroads did for the second half of the last century, and the automobile for the first half of this century, may be done for the second half of this century by the knowledge industry: that is, to serve as the focal point for national growth."

The central role that universities played in this new kind of empire inspired Kerr to brand it with a new phrase: "the multiversity." He paid considerable attention to the role of a university president such as himself in this brave new world, describing college leaders as wise mediators between "a delicate balance of interests" involving not just the students and faculty on campus but a plethora of politicians, donors, and corporations.

Not everyone applauded Kerr's speech. Back in Berkeley, a university librarian named Hal Draper, who was a leading socialist, criticized the analogy that made higher education sound like a factory in which students were the widgets and the newly named military-industrial complex was the chief investor.

In those last final months of "Camelot" optimism before JFK's assassination in November 1963, few could have imagined that at that moment the hard, idealistic morality of the younger generation was rising, that Kerr's frictionless world of savvy compromise was crumbling, or that the politicization of college in America was about to begin. Clark Kerr's machine was already making odd rumbling noises, but the explosion was still a year off.

Back on the East Coast, Don Balfour was entering his forties around the time that the postwar college boom that he'd helped to initiate reached its zenith. Ironically, even as he stayed in the government-dominated D.C. region, he'd never really made a career in the field of his college major, international relations. Instead, he quickly saw an opportunity tied closely to the other major component of the G.I. Bill, the mortgage breaks for veterans that fueled a U.S. housing boom in the late 1940s and '50s. Balfour started a long and successful career as a builder, involved in the rise of Washington's suburbs like Silver Spring.

Balfour died in 2009. On a winter's night a dozen years later, I spoke with his children, Brad and Marla. We relived the legend of their dad's pluck in 1944, but I also wanted to talk about his life in the postwar world, and theirs. And about that American Dream of knowledge as the way to do better than one's parents.

"It was just kind of a given," said Brad, noting that—while it took some time—both he and Marla greatly pleased their father by earning graduate degrees. They said their dad lived a life of the mind and started encouraging them to do the same at an early age, with piles of puzzle books and math shortcuts. "At the dinner table, he would get the Mensa magazine"—from the high-IQ organization—"and start reading off the questions, and ask you to sit down and figure them out."

That level of preschool college prep wouldn't be unfamiliar to today's parents, but there was another nugget buried in Don Balfour's American life. When his hometown of Washington erupted in violent riots after the Reverend Martin Luther King Jr.'s assassination in April 1968, many whites fled the city for the suburbs. But Balfour went in the other direction. Midcareer, he switched from the building business to selling insurance, and he set up shop near 14th Street NW and Rhode Island Avenue NW, not far from the epicenter of the riots. "He sold a lot of insurance to people who otherwise couldn't get regular insurance," his son Don recalled. "People asked him, 'Why don't you move to the suburbs?' He replied simply that it was important for him to serve that community."

The first American to benefit from a taxpayer-funded free college education felt the urge to give something back.

CHAPTER 3

WHY THE KENT STATE MASSACRE
RAISED YOUR TUITION

On February 1, 1960, just thirty-two days into a bright new decade, an eighteen-year-old college freshman known as Ezell Blair Jr. did something radical that would change the world. But before he did, this son of an African American high school teacher in North Carolina wanted to make sure he had one thing: his mom and dad's permission.

"If my mother and father said 'no,' then I wasn't going," the man who later changed his name to Jibreel Khazan would say. In fact, he said he voted against the audacious plan for four Black undergraduates at North Carolina A&T to sit in at a segregated Woolworth lunch counter—but he was outvoted and, in the end, went along with it. "I had fears of the unknown. I'm not going to tell anybody I was a brave guy, because I wasn't."

Khazan is far too modest. The reality is that he stood at the vanguard of a new generation of Black youth in America—just as eager as their white counterparts to chase the American Dream, but unable to ignore the contradictions of a superpower selling itself to the world as a beacon of democracy while maintaining apartheid in the former Confederacy. Yet there was a kind of a space-age optimism embedded in this burgeoning freedom movement, as Khazan later recalled the civics teacher who'd told him en route to college: "We're preparing you for the day you have civil rights."

"We wanted to find out if what was written in the Constitution and the Bill of Rights was true," Khazan said in 2020, echoing a familiar refrain of young people raised in the afterglow of World War II. "It looked good on paper, but in reality it wasn't true for all of us." At 4:30 p.m. on that Monday, the future Khazan was joined by schoolmates David Richmond, Franklin McCain, and Joseph McNeil as they sat down at the stainless-steel lunch counter and asked a white waitress for a cup of coffee. "We don't serve Negroes here," the woman replied, but the manager didn't ask them to leave. So more students returned to sit in the next day.

The Greensboro protests electrified campuses across the nation—initially at other HBCUs in the Deep South but also as a source of wonder and inspiration at a growing number of predominantly white universities. The protests spread in a matter of weeks to other Southern cities, including Nashville, where a pastor named James Lawson had launched a workshop to teach protest tactics to eager young college students. Lawson knew of what he taught; he'd served a year in prison as a conscientious objector to the Korean War, then traveled to India where he studied the nonviolent protest techniques of the late independence leader Mohandas Gandhi. Working with future icons of the 1960s civil rights movement like eventual congressman John Lewis, Diane Nash, and James Bevil, the Lawson-connected Nashville Student Movement desegregated lunch counters in the Tennessee city by May and—perhaps more important—sparked a conference at which leaders from a web of college campuses agreed to form the Student Non-Violent Coordinating Committee, or SNCC.

Lynne Hollander Savio was an undergraduate at Pennsylvania's Bryn Mawr College when the Southern sit-ins occurred. Prior to

Greensboro, young Lynne Hollander had been only mildly interested in politics, but soon she and her classmates were protesting at a nearby Woolworth and working for a student-senate resolution in support of the burgeoning Black student movement. "When the Black students sat down at the lunch counter," she recalled sixty years later, "we were like, 'Oh, wow. Here is something that is moral—here is something that is real and you can care deeply about.' It was like lighting a fire."

Hollander, like many of her peers, grew up a seeker. Raised on the west side of the Bronx, her parents—college-educated Jews who'd been young socialists, then New Deal Democrats—made her education their top priority, as did most parents in her working-class neighborhood, which was divided fairly equally between Catholics and Jews. But she found the elite, somewhat WASP-y Bryn Mawr to be unsatisfying, and she left after her sophomore year.

"I left and I went to Boulder for the summer with some friends and there I met a lot of cool hippie, beatnik-y people," she recalled. Hollander followed her inner muse to New York and finally west to San Francisco, the capital of beatnik poetry and rebel culture of the late 1950s and early '60s. She felt the gravitational pull of "what was happening with [Jack] Kerouac and [Allen] Ginsburg, that was the vibe."

She finally decided it was time to finish college and enrolled in Berkeley in the fall of 1964, with little sense of the political earthquake that was just weeks away. It's only striking with the jaded wisdom of the 2020s to look back on how easy it was for young people to move in and out of top universities without worrying about fraught admissions or taking out a five-figure loan. Hollander got the out-of-state tuition waived and recalls being charged less than one hundred dollars in fees. "And you got an apartment for sixty to eighty dollars a month—it was easy to live," she added. "You could work for a few hours a week."

Berkeley also put Hollander on a collision course with a shy yet oddly charismatic student leader who years later would become her husband: Mario Savio. Born in Manhattan on December 8, 1942—or, one year and one day after Pearl Harbor—Savio was very much a child of World War II. Indeed, his dad—a Sicilian immigrant—was off fighting for the U.S. Army during his infancy. But more than the war, or the role of his strong-willed grandfather—who, ironically, had supported Mussolini's rise in Italy before coming to America—young Mario's outlook on life would be shaped by his encounters with the Catholic Church, and what he later called "a somewhat dreamy sense of religiosity." Years later, after Savio became famous and had rejected Catholicism and its rituals like the confession booth, he claimed to have developed "a secularized liberation theology"—a mission to uplift the poor and oppose modern materialism.

Like so many children of the 1950s, Savio—whose parents both regretted not being able to afford college for themselves—was pushed hard to become the first in his family to earn a diploma. He probably didn't need much of a shove, though, because young Mario—despite struggling to overcome a stutter—was brilliant, and especially at math and science, right as America was having its mass freak-out over Sputnik. He was a national finalist in the Westinghouse Science Talent Search (he'd later criticize the search as "preparedness for the Cold War") and high school valedictorian, and attended a nearby Catholic institution, Manhattan College, because it offered a full scholarship, before transferring to the public and fully free Queens College. Increasingly, though, Savio felt caught between his science classes and his political beliefs. A summer project building a laundry for a poverty-plagued village in Mexico, after which he spoke out against "the socially unjust situation," fueled his new trajectory. Still, when Savio's family relocated west and he enrolled in the also-tuition-free University of California main campus at Berkeley in the fall of 1963, few would imagine that he was on a collision course with the colossus of the modern American university.

Hollander understands the yearnings of her late husband because in many ways she felt them herself, growing up not far from him in a nearby Bronx neighborhood and also taking a circuitous route to sunny California and to Berkeley in the early 1960s. She spoke in an interview for this book about her "very alienated generation, and we had this sense growing up in the '50s of seeing the whole Organization Man, The Man in the Gray Flannel Suit, 'plastics'—the famous jab at business careers in 1967's *The Graduate*—"and is that what was aiming for us? I think there was a deep hunger in the people of my generation—or a significant number, anyway—for something to believe in, to make our lives not gray."

Lynne Hollander wasn't alone in sensing that things were changing rapidly on campus, as the mission-driven, Depression-reared G.I.s of the late 1940s gave way to a new wave of younger students raised in postwar prosperity. At a bulging public institution in the American Heartland, the University of Michigan, Tom Hayden, the editor of the campus newspaper, found himself increasingly drawn toward political activism. The son of a white-collar accountant for Chrysler, perhaps mindful of his own youthful rejection of the Catholic Church, Hayden reflected in the mid-1960s that campus radicals "come from middle- to upper-middle-class professional homes. They were born with status and affluence as facts of life, not goals to be striven for. In their upbringing, their parents stressed the rights of children to question and make judgments, producing perhaps the first generation both affluent and independent of mind."

The new leisure time and the ethos and popularity of liberal arts education offered something that had come only with great difficulty to previous generations—freedom of thought. The result would be a new kind of politics, a revolution that is still felt today in ways the movement's founders could never have imagined. The movement that came to be called The New Left united many of the vague stirrings caused by the psychic whipsaw of Cold War anxiety and the comfort-craving materialism of the 1950s. "The government lied to people and this image that we were fed in school—our great forefathers and this great democracy and we're the greatest country in the world, blah blah—when you're confronted with other things," said Hollander, referring to segregation and McCarthyism. "Plus the insecurity of feeling that nuclear war might break out at any time, and these crazy people thinking you could duck under your desk. All of these things came together."

They came together in one of the most remarkable documents of the twentieth century: the Port Huron Statement. It was the foundational work of a new group called the Students for a Democratic Society, or SDS, which ironically arose from the ashes of a leftist youth group backed by the powerful United Auto Workers Union, only to reject the labor-driven brand of liberalism that had defined the Industrial Revolution. The first leader of the SDS was the University of Michigan's Hayden. In June 1962, he and his fellow founders of the SDS gathered for a retreat at a UAW summer camp in Port Huron, Michigan, north of Detroit, where they drafted a statement that shunned the old fights over communism in favor of a new politics that rejected both middle-class conformity and Cold War angst. Most significantly, it identified American college campuses as the nexus of a new political and social revolution.

"We are people of this generation, bred in at least modest comfort, housed now in universities, looking uncomfortably to the world we inherit," the Hayden-drafted Port Huron Statement begins famously. "When we were kids the United States was the wealthiest and strongest country in the world; the only one with the atom bomb, the least scarred by modern war, an initiator of the United Nations that we thought would distribute Western influence throughout the world." Their childhood bred complacency, the statement argues, which would be shattered by growing awareness of the destructive power of the atom bomb and the moral indefensibility of racism, especially segregation.

The 25,700-word statement embraces a newish concept that it labeled "participatory democracy," which would give individuals more of a say, in politics and over their own lives. It was a "New Left" because in pursuit of progressive goals, it rejected the collective action of worker-based early-twentieth-century leftist movements for a kind of personal freedom, made possible—ironically—by the liberation of union-aided postwar affluence, and boosted by the free thought of liberal education. It would have been impossible to predict from a 1962 perspective how the desires for personal freedom might someday metastasize—steered by the generations coming up right behind them—into things like open-carry gun ownership or refusing to wear a mask during a pandemic. At the peak of JFK's soon-to-be-shattered "Camelot," participatory democracy instead was seen as the vehicle that would finally bring about goals like integration, peaceful use of atomic energy, and an end to overseas imperialism.

In other ways, the Port Huron Statement is a kind of a yin to the yang of Kerr's Uses of the University lectures. While the University of California president saw his modern "multiversity" as the humming factory of a knowledge economy that was making the United States the essential world superpower, Hayden and the SDS saw the university as the last place where a democratic America could be saved—if students and faculty were allowed to convert their knowledge into political power.

With labor unions compromised by the Cold War and other key groups such as southern Blacks struggling on the margins, the statement argued that the nation's booming universities were now the last best hope for progressivism as "the only mainstream institution that is open to participation by individuals of nearly any viewpoint." College campuses, it continued, could be incubators of democracy, exactly as the New Deal technocrats of the Truman Commission era had imagined—but a true version of democracy, not the corrupted Cold War model. The Port Huron Statement urged that both students and faculty "wrest control of the educational process from the administrative bureaucracy" and integrate more real-world issues into the curriculum—the 1950s notion of college as "general education," but on steroids. Students could use the new American way of college as "a base for their assault upon the loci of power."

This was a radical notion. In the short term, this key argument of the Port Huron Statement set the stage for a decade of youthful political energy and revolutionary ideas unlike anything that America has seen before . . . or since. Needless to say, the so-called Establishment had no idea what was coming. The newspapers of 1962 didn't bother to dismiss the statement as the sophomoric ramblings of idealistically naive youth, because the newspapers didn't even think this was news. Only when the seeds that were planted near the shores of Lake Huron began to bloom on campuses from Berkeley to Columbia would the postwar Establishment begin to wonder whether its great experiment in taxpayer-subsidized liberal education and free thought had run amok and created a monster. The coming battles that would be waged from the streets of Chicago to Woodstock Nation were only the first shots of a war that has lasted until today. The youth power of the student movement sparked by groups like SNCC and the SDS gave rise to a powerful opposing force—the backlash that gave voice to Ronald Reagan, then Rush Limbaugh, then Donald Trump.

A KEY TURNING POINT IN THIS EPIC CHAIN OF EVENTS WAS A CAMpaign called Mississippi Freedom Summer that took place in 1964, a joint effort involving the now-flourishing SNCC as well as Dr. Martin Luther King Jr.'s Southern Christian Leadership Conference and established groups like the NAACP and the Congress for Racial Equality, or CORE. Under the charismatic leadership of Bob Moses, a brilliant high school teacher with a master's degree in philosophy from Harvard, the Freedom Summer aimed to swarm the state that in the mid-1960s had the lowest percentage of Black voters registered. The project recruited kids, mostly white, from top universities all over the country, in the hopes that white volunteers might be a buffer against the violence that Black civil rights activists typically encountered. About one hundred such students were expected, but closer to one thousand underwent the training in nonviolence and organizing at a rural Ohio campus. One of them, not surprisingly, was Mario Savio.

During his first full year on the Berkeley campus, Savio had been increasingly active in a group called University Friends of SNCC, a chance to address some of the stirrings about poverty and repression he'd felt during his summer in Mexico. Through the group, Savio created a tutoring program for African American kids in nearby Oakland and then got arrested for the very first time as part of an interracial coalition protesting hiring discrimination at the Sheraton Palace Hotel in San Francisco. In SNCC, Savio finally found the meaning and purpose he'd been seeking from the college experience, writing later that "you're just drawn . . . like a moth to light." Just weeks after his arrest, Savio volunteered for the Freedom Summer project and was approved, despite organizers' qualms about his earnest but subdued nature.

Before he even arrived in Mississippi, Savio learned the shocking news that three of the Freedom Summer activists—two of the white participants, student Andrew Goodman and organizer Michael Schwerner, and Black Mississippi activist James Chaney—had vanished after being released from a jail near Philadelphia, Mississippi. Foul play was suspected. Still, the twenty-one-year-old Savio was more determined than before to join the project, and he would be in Holmes County, Mississippi, trying to register Black voters at the courthouse and teaching kids in a Freedom School by the time the bodies of the three murdered civil rights workers were discovered in an earthen dam.

These existential threats soon reached Savio himself, as he walked with a Black activist and a white activist down a street in Macomb, Mississippi, and two members of the local Ku Klux Klan jumped from a car, swinging clubs. Savio was hit in the shoulder but not hurt, but his white colleague sustained more serious injuries. By the time he returned to Berkeley, Savio felt the things he'd seen in Mississippi—especially the constant threat of violence against the Black community there—compelled him to remain active in the cause.

Neither Savio nor anyone else who was politically active on the Berkeley campus was ready for the surprise that greeted them that fall. Although overt political activity had long been banned on campus—a hangover from McCarthyism and the acquiescence of the "Quiet Generation"—there was a row of political tables just outside the university's main gate, on Bancroft Street. But a growing uproar over student activism—including the Sheraton Palace arrests and protests at the Republican National Convention that nominated Barry Goldwater in San Francisco that summer—led to a belated discovery that the Bancroft site was actually university property, which led to a ban on the tables. This united everyone from campus socialists to the Young Republicans in anger. Their rage became a movement: the Berkeley Free Speech Movement.

Apparently, Clark Kerr's list of uses of the university didn't include students engaging in politics. The University of California president had made clear in a speech on the UC-Davis campus that spring that civil disobedience of the kind moving north from Mississippi was not compatible with liberal education. Kerr said such protesters "may be paying merely lip service to democratic ideals while in actuality serving the cause of anarchy or some other cause."

But on the Berkeley campus, events moved rapidly in the fall of

1964. A so-called United Front of political groups objecting to the ban—covering the entire spectrum from right to left, including Savio's University Friends of SNCC—held a series of protests and sit-ins and attempted to set up tables as an act of civil disobedience. The momentous events of October 1, 1964, were a turning point. The university launched disciplinary action against eight students who were defying the ban, which caused another protest, which caused Berkeley to call in police to break up the event. Jack Weinberg, a twenty-four-year-old math dropout who'd remained an activist on campus and spoke at the October 1 rally, was dragged, limp, into a police car—which was promptly surrounded by a few dozen students, then several hundred. Over a number of hours, a remarkable scene ensued as Savio and other protesters—taking off their shoes, so as not to be charged with vandalism—climbed atop the immobilized cruiser and delivered fiery speeches. For the first time, the world was seeing that political and social unrest among college youth wasn't just a fringe, but instead that these radical stirrings were widely felt.

The true highlight of the movement, however, came just over two months later, in a speech delivered by Savio. The young man who'd struggled to overcome a persistent stutter since grade school and had been seen as possibly too milquetoast by the Freedom Summer organizers just months earlier had now found his calling and his voice. The vision Savio would offer was in sharp contrast to Kerr's "multiversity" where students emerged from the assembly line. Rather, in the words of Savio's biographer Robert Cohen, "there was a new political reality in which university students had to be seen as citizens with rights rather than as children in need of guidance."

On December 2, 1964, several thousand students showed up to sit in at Sproul Hall, the main administration building. Not long after singer Joan Baez had performed "Blowin' in the Wind," Savio stood on the steps and delivered the speech that would define a decade of student activism in America. He seemed to be especially triggered by a comment from Kerr in which the university president spoke as if he were the CEO of a big corporation. The crystallizing critique of the American way of college—the one that had been laid out in Kerr's lectures and countered by Hal Draper as a "knowledge factory" in service of a militaristic empire—poured out with anger and emotion.

Savio said, "If this is a firm, and if the Board of Regents are the board of directors, and if President Kerr in fact is the manager, then I tell you something—the faculty are a bunch of employees and we're the raw material!" Here, Savio—his accent still with traces of his native Bronx—stammered slightly. "But we're a bunch of raw materials that don't mean to be—have any process upon us. Don't mean to be made into any product! Don't mean—don't mean to end up being bought by some clients of the university, be they the government, be they industry, be they organized labor, be they anyone! We're human beings!"

Then, famously:

And that—that brings me to the second mode of civil disobedience. There's a time when the operation of the machine becomes so odious, makes you so sick at heart that you can't take part! You can't even passively take part! And you've got to put your bodies upon the gears and upon the wheels, upon the levers, upon all the apparatus—and you've got to make it stop! And you've got to indicate to the people who run it, to the people who own it—that unless you're free the machine will be prevented from working at all!!

That night, following Savio's speech the police literally dragged protesters out of Sproul Hall, bouncing them down the hard steps. But the young organizer's point had been made. The protesters won overwhelming support from Berkeley's faculty. Soon, Kerr and the other administrators largely backed down, giving new freedoms to student activists to speak out, which in weeks they began to funnel into a fast-growing protest movement against the Vietnam War.

The battle for the soul of the new American university had been joined. Few would argue that the ability of these still-fast-growing high-rise campuses to produce intelligent citizens was something the world had never really seen before. But would Kerr's "knowledge economy," backed by Big Business and the political establishment, continue to use the university on behalf of American superiority? Or would college become "the loci" of a moral awakening that would undo the military-industrial complex, as envisioned by the Port Huron Statement?

The events that flowed in the immediate aftermath of the Berkeley Free Speech Movement—a dramatic narrative in their own right, including the massive anti-Vietnam War protests, the infamous 1967 attempt to "levitate" the Pentagon, the 1968 student strike and take-over at Columbia, the "police riot" against demonstrators at that same year's Democratic National Convention in Chicago—certainly looked and felt like a revolution at the time, even if in hindsight it was more of a short-lived supernova.

The conflict in Vietnam—and the prospect for male college students that they would be drafted to fight in the deadly conflict once their student deferments expired—was a big driver, but as the unrest expanded, other aspects of modern college also came under fire. Some struck at the heart of the relationship between universities and the Cold War military-industrial complex, such as the October 1967 sit-in by University of Wisconsin students that aimed to block campus recruiters for Dow Chemical. The protest against Dow, who made the napalm used to firebomb villages in Vietnam, devolved into a riot after Madison police officers fired tear gas at peaceful demonstrators.

And increasingly, the definition of "liberal education" came under fire from students who believed the current curriculum reinforced white, Western values—a complaint that led to passionate protests for Black studies, more of a focus on non-Western cultures, and—eventually—programs around gender equity. At what is now San Francisco State University, a group called the Third World Liberation Front led a five-month strike, marked by violent clashes on campus with police, over increasing both African American studies and the number of Black professors and students. The movement, copied on other campuses from coast to coast and reflecting trends in the broader society, like the Black Power movement and increasing Black separatism, can be seen in retrospect as the earliest stirrings of what's now known as "identity politics."

That unrest would occur on a campus such as San Francisco State—once a small teachers' college that was expanding rapidly with middle-class students and would soon become a full-fledged urban university, a common evolution in the 1960s—was fitting. The heyday of campus protest also marked the height of the government's commitment to an expansive, taxpayer-funded role in public education. The first wave of baby boomers—those born in 1946, right after the war—hit campuses in the fall of 1964, the semester that had produced the Berkeley Free Speech Movement. Just from 1950 to 1965, the number of undergraduates at public four-year universities nearly tripled, and public universities that had once educated about half of all undergraduates at the end of World War II saw their share rise steadily to 59 percent.

Although the popular mythology of the 1960s focuses on the action at elite campuses like Columbia, or the children of wealthy executives who joined radical groups like the bomb-manufacturing Weather Underground, the role of these fast-growing public campuses in radicalizing the kids of culturally and politically conservative Middle America is a forgotten flashpoint.

As chronicled by education historian Kenneth J. Heineman, the growth on some public campuses was explosive. At Michigan State University in East Lansing, administrators embarked on the largest on-campus dorm construction in the nation as undergraduate enrollment soared from 15,000 in 1950 to about 38,000 by 1965—aided by a virtually open admissions policy and low tuition. Many of these booming public campuses had started with a focus on teaching or engineering only to shift sharply toward liberal education after World War II. MSU was no exception; over the course of the 1960s, students majoring in social sciences or liberal arts soared from 20 percent to 54 percent.

Ironically, the federal government's interest in hard research, especially for the military, was paying for all these new dorms and liberal course offerings. Under Michigan State's Republican and staunchly anti-Communist president of that era, John Hannah, MSU saw a whopping 69 percent of its overall appropriations covered by federal taxpayers. Most significantly, Hannah's MSU Advisory Group hired one thousand people after the Eisenhower administration tasked it in the 1950s with remaking the government security forces in Vietnam; in 1955, the university was even involved in shipping weapons like grenade launchers and tear-gas canisters to our South Vietnam allies, and the MSU group worked closely overseas with the CIA. In a 1955 speech, university president Hannah had said, "Our colleges and universities must be regarded as bastions of our defense, as essential to the preservation of our country and our way of life as supersonic bombers, nuclear-powered submarines, and intercontinental ballistic missiles."

But a decade after Hannah uttered those words, this remarkable contradiction—a U.S. war machine underwriting the cost for thousands of young Americans to attend college virtually for free, to major in liberal subjects such as philosophy and then question the military, and authority in general—was, inevitably, imploding. The wave of campus protest was accelerating right at the exact time that Washington was—amid a flurry of social-welfare laws enacted at the height of Lyndon

Johnson's "Great Society" agenda—passing the Higher Education Act of 1965. The act was a tentative start down the road envisioned by the 1946–47 Truman Commission of a wider role for the federal government beyond the Pentagon or atomic R&D. It expanded federal programs such as student loans and work-study arrangements to bring college to more low-income families, and also dangled money for universities to expand their course offerings. It seemed an endorsement of the optimistic, if technocratic, vision backed by America's Clark Kerrs and John Hannahs.

But as student unrest became front-page news in 1965 and beyond, a powerful backlash was brewing. A new generation of conservative politicians, running under a banner of "law and order," was coming to question the basic assumptions of the so-called Liberal Hour in America that peaked with LBJ's Great Society. The consensus around taxpayer support for higher education and a liberal curriculum would start to collapse. At the vanguard of this movement was a former Hollywood film star who'd become a rabid anti-Communist and an outspoken opponent of government social-welfare programs such as Medicare: Ronald Reagan.

REAGAN'S POLITICAL EMERGENCE HAPPENED—COINCIDENTALLY, AT first—just as the Berkeley Free Speech Movement was peaking in the autumn of 1964. That October, Reagan delivered a nationally televised endorsement of GOP presidential nominee Barry Goldwater called "A Time for Choosing." Soon, wealthy GOP power brokers were urging the former actor to launch a long-shot 1966 challenge to incumbent California governor Pat Brown. Brown was an icon of the domestically liberal Cold War consensus, and had strongly supported Kerr in the University of California expansion. But Reagan's unlikely crusade seized on two seemingly different political earthquakes—the ongoing student unrest and emergence of a youth counterculture at Berkeley, and the July 1965 Black uprising that burned through the Watts section of Los Angeles and left thirty-four dead—to forge a winning narrative about moral decline and the need for law and order.

On May 12, 1966, Reagan bounded onto the stage at San Francisco's Cow Palace arena—the same spot where Goldwater had famously accepted the GOP nod and declared that "extremism in defense of liberty is no vice!"—to deliver a major address on what he dubbed "the morality gap." By now, the counterculture that Savio's speech had foreseen had fully sprouted at Berkeley and other campuses, signified by longer hair, wilder clothes, and the popularity in the Bay Area of still-underground bands like the Grateful Dead and Jefferson Airplane, as well as a small but much more radical successor to the FSM called the Filthy Speech Movement that had shocked California's conservatives.

Reagan spoke of how "a small minority of beatniks, radicals, and filthy speech advocates have brought such shame to and such a loss of confidence in a great university" and said that the failure of Kerr and other administrators to crack down on the Free Speech Movement had led to a rapid decline in values. If the events at Berkeley hadn't yet fostered widespread moral panic, the Gipper worked hard to create it. Using language that would have shocked a 1966 audience, he related a tale about a campus rally–turned-party where "the nude torsos of men and women were portrayed from time to time in suggestive positions and movements" as the smell of marijuana lingered in the air, adding: "There were indications of other happenings that cannot be mentioned here."

Asking, "What in heaven's name does academic freedom have to do with rioting, with anarchy, with attempts to destroy the primary purpose of the university which is to educate our young people?" Reagan called for public hearings into what he called communism and sexual promiscuity at UC and a clean sweep of its leadership. This wasn't the only cornerstone of Reagan's first gubernatorial campaign—he also, in the wake of the riots in L.A., railed against "welfare bums"—but in many ways Berkeley and Watts were part of one big fear campaign. Reagan argued that white middle-class values—harsher critics might call it white supremacy—were suddenly under assault. In going hard after the campus "hippies" he described as "someone who looks like Tarzan, walks like Jane, and smells like Cheetah," the future 40th president of the United States was firing the very first shots of what only much later would be called America's "culture wars." On November 8, 1966, Reagan defeated Brown by nearly 1 million votes, a landslide.

Reagan's election in many ways ended the post–World War consensus that higher education should be liberal in outlook and accessible to everyone. Almost immediately, he made good on his implied promise to force Kerr out as the UC president, and as protest movements grew ever more radical he also delivered on the harsh crackdown he'd promised voters. That culminated on "Bloody Thursday"—May 15, 1969—when the governor dispatched state troopers to Berkeley who fired birdshot and even live rounds at students who'd created a "People's Park" on campus property. One young man, James Rector, was killed. Five days later came a shocking helicopter tear-gas attack against a rally on campus. But the Reagan move that continues to echo more than a half century later was his push to end free tuition, the bedrock principle of the postwar college revolution.

In fact, Reagan's very first act upon becoming governor was a proposal to impose tuition in the UC system—$400 a semester at the top-tier universities and $200 at the mid-level schools—with the state's savings to go as a tax refund for the middle-class voters who'd just elected him. The numbers seem ridiculously small when compared to today's five-figure college bills, but if enacted, UC students—who already paid a grab bag of fees that averaged $220 a semester—would have been suddenly paying the highest public-university costs in the

United States, $1,240 for a full year. UC's lobbyists, however, were able to kill the plan in Sacramento. So Reagan got creative, spending his next eight years in office eating away at the UC system with ever-higher student registration fees. By the time he left office at the end of 1974, these fees made a mockery of the state's no-tuition pledge (at a time when the average annual cost of attending a four-year public university was $510, according to the National Center for Education Statistics). He also used his bully pulpit in the nation's largest and fastest-growing state to change the way that voters felt about college and their tax dollars. At a February 28, 1967, news conference, Reagan said famously that the main purpose of college should be workforce development, that "taxpayers shouldn't subsidize intellectual curiosity." This radical notion—the 180-degree opposite of what postwar leaders had argued in the aftermath of Hitler and of Hiroshima—was several years ahead of the rest of the nation.

America would soon catch up.

THE EXPLOSIVE GROWTH OF KENT STATE UNIVERSITY, SITUATED near the belching tire smoke of Akron and drawing the offspring of working-class boomtowns like Cleveland and Youngstown, was typical of the 1960s. A small teachers' college until the late 1950s, Kent State moved in 1959 to offer doctoral degrees, took money from the Pentagon for a research institute that designed liquid crystals that helped the Army trace enemy tank movements along the Ho Chi Minh Trail in Vietnam, and saw its enrollment skyrocket from 5,000 in 1954 to more than 21,000 by 1966.

Many of those 16,000 extra kids were the offspring of Ohio's thriving factory towns who'd already learned to question authority from an unexpected source—their dads, who'd in many cases walked the picket lines in chaotic and sometimes violent labor unrest that spread across

America in the 1930s and '40s. Most families in Akron, the center of the American tire industry, just west of Kent State, were shaped by the dramatic events of 1936, when thousands of workers staged sit-down strikes or walked picket lines in the midst of the Great Depression to unionize the big plants like Goodyear Tire and Rubber. Now, undergrads like Alan Canfora, whose father was a local leader in the United Auto Workers who'd clashed with the tire company's Pinkerton guards, arrived at Kent in the late '60s feeling that protesting The Establishment and supporting liberal causes like Black civil rights were in their blood.

"The New Deal had saved my family," Thomas Grace, who became Canfora's roommate in the fall of 1968 when Canfora transferred to Kent State, said, recalling the government coal deliveries and his uncle's work in the Civilian Conservation Corps that were now the stuff of family legend. Grace's grandfathers—on his mom's side, an immigrant from Slovakia—had both worked on the railroads in upstate New York. His parents, though, were college-educated. And a diploma was their only demand of all four children growing up near Buffalo. Grace chose to head for Ohio because Kent State's history department has an outstanding reputation for teaching the Civil War.

The roommates Grace and Canfora were torn in the tumultuous year of 1968 between the New Deal, trade-union liberalism of their parents—when an icon of that movement, Hubert Humphrey, was the Democratic presidential candidate—and the radicalism that was brewing at Kent State. In the end, neither young man could shake the images from that summer of helmeted police officers in Chicago—under Humphrey ally Mayor Richard Daley—beating up peaceful anti-war protesters. That fall, the two went alone to protest Richard Nixon at a rally in Ohio, but they were drowned out by several hundred rowdier kids from SDS.

"Alan said to me, let's go with these guys!" Grace recalled with a laugh, but he recalls that the SDS's antics—like carrying a coffin around campus and into classrooms to protest the seemingly endless Vietnam conflict—captured the moral outrage he and his peers felt. "There was just a powerful sense of the importance of political work against war and racism," he explained. "They disdained complacency."

But it would be Nixon who was narrowly elected that November. He had borrowed heavily from Reagan's California playbook by centering his campaign around "law and order," punctuated by a TV ad showing bloodied college-aged protesters and youths flashing peace signs as the candidate intoned, "the first American civil right is to be free from domestic violence." The new government's tougher stance against protests—dramatized by trumped-up federal charges against eight leaders of the 1968 Chicago demonstrations—was headed for a collision course with the increasing radicalism of campus groups that inherited the fight from the SDS, which had collapsed due to infighting and a heightened argument over whether violence was needed to bring revolutionary change to America. When Nixon announced on April 30, 1970, that instead of ending the war he would widen the conflict by sending U.S. troops on a mission into neighboring Cambodia, Grace recalled that "it seemed like throwing a match into a dynamite shed."

At first, few Americans were paying much attention to the unrest at Kent State, just one of scores of campuses from coast to coast that erupted that weekend. Nixon himself seemed to throw even more gasoline onto that flaming dynamite shed—and summed up the growing conservative viewpoint that state university students were unworthy ingrates—when he told some civilian employees he encountered after a Pentagon briefing: "You see these bums, you know, blowing up the campuses. Listen, the boys that are on the college campuses today are the luckiest people in the world, going to the greatest universities, and here they are burning up the books . . ."

It was such a turbulent era that events which might have been top-of-the-hour cable-TV news in the twenty-first century—a student rampage that broke store windows on the main street of Kent, a conservative town where many locals detested the constant protests, followed by the burning down of the small Army ROTC building on campus—didn't get a lot of press. They did, however, get the attention of Ohio's ambitious "tough-on-crime" Republican governor, James Rhodes, who blamed Communist influence and said, chillingly, "We are going to eradicate the problem." In an ironic reminder of the ties between the labor movement and the radicalism of its middle-class kids, Rhodes had already activated the state's National Guard to deal with a Teamsters strike, but now he diverted these armed troops to Kent State.

An anti-war rally planned for noon on May 4, 1970, was banned by the university, but Alan Canfora wasn't going to miss it for anything. Just a couple of days earlier, he'd attended the funeral of a childhood friend who'd been killed in combat, and so now he stood in front of about five hundred other protesters and onlookers, waving a black flag. For the first twenty minutes, the events moved slowly to a choreography that probably felt numbingly familiar to veterans of Vietnam-era protests. No one was surprised when the National Guard troops fired tear gas into the gathering, or when some students lobbed the canisters back, or even when the soldiers marched in formation to push protesters up a hill and into a nearby parking lot. No one expected that college life in America was moments away from changing forever.

But at 12:24 p.m., two rows of Guardsmen—suddenly, with no real warning—kneeled down and fired live bullets toward the protest, getting off as many as sixty-seven shots in a thirteen-second barrage. Canfora, who was among the closest to the shooters, dove behind a narrow nearby tree trunk for cover as one bullet tore into his right wrist and several others pinged off the tree. It was then he realized his friend Tom Grace was just ten feet away, bleeding and in pain from a bullet that struck his left ankle, and he yelled at Grace to keep his head down.

But in the parking lot behind them, four students—Allison Krause, Jeffrey Miller, Sandra Scheuer, and William Schroeder—lay dead or dying. The moment would be labeled decades later by documentary filmmakers and others as The Day the Sixties Died.

While tens of thousands of students from coast to coast went on strike, the winds of backlash were stronger. Eleven days after the massacre, white Mississippi State Troopers fired a thirty-second fusillade into dorms at an HBCU, Jackson State University, killing two Black youths. It was telling that students at Ivy League campuses and other universities heavily populated by children of the elite were spared the state-sponsored bloodshed unleashed at the public Kent State or the predominantly Black Jackson State, dramatizing a perception that radicalized working-class kids—especially nonwhites—were what really threatened The Establishment. That same month, a youthful anti-war protest in lower Manhattan was descended on by fist-swinging construction workers from the nearby World Trade Center project in what became known as the Hard Hat Riot. Nixon invited the leaders of their union to the White House and hailed them as if conquering heroes.

A Gallup Poll taken immediately after the May 4 shootings found that 58 percent of Americans blamed the Kent State students for their own deaths and only 11 percent blamed the National Guard that had opened fire upon them. The finding seems shocking today—only 13 percent blamed students in a poll for 2020's fiftieth anniversary—but reflects not only initial misinformation but also sweeping resentment of campus protests by older Americans. The writer Rick Perlstein, in his book *Nixonland*, found that bitter sentiments were given voice right there in Kent by townspeople who chanted "Kent State Four! Should have studied more!" to drown out a memorial event. Others wrote letters to the local paper asking, "Why do they allow these so-called educated punks, who apparently only know how to spell four-lettered words, to run loose on campuses tearing up and destroying that which good men spent years building up?" The feelings were not confined to Kent. At Northwestern University, he wrote, a man in work clothes grabbed an upside-down American flag carried by protesters and screamed: "We will have to kill you. All I can see is a lot of kids blowing a chance I never had."

That cry—in one form or another—would only grow louder and louder over the next fifty years.

Nixon's appeal to what he called "the silent majority" of middle-class, Middle American homeowners who weren't protesting or carrying upside-down American flags would result, in the 1972 election, in the largest presidential landslide ever. Under his watch, the backlash politics of the early 1970s would change the American way of college and crush the egalitarian dreams of the postwar planners. The emotional cries of the angry hardhats and their political protectors like Reagan, Nixon, and Nixon's vice president and "hatchet man," Spiro T. Agnew, would become the intellectual underpinning of a new conservatism.

One particularly influential voice was that of James McGill Buchanan, an ultraconservative economist who would win a Nobel Prize in 1986. Buchanan had a decades-long run as a behind-the-scenes player in movements ranging from the Southern resistance to school integration in the late 1950s to covert U.S. support in the 1970s and '80s for Chilean dictator Augusto Pinochet to the pro-business libertarianism of oil billionaires Charles and David Koch. As documented in Nancy MacLean's award-winning 2018 book *Democracy in Chains*, the right-wing movement funded by the Koch brothers and advised by Buchanan would eventually dominate much of American politics in the twenty-first century, but that was still decades in the future. At the dawn of the 1970s, Buchanan was busy focusing on "the college problem."

In fact, the "college problem" was right in Buchanan's face after he left the familiar confines of his native South to teach at UCLA, just in time for the tumultuous academic year of 1968–69. In the months after his arrival, two activists were murdered on campus in a dispute between rival Black Power groups, a bomber attempted to blow up the economics department over its lack of Black faculty, and the campus was in turmoil over the attempted firing of radical professor Angela Davis. Demanding "law and order," even if that seemed to conflict with his libertarian worldview, Buchanan in 1970 coauthored a book titled *Academia in Anarchy* which—while not a bestseller—did anticipate a radically new deal for American higher ed.

Simply put, Buchanan and his co-author Nicos Devletoglou saw college not as a public good but as "a unique industry," a kind of a callback to Clark Kerr's Uses of the University lectures that must have already seemed from another era. In applying a capitalistic worldview to the American university—that higher education was to train labor for the workforce, not produce free thinkers—they argued that the moral framework of the 1960s made no sense, and that low or, in the case of California, free tuition provided little incentive to keep kids from becoming revolutionaries. "Is it to be wondered," they wrote of the modern undergraduate, "that he treats the whole university setting with disrespect or even contempt?" As Nancy MacLean summarizes: "The cure flowed from the diagnosis. Students should pay full-cost prices, and universities should compete for them as customers. Taxpayers and donors should organize 'as other stockholders do' to monitor their investments." The consequences of such a philosophy would make it harder for low-income students to attend college. It would also establish a framework where the money to pay tuition would be borrowed against future earnings—committing graduates to the service of capitalism.

Other, more powerful players were coming over to Buchanan's cause—particularly Big Business, which had been rattled by the events at Berkeley, Kent State, and elsewhere. In 1971, a prominent Richmond, Virginia, corporate lawyer named Lewis Powell was asked by leaders of the U.S. Chamber of Commerce to assemble a document called "An Attack on (the) American Free Enterprise System," better known as the Powell Memorandum. Powell shared Buchanan's growing alarm over campus protest—arguing in a 1970 speech that radical professors, especially in the social sciences, abused academic freedom and nurtured in their students the idea that America is "a wholly selfish, materialistic, racist and repressive society."

In the Powell Memo—which was intended to be confidential but was leaked after Nixon appointed Powell to the U.S. Supreme Court in October 1971—he called the campus-based New Left "the single most dynamic source" of an assault on capitalism. The memo runs through a now-familiar litany of conservative indictments of the college environment at the dawn of the 1970s, but also complains about the growing impact in the wider American society as graduates "seek opportunities to change a system which they have been taught to distrust"—as journalists, or by working in education, or by entering government or elective politics. Unlike Buchanan, Powell avoided the low-tuition issue but instead urged business leaders to use their influence and wealth to push for "balance" that would put more conservatives on the faculty at their alma maters, or to bring more pro-business outside speakers to campus.

The new corporate-friendly environment that Powell conjured up—with outposts of conservative ideas that were becoming known as "think tanks," a right-wing media infrastructure in print, on the radio, and maybe even on TV, and wealthy capitalists funding on-campus programs around the promotion of free enterprise—must have seemed fantastical to those who saw the confidential memo in the early 1970s when it was written. A half century later, academics still debate how influential the Powell Memo actually was. But a quick look at the twenty-first-century landscape—populated by the Heritage Foundation, Rush Limbaugh, Fox News, and the flow of cash from the Koch brothers to the economics department at Florida State—suggests the seeds planted then by Buchanan, Powell, and their allies bore a bitter fruit.

But these ideas wouldn't fully flower right away. Baby-boom births didn't hit their peak until 1956—which means that the largest potential freshman class wasn't arriving until 1974. Despite the political discomfort, college enrollment was still growing in the early 1970s—albeit not at the moon-launch pace of the 1950s and '60s—and, partly as a result of a decade of protests, aggressive efforts to make campuses more diverse were paying off in rising Black and female student populations.

College remained the only slightly tarnished American Dream in the 1970s. Recall that even Reagan—for all his political popularity and charisma—was never able to fully follow through on his threats to impose tuition at the University of California during his eight years in office. Meanwhile, campus activism—which never fully disappears—declined in the early years of the decade for a variety of reasons. Part of it was growing fear and disgust over the violence, not just by the authorities at Berkeley's People's Park or Kent State but also by increasingly extreme radicals like the University of Wisconsin students who blew up the Army Mathematics Research Center on campus in August 1970—and inadvertently killed a grad student who was pulling an all-nighter. Some pullback was inevitable as the Vietnam War ended and the moral clarity of the early 1960s' civil rights movement gave way to complicated Black Nationalism. But there was also a strong countervailing wind blowing from the right that would alter everything from state budgets to students' choice of their major.

THE POSTWAR ECONOMIC BOOM—THAT VIRTUOUS CYCLE THAT PAID for all those new dorms and labs from overflowing tax coffers, and that encouraged idealistic planners and those "intellectually curious" young people to major in philosophy or literature or the social sciences because jobs were so plentiful—was ending. By the summer of 1971, when Lewis Powell was drafting his memo about saving U.S. capitalism from the campus infidels, Richard Nixon in the White House was secretly concluding, in the words of Rick Perlstein, that the nation faced "the imminence of America's decline as the world's number one power." The radical actions that Nixon took—breaking the bond between gold and the value of the U.S. dollar, a wage and price freeze and a tax on imports—provided a short-term boost that carried him through his landslide reelection in 1972, but didn't stave off the long-term consequences that were compounded by a loss of American prestige over the Vietnam debacle. The shocks that followed—Arab oil embargoes and long lines for no-longer-cheap gasoline, runaway inflation followed by the "stagflation" of unemployment and higher prices, the closing of rust-bitten factories, and Nixon's Watergate scandal that accelerated eroding faith in institutions—changed the mood of the nation, especially on college campuses.

In 1971, more U.S. graduates earned bachelor's degrees in the social sciences than in the business categories—but those numbers were about to invert. One survey found that the annual number of business diplomas rocketed upward by 92 percent from 1972 to 1985, while degrees in English dropped by 54 percent and history diplomas by 63 percent, with a 61 percent decline in sociology degrees. Some of the shifts can be attributed to the more rapid increase in women attending college, as many looked to bust out of the narrow career pathways, especially teaching, to which they'd once been confined, and thus turned to more practical and higher-income career paths. But according to surveys of incoming freshmen, 82 percent in 1969 said it was very important to "develop a meaningful philosophy of life"—which plummeted to 43 percent by 1985. During those same years, incoming students aspiring to be "very well-off financially" soared from 40 percent to 71 percent. This surge in careerism—inspired by the suddenly tough job market—played right into the reactionary scheme envisioned by Reagan, that college is for job training and not intellectual growth.

Ironically, as the nation suffered through one of several recessions, it fell to Reagan's Democratic successor as California governor—Jerry Brown (yes, Pat Brown's son)—to impose the first official UC tuition, which in 1975 with related fees came to six hundred dollars a year. But the Golden State, which had once been the leader in moving toward a universal higher education, would soon be facing a taxpayer revolt that in 1978 resulted in voters approving Proposition 13, a hard cap on annual property tax increases—having ramifications to this day. Broadly, this landmark vote was a pivot point away from activist government and toward a Western philosophy of rugged individualism, which came to include paying for college. In politics, the Proposition 13 vote felt like a validation of America's turn to the right, which was cemented two years later when Reagan, on his third try, was elected president. Reagan's first term, some forty years later, is remembered for its huge income tax break that particularly favored the wealthy, and for its cuts in government services that accompanied them. With so many programs on the chopping block in the early 1980s, Washington's sharp right turn on higher education flew under the radar.

IN 1978, CONGRESS HAD PASSED THE MIDDLE INCOME ASSISTANCE Act, which "assisted" the middle class by removing limits on the amount of federal Guaranteed Student Loans they could take out. As Roger Geiger observes, this was "the first step toward opening a new source of income for colleges and universities—the future income of students." After less than a decade, Buchanan's transactional vision for academia was becoming a reality, and now the Gipper was here to finish the job.

The 40th president's budget hatchet man, David Stockman, described college students as "tax eaters" in testimony before a House hearing on higher education, in which he declared that student aid "isn't a proper obligation of the taxpayer." During Reagan's first term, the philosophical notion that "government is the problem" and that success—including a college diploma—was a question of personal responsibility were translated, harshly, into U.S. fiscal policy.

During that 1980–85 stretch, overall federal spending on higher education fell by roughly 25 percent, with reductions to student aid—including the Pell Grant, which had been the cornerstone of federal policy for helping lower- and middle-income families send their kids to college since LBJ's Great Society in 1965—totaling about $1 billion. Many of these reductions were achieved by converting what had once been direct aid into loans that students would need to pay back. The Pell Grant program grew in popularity during the 1980s but the new template would fall further and further behind rapidly rising tuition. In 1980, a Pell Grant covered 75 percent of the cost of attending in-state public university, but today it's roughly 30 percent. That means college would become financially out of reach for many of the kind of blue-collar kids who had swelled the population of the new high-rise dorms at Kent State or Michigan State in the 1960s.

Thus, every generation or so, America's leaders made a consequential decision that moved the nation further and further from the G.I. Bill's promise that higher education could be a public good. In 1947, the failure of high-minded technocrats and college leaders to commit Washington to a federally funded push for universal higher ed would make it easier for future leaders like Reagan to undo their more tentative commitments. In 1965, when the federal government was enacting other sweeping programs such as Medicare, the decision that dollars for college would be attached through Pell Grants would lock in the idea of personal merit over taxpayer-funded access for all. And in 1981, that framework made it much easier for Reagan to further privatize the idea of college as a complex and expensive meritocracy that wasn't for everyone, the 180-degree opposite of America's approach to K-12 learning.

These policy decisions matter for one simple reason: College started becoming more expensive and less accessible right at the very moment it became critical for getting a good job. For one thing, the end of the industrial economy on U.S. soil accelerated rapidly in the 1970s and early 1980s. Factory closings were at the center of the national zeitgeist—if you weren't there, listen to a few Bruce Springsteen LPs—and the type of union job in which a man without a college diploma earned enough at the plant to eventually buy a vacation cottage or a fishing boat was the prime casualty. Stability, if not growth, was to be found within the knowledge economy that Clark Kerr had announced to the world in 1963—not only the computer work that was evolving into a new term, "high tech," but also in fields like journalism or law or academia that were the outgrowth of all those social sciences majors in the 1960s and '70s.

One of the many, perhaps unintended, consequences of the post-war boom in college enrollment was the birth of what became known as "credentialism"—essentially the notion that, in a much tighter employment market, a college diploma became a shortcut for job recruiters looking to hire the best candidate. This trend was well underway by 1979—the year that sociologist Randall Collins published the seminal work on the concept, *The Credential Society*—and "credential inflation" has only become more entrenched in the forty-plus years since then. Would-be employers increasingly demand a college diploma for all sorts of jobs—everything from data entry to funeral-home management to dental lab technician to my own chosen profession, newspaper reporter—that at one time didn't require one. So by the 1980s, government policy was making families bear more of the cost of college education at the same time that a diploma was the only way to meet the American imperative of each generation doing better.

The American Dream of college—as reinvented in the 1940s, '50s, and '60s—hadn't changed in most households, but the tectonic plates beneath were shifting, powerfully. It took roughly forty years for the idealism of higher education as a tool for molding smarter citizens committed to liberal democracy and international understanding to instead become the rough show-us-your-papers demand for clinging to the middle class. For the millions who still dreamed, this transformation brought a willingness to borrow whatever it took—even from the increasingly privatized loan sharks who began circling in the Reagan years—to complete this paper chase. But millions of others began to internalize that America in the college age was now a "meritocracy," and that their failures to keep up weren't because the deck was stacked against them, but because of arrogant eggheads who didn't know how to screw in a lightbulb telling them they lacked "merit." And the smart elites who promoted this myth of a meritocracy apparently weren't bright enough to see that that resentment would become the driving political force of the twenty-first century.

THIS SHARP U-TURN WAS REFLECTED IN MARIO SAVIO'S LONG AND winding road after the bright intensity of the 1964 Berkeley Free Speech Movement. Alienated by the demands of instant fame and confronted with his own personal mental health demons, he largely disappeared from the public eye as both youth radicalism and the backlash against it intensified in the late 1960s and early '70s. But by the time of Reagan's presidency, Savio found his footing with his marriage to Hollander, with a career doing what he'd initially set out to do, teaching philosophy and math at Sonoma State University, and by speaking out against reactionary politics, including U.S. imperialism in Latin America—so similar to what had motivated him at the dawn of the 1960s.

The very last fight of his life, though, tied together the link between social change and access to higher education. In the fall of 1996, some thirty-two years after the FSM, Savio found himself leading faculty and students at Sonoma State in a campuswide protest against a plan to impose a three-hundred-dollar fee that Savio saw as a backdoor tuition hike that would make the school inaccessible to low-income kids. "A university education is as necessary to a decent life as a high school diploma was seventy-five years ago," he said. "What is necessary should be free . . . Fees should be coming down, not going up." In the middle of that pitched battle, on November 2, 1996, Savio suffered a massive heart attack, and died four days later. He was just fifty-six, lost right at the moment when the voices calling for a free and more democratic higher education in America were growing both fewer and fainter.

CHAPTER 4

YUPPIES, DITTOHEADS, AND A "BIG SORT": COLLEGE AND THE CULTURE WARS

Looking back and knowing everything that's happened over the last three decades, it's hard to summon the breathlessness expressed by the *New York Times* on January 29, 1993, about the growing power in Washington of a populist phenomenon sweeping through Middle America: talk radio. In her piece, headlined "The People Are Heard, or At Least Those Who Call Talk Radio," the *Times*'s Elizabeth Kolbert traces how these angry, random callers had fomented an uproar over new president Bill Clinton's plan to allow gay people to serve in the military, and how Republicans on Capitol Hill were increasingly afraid not to follow the lead of this strange new force. "Congress believes in the interactive phenomenon," said Michael Deaver, the former Ronald Reagan aide. "They feel the people feel this may be their new franchise." A middle-of-the-road GOP senator, James Jeffords of Vermont, agreed, adding: "Rush Limbaugh is a factor now."

Rush Limbaugh was indeed a factor. As unfathomable as this would seem to political reporters of the early 1990s, this then-320-pound college dropout who'd never held elected office was already becoming the defining force of post-Reagan American conservatism. Limbaugh achieved this with an innate understanding that once the revolutions of the 1960s and '70s had petered out, the political battlefield was in reality a cultural one—defending Heartland traditional values against the campus-bred libertines banging at the gates. Limbaugh arguably didn't start the "culture wars" (a phrase that didn't appear in the *Times* until late 1991, and then by a book critic who wasn't sure it was even real) but he sure knew how to widen them. His three-hour radio show beamed to hundreds of stations may have ostensibly been "a political show," but nothing energized Limbaugh or his like-minded callers—who proudly self-identified as "dittoheads"—more than going after cultural targets like "tree hugging" environmentalists, animal-rights activists, the homeless, or, especially, the women he dubbed "feminazis." His raw start in the late 1980s had coincided with the peak of the AIDS epidemic, and Limbaugh actually had to apologize—a once-in-a-lifetime event—for a briefly recurring "AIDS Update" segment that literally mocked a list of that day's dead with songs like "I Know I'll Never Love This Way Again."

This was right after the release of the 1990 census showing that—after four decades of rapid growth—some 45 percent of adults now had at least some college education, a rising tide but not yet a majority. Limbaugh was arguably the avatar of the other 55 percent, an increasingly not-so-silent-anymore majority. The radio talker had inherited the politics of his prominent right-wing attorney father but not his dad's educational attainment; the younger Rush flunked out of Southeast Missouri State University after just three semesters, too eager to begin working as a radio DJ.

Yet Limbaugh would keep revisiting the subject of college to collect the kindling he needed to light his cultural fires. In the days following that 1993 *Times* article, Limbaugh balanced tirades against the new Democratic president with updates on an obscure campus controversy at the University of Pennsylvania, in which an Israeli undergrad had been expelled for yelling out his window at noisy Black sorority members and calling them "water buffalo." For Limbaugh's heavily working-class, heavily male audience, a strange racial controversy at an Ivy League school and a president who'd protested Vietnam and (sort of) tried pot was all part of their growing mood that nothing in America made sense anymore.

That 42nd president of the United States, William Jefferson Clinton, was in fact the perfect foil for launching this shiny new culture war. Born in the first year of the baby boom in 1946 and the product of a difficult childhood in rural Arkansas, Clinton was the poster child for the notion of meritocracy. He had been the first in his family to attend college—on a scholarship to an elite East Coast campus in Georgetown—which exposed him to 1960s anti-war politics, the sweet smell of marijuana, and finally, at Yale Law School, to his feminist wife, Hillary Rodham Clinton. In theory, Clinton's rise from his liberal college education all the way to the White House made him the person Ronald Reagan tried to warn you about back in the '60s. The reality was more complicated—that any lingering campus idealism in Clinton's rhetoric was subsumed by vaguely conservative politics around small government and "ending welfare as we know it."

Yet the symbolic contrast between Clinton and Limbaugh was almost too perfect. Limbaugh was the ideal figurehead for the no-diploma school-of-hard-knocks crowd, who made it on their own terms, stayed rooted in the hometown values of Middle America, and could only laugh at the less-than-macho inanities of the college crowd. Clinton, who grew up just a couple years ahead of Limbaugh and just a couple hundred miles on the other side of the Ozarks, was a man forever changed by college.

By the dawn of the 1990s and into our tangled present, the changes in America that motivated millions of young people to become the first generation in their family to attend college, to learn about new things or chart an adventurous career, brought all sorts of unintended social consequences. Leaving home for a campus dorm was often the start of a lifelong odyssey to make new friends, experience new bands or exotic foods, and gravitate toward cities where all the cool jobs are. It also meant leaving behind increasingly empty church pews and shrinking bowling leagues. The excitement of the university-bred life triggered an equal and opposite reaction of resentment coming from the left behind, who hadn't been told that the rules of the American Dream were changing. This cultural shift that began to harden in the late twentieth century was so profound that millions sorted themselves into communities of like-minded people. They formed what University of Maryland political scientist Lilliana Mason called "mega-identities" which brought shared values within these competing groups about religion, about the importance of family, about diversity and gender roles, and even around favorite TV shows or movies or pop bands.

And, of course, around politics.

America's college-driven cultural crack-up took place through a series of seemingly discrete happenings—mostly in the latter twentieth century—that often looked in real time like mere cultural fads or brief economic fires. In fact, they were all tied to sweeping societal change around educational attainment. In the moment, no one imagined that things like "identity politics" on college campuses, or a new rural class consciousness, or the rise of yuppies rediscovering American cities, or the so-called Big Sort where residential neighborhoods increasingly reflected shared values would lead to a national political crack-up—one so pronounced it ultimately elected a rogue character like Donald Trump as president and pushed U.S. democracy to the brink.

The culture war that was poo-pooed by the *New York Times* thirty years ago somehow grew from a quirky sideshow of American politics into the main attraction. How? To better understand, let's take a brief step backward in the timeline. In the last chapter we focused on how the new American way of college started to change our politics—and vice versa. But while the direct political impact of protests and other campus activities began to fade as the 1960s melted into the '70s, the lasting cultural influence of the new mass university education was just beginning—in a lifestyle that would last well after commencement.

IT STARTED AT THE END OF THE 1960S. THAT DECADE HAD SEEN STU-dents hoping to both change the world through political protest, but also change the academy, to liberalize academics itself and to broaden the lens beyond a white male—dominated Western view of learning. The former mission faded in the wake of Kent State, the Army Mathematics Research Center bombing, and the U.S. withdrawal from Vietnam, but the changes wrought by the latter movement—creation of programs in Afro-American and women's studies, or so-called Third World cultural centers on campus—not only survived into the 1970s and '80s, but flourished. Perhaps understandably, as the outside America seemed to move further and further to the right, college campuses—their faculty comprised of the product of the 1960s "Liberal Hour," and their young students still hormonally driven to question authority—remained islands of progressivism.

What became known as "identity politics" certainly started as a direct outgrowth of events such as the Black-led strike at California's San Francisco State in 1968—69. Black Nationalism had pushed aside the more integrationist approach of efforts like the Mississippi Freedom project that had so energized the likes of Mario Savio and his mostly white peers. And their movement for some version of Black equality inspired other groups—the Indigenous people of the American Indian Movement, the women's liberation movement, and the push for gay rights that burst into consciousness with the 1969 Stonewall riot—to seek their own visions of equity.

By the late 1970s, the energy of these movements felt less like the rocket of a unified, college-led New Left movement for social change, as envisioned in the Port Huron Statement, and more like the splintered pieces after a cultural explosion. In 1977, a groundbreaking movement of predominantly Black lesbians called the Combahee River Collective published a now-historic statement that declared "focusing upon our own oppression is embodied in the concept of identity politics. We believe that the most profound and potentially most radical politics come directly out of our own identity, as opposed to working to end somebody else's oppression."

These years were also my own moment as a college student, as an undergraduate at Brown from 1977 to 1981—and the rise of identity politics was a palpable force on campus in Providence, as elsewhere. Protest movements led by Black, Brown, and Asian students in 1968 and again in 1975—addressing the threat of budget cuts in the downsizing economy—had led to the establishment of what became known as Third World Transition Week, an extra first-year orientation week for students of color. When I arrived as a freshman, I was surprised how few (if any) Black-white roommate pairings had been assigned by Brown's supposedly newfangled computers—but I was told that nonwhite kids who'd made friends during that extra Third World week had asked to switch their initial pairings. This flowed into what seemed like a running, four-year-long debate about social segregation at Brown, whether it was the large all-Black table at the main dining hall, or the separate dining rooms that mostly white fraternities clung to. In a quiet era, the loudest dissent often came from Brown's Third World Center, where I had my most memorable experience as a student journalist—covering a forum on U.S. imperialism during the depths of the 1979–80 Iran crisis, as angry white frat brothers screamed, "What about the hostages?!" It was my introduction to a politics of talking-past-each-other I'd be writing about for the next forty years.

In hindsight, the rise of identity politics can also be seen as a kind of defensive posture. The end of the 1960s had seen a brief consensus in favor of affirmative action, the idea that essentially giving preference to Black and Brown applicants for competitive college slots, or college faculty positions, as well as an array of jobs and programs in the outside world, was needed to reverse a legacy of discrimination. But the increasing conservatism and tight job market of the 1970s brought a backlash, punctuated by the Supreme Court's 1978 decision in the so-called Bakke case (involving a medical school in the always-contentious University of California system) that preserved the broad idea of affirmative action but banned numerical quotas, and thus further raised tensions.

Despite the legal challenge and growing criticism from conservative politicians, the 1970s were a time when societal trends—aided, to some degree, by affirmative action—brought a steep rise in African American college enrollment. The Census Bureau found that not only did Black college matriculation double during the 1970s from 522,000 to more than 1 million, but by 1976 the rate of Black students in higher education had equaled their percentage of the college-aged population. In the same vein, 1979 was the first year that more women than men were attending college, reversing the large advantage for male students created in the 1940s and '50s by the inequity of the G.I. Bill—and this gap would continue to grow.

The pride felt by this surge not just of Black students and women but by other previously underrepresented groups—including gay students, who'd been virtually invisible prior to the 1970s—created a campus culture of conflict with entrenched white male norms, from fraternity row to the classics department. In these clashes, one sees the green shoots of a symbiotic relationship between campus "identity politics" and matriculation into the Democratic Party, which was more supportive of gender and racial equity, thus making identity politics increasingly embedded in the party's DNA.

In 1980, just one year after female college attendees surpassed men, political pundits first began to notice a gender gap in American politics. Historically, there had been little difference in how men and women voted for president. Not so with Ronald Reagan. Among female voters, Democratic incumbent Jimmy Carter lost by just 1 percentage point—compared to a Reagan blowout of 17 percentage points among men—and analyses of the 1982 midterm election that followed showed women voters were critical in a gain of twenty-six House seats for the Democrats. The reasons for this are complicated; some experts point to the huge rise over the 1970s and '80s of single households headed by women—partly because of female college grads deferring marriage but also because of the skyrocketing divorce rate. The GOP platform under Reagan also gave women voters plenty to dislike—opposition to affirmative action and abortion, as Republicans rallied around this looming culture war, but also harsh economic policies that fell heavily on single mothers.

The gender gap at American universities and in the voting booth grew hand in hand. On campus, female matriculation continued to grow and outpace stagnant rates of men attending college; by 2020–21, nearly 60 percent of current college students were women, and overall there were now more women with college diplomas in the workforce than men. At the ballot box, the gender gap also grew steadily larger over time so that women now reliably vote 10–12 percentage points more Democratic in a typical presidential election. As these two trends solidified into the twenty-first century, it's no wonder that pollsters began seeing a new gap in U.S. politics: the college/noncollege divide.

THE HAND-IN-HAND FEMINIZATION OF RISING COLLEGE ATTAIN-ment and the Democratic Party wasn't the only cultural change that would ultimately rock American politics. But it wouldn't be until the turn of the millennium that demographers and other experts took note of some unexpected trends that took off around 1965—that critical year when the first baby boomers had just arrived on college campuses and Reagan announced his reactionary campaign for governor. The change they saw was that Americans were now moving not just because of economics, or racial tensions in big cities. Now there was a new brand of U.S. mobility: creating new communities around a shared culture.

The first real notice of these stirrings took place with the "fad" coverage that launched a thousand magazine covers in the mid-1980s—the cultural phenomenon known as "the yuppie." Derived from "young urban professional," these yuppies—twenty- or thirtysomething college grads who seemed more interested in winning at capitalism than overthrowing it, and who gentrified recently hollowed-out city zip codes with their exotic restaurants and coffee shops—had a man-bites-dog quality for headline writers numbed by a generation of "white flight" to the suburbs. Perhaps not ironically, one of the early champions of yuppies was the former "yippie" political activist Jerry Rubin, who hailed what indeed seemed like a logical extension of the New Left—taking the mantra of personal freedom and turning it toward tech entrepreneurship and, thus, wealth . . . now that the political clouds of Vietnam and segregation had dissipated. The yuppies even came with a political wing dubbed "the Atari Democrats"—young white intellectuals like Colorado senator Gary Hart who believed in the social progress of identity politics but also a high-tech capitalism that they promised would raise all boats.

One urban affairs guru who captured this new zeitgeist is Richard Florida. Much of Florida's work revolves around the role of a new "creative class" in American life—computer whizzes, scientific researchers, designers, writers, and artists—in creating the modern postindustrial city. Florida argues that this creative class moves around because it's looking primarily for a lifestyle, with a job as only one part of that. And in the culture of start-up companies that employ many of these creatives, new companies locate where they think these hip workers already are, instead of the other way around. The core values of these "creatives"—individuality and diversity and tolerance of other lifestyles—made them more receptive to the modern Democratic Party, but as practitioners of this new culture grew in number (Florida pegs its size at 30 million Americans and growing), money and influence, they also bent the Democratic Party to look more and more like them.

In *The Big Sort*, author Bill Bishop notes that in the 1960s there was very little difference between Democratic-leaning counties and Republican ones in measuring higher education. But by the turn of the millennium, there were not only more counties that voted for one party or the other with predictable regularity, but 29 percent of voters in the Democratic counties had college diplomas compared to just 20 percent in the Republican counties. This happened because educated people were packing up and moving to those more liberal places. According to one study that looked at U.S. mobility in the 1980s and '90s, only 19 percent of Americans with a high school degree or less had moved between states, while 45 percent of those with college degrees did so. That changed the look of the hottest communities like Bishop's hometown of Austin, Texas—a college-oriented city that became home of Tex-Mex restaurants, country-fried music, and microchips as the number of bachelor's degree holders there rose steadily to 45 percent by the 2000s.

Of course, "the Big Sort" is more complicated than just philosophy majors following their inner Zagat guide to foodie bliss. The Democratic slant of big cities isn't only because of white gentrification but also the twentieth-century legacy of de jure housing segregation that kept many Black residents confined to certain neighborhoods. At the same time, the conservative instincts that drove "white flight" to the suburbs after World War II found a new momentum to create the so-called exurbs—where more affordable land allowed a certain breed of folks to keep their distance. The exurbs became home to a new phenomenon called a "megachurch," where arena-sized houses of worship also offered a new lifestyle, albeit around Bible class and choir practice instead of alt-rock nightclubs. Weirdly, there was an ethos around personal freedom that mirrored that of the creative class, but more centered on property rights, gun ownership, conservative social mores, and shunning the types of diversity that were celebrated in the dense cities. Like the suburbs that came before them, these new exurbs voted heavily Republican and provided winning margins for candidates like Reagan, for George H. W. Bush in 1988, and for the GOP wave that overwhelmed Congress in 1994.

But there's another piece of the Big Sort that, frankly, gets shorter shrift from Bishop. While human nature is to watch the sorters—i.e., the trendy urban yuppies—no one was watching who the sorters had left behind: the web of small towns and midsized cities across Middle America that started to erode once the downside of the Industrial Revolution accelerated in the 1970s and beyond. The most highly motivated young folks in these places tended to leave for college and—lacking hometown job opportunities—never returned, while some blue-collar residents also left, searching for new work. Losing what the elite egg-heads were starting to call "human capital" only compounded the despair in small town America or once-thriving places like Youngstown or Flint.

ANOTHER SOCIAL PHENOMENON THAT ONE MIGHT CALL THE FIRST cousin of *The Big Sort* was chronicled by the Harvard sociologist Robert Putnam in his 2000 book, *Bowling Alone*. The title stems from a rapid decline in people joining community bowling leagues, but it's just the most dramatic example of a steep drop in civic participation in all sorts of groups that began—of course—in the 1960s. There have been enrollment drops in parent-teacher associations, fraternal orders like the Kiwanis Club or the Elks Lodge and religious orders like Knights of Columbus, as well as an array or organizations ranging from the Boy Scouts to the United Way. Putnam's data is compelling although he struggles somewhat to find a reason for the sudden change. The new atomized media landscape—the hours spent watching TV or using the internet, which had just caught on when Putnam was researching the book—obviously played a role, as did the increasing hours that adults spent commuting and at their jobs, in the era of two-income parents. But the passion of Richard Florida's "creative class" for new experiences over familiar conformity had surely played a role.

Of course to some extent, Americans in small towns kept bowling, meeting every week at the Rotary luncheon, or bonding with like-minded neighbors in Sunday school. There were just fewer of these folks every year, as their ambitious offspring moved away and the ones who stayed around sunk into McJobs, YouTube rabbit holes, or the dangerous trapdoor of opioids. The conventional wisdom is that civic engagement makes people happier, better adjusted, and more successful. In *The Big Sort*, Bishop was somewhat surprised to find that U.S. communities that score high on what sociologists would call civic health actually fared worse when it comes to economic health. New inventions and rising profits came from cities where young college grads built a life around work, not their neighbors.

This unhealthy unraveling of community bonds coincided with an era of economic turmoil. In the 1950s and '60s, the societal push for greater college attainment was expected to create only winners, not losers. The nation was in the midst of what modern economists now call the Great Compression, a period in U.S. history where economic differences between the wealthy and the vast middle-class still existed, of course, but had been flattened out by across-the-board prosperity. In an era of consistently low unemployment, the standard of living for the American working class nearly doubled from 1947 to 1973. The American Dream was that the children of the next generation would do even better with their diplomas, and few imagined that a thriving "knowledge economy" would happen at the expense of a sinking industrial sector.

But the industrial age had already plateaued by the dawn of the 1970s. Middle-class families would be rattled again and again—especially by the Arab oil embargo of 1973–74, with hours-long lines at gas station and prices soaring toward the unthinkable $1-a-gallon that jolted the car-crazed suburbs, but also by the so-called stagflation of rising prices amid higher unemployment, with astronomical mortgage rates. The number of manufacturing jobs in the United States finally peaked in 1979. It would be over the course of the 1980s and '90s that factory closures accelerated and the trends that have shaped the modern American economy—such as the rise of cheap foreign labor and the outsourcing of U.S. factory jobs—began to take root.

In 1991, two Pulitzer Prize–winning journalists for the *Philadelphia Inquirer*—Donald L. Barlett and James B. Steele—wrote a major series with the plaintive title "America, What Went Wrong" that both exposed the agony of the industrial Heartland and looked at government policies during the Reagan years that had accelerated the loss of factory jobs. Their thesis had been unthinkable during the postwar boom years, that "for the first time in this century, a generation entering adulthood will find it impossible to achieve a better lifestyle than their parents." They blamed political leaders, especially in Washington, for placing more of the nation's tax burden on the middle class while dramatically lowering rates on the wealthy, doling out tax breaks or advantages to corporations that shipped jobs overseas, and making it harder for workers to buy a home and, yes, pay for college.

One other thing that government had promoted during the 1980s was the decline of unions. Along with his tax cut that so heavily benefited the upper brackets, the signature achievement of Ronald Reagan's first year in office, 1981, was his firing of the nation's unionized air traffic controllers when they walked off the job in a labor dispute. The president's harsh but successful crackdown on a public-sector union—which would have been unthinkable during those Great Compression years when labor-management teamwork was seen as a path to prosperity—was a signal to the private sector that the general public now backed a tougher, anti-union posture. In tandem with manufacturing jobs, the total number of union members in America peaked in 1979, at 21 million (although the rate of membership had started slipping in the mid-1950s, as white-collar work expanded). The ever-shrinking power of unions drove the falling standard of living for the working class, even as pay for CEOs and other top executives—no longer impeded by high marginal income-tax rates—began to skyrocket. It's important to realize that not only did weaker unions mean less bargaining power and less political power for the working class, but added to the fraying of the social bonds that Putnam described in *Bowling Alone*.

But if rank-and-file blue-collar workers in America were increasingly both angry and isolated, who would they blame for their plight? The reaction to Barlett and Steele's "America, What Went Wrong" project is instructive. The massive series, which was soon repackaged as a bestselling book, instantly struck a chord with middle-class readers who were thrilled to learn that they weren't going crazy, that someone understood and gave voice to their plight. (Big-time journalists, perhaps drunk on the Kool-Aid of the era's top-line profit numbers, were less impressed, as the series wasn't even a finalist for the Pulitzers that year.)

Yet to many social observers, but especially those who clung to the political left, it seemed obvious by the dawn of the 1990s whom the displaced and disillusioned American middle class ought to be hating on: Big Business, with the rise of a generation of ruthless CEOs like General Electric's "Neutron Jack" Welsh or Sunbeam's notorious "Chainsaw Al" Dunlop, who lopped off thousands of blue-collar jobs to reward their wealthy shareholders, or the new generation of finance vultures as portrayed in popular films like *Wall Street* or *Other People's Money*, or the politicians like Reagan who had empowered their greed while all but declaring war on organized labor. That wasn't where their anger went. Instead, middle-class rage was steered toward the urban avatars of the new college-educated "creative class"—liberal Hollywood actors, big-name journalists, and college professors, or lesser members of a new aristocracy dubbed "the professional and managerial elite."

Although it received little or no attention at first, the vast American middle class of the generation that immediately followed World War II was dividing in two—into a noticeable split between a mostly college-educated upper middle class and a blue-collar lower middle class. Economists point to a measure of income inequality called the Gini co-efficient, a curve that does a particularly good job in noting disparities within the middle class. The Gini curve—a statistical tool for measuring the distribution of wealth—in the United States rose sharply over the course of the 1980s and remained at high levels during the 1990s. As the writer Noah Smith pointed out, this divergence spiked almost in tandem with the premium that employers were now paying to those with a diploma; a Brookings Institution project showed that the wage premiums for college degrees as well as graduate degrees rose from about 40 percent in 1979 to more than 200 percent by the mid-1990s.

In blue-collar communities, especially among the white working class, the diverging outcomes created by the new knowledge economy created a backlash storyline that college-educated workers were lazy or pampered and lacked the skill or even the brains for manual tasks, such as changing the oil in their cars. "There ain't very many of 'em that sweat," a rural Wisconsin man told the academic Katherine J. Cramer for her book *The Politics of Resentment*, referring to state workers he saw as spoiled. "I still know how to work. I'm eighty-two years old and driving a semi!"

Other social critics have noted that while billionaire CEOs getting rich off cheap overseas labor seem to be a million miles away for the rural working class, the condescending know-it-alls of the new upper middle class were often in their face, whether it was a pompous state bureaucrat or a crusading journalist for the hometown newspaper. In 2017's *White Working Class*, Joan C. Williams writes of the "class cluelessness" of the managerial and professional elites when it comes to understanding the issues and worldview of the lower middle class. Everyday workers suffer slights, Williams writes, such as "the doctor who unthinkingly patronizes the medical technician [or] the harried office worker who treats the security guard as invisible."

Of course, the growing resentments of rural working-class life, and the increasing mocking of lazy, clueless elites, masked real pain over the changes in the American economy that suddenly made life harder for people who'd grown up in a world where a diploma wasn't necessary for a comfortable lifestyle—until suddenly it was. In 2020, two psychologists published a survey of the American class divide when it came to happiness; in 1972, the difference between people with or without bachelor's degrees had been very small, but it had steadily grown to a huge gulf by 2016, the year that, coincidentally or not, Donald Trump was elected president of the United States.

But it's critical to remember that in channeling their anger and unhappiness away from CEOs and certain political leaders and toward those folks that Spiro Agnew had once dubbed "pointy-headed intellectuals," America's working-class whites had prominent outside help. Remember the 1971 Powell Memo, which imagined a parallel universe of pro-capitalism think tanks and a right-wing media that would counter the progressive tilt of working journalists? At first, those most enthusiastic about these ideas—such as Roger Ailes, a political strategist who managed an image makeover for Richard Nixon in 1968 and had visions of a conservative-leaning TV network—faced significant technological and legal obstacles. Cable TV was still in its infancy, and over-the-air television and radio were heavily regulated by their licensing body, the Federal Communications Commission, bound by a so-called Fairness Doctrine to present both sides of political issues. This ensured that politics would be largely avoided.

Here, again, the changes were wrought by Ronald Reagan and his administration. But even the Gipper probably couldn't have predicted the political earthquake he was unleashing when, in 1987, an FCC led by his appointee Mark Fowler killed off the Fairness Doctrine. Coincidentally, the move came just as hundreds of once-thriving AM radio stations were desperate to find the next new thing as music fans flocked to FM stereo. In 1988, an obscure, itinerant jock named Rush Limbaugh launched a politically conservative talk show on an equally obscure AM station in Sacramento. Within just a few years he'd gained as many as 20 million listeners on hundreds of stations.

Indeed, while America only had two all-talk radio stations at the dawn of the 1960s, by 1995 there would be a whopping 1,130—and almost all of these would be all conservative, all the time. Again, the nation's politics were being driven by culture, and by the growing tribalism of the Big Sort era. It's not so much that the United States was dominated by the right wing in the late 1980s and '90s; polls showed most Americans favored pursuing center-left policies on everything from the environment to civil rights. But while the left—especially its nascent base of cosmopolitan urbanites—gravitated toward traditional news sources like the *New York Times* or National Public Radio, people on the right were galvanized by this new place to air their boiling grievances and resentment. Especially one group in particular—white middle-class men. They often worked in jobs—truck driver, contractor, small business owner—where they could easily listen all day to the radio, and shows like Limbaugh's gave them the power of knowing that, in resisting rapid cultural change, they were not alone.

The new right-wing talk radio was ostensibly a political movement and at times it was—most notably in 1990 when an angry populist backlash to congressional pay raises amplified by these new AM megaphones caused several incumbent members of Congress to lose their seats. But on a typical day, traditional politics didn't light up the phone lines for Limbaugh nearly as much as did cultural grievances—the latest ridiculous examples (to them, anyway) of nonsensical things happening somewhere in America in the name of women's liberation or affirmative action or some other assault on the nation's dominant white patriarchy.

In a way, Limbaugh was surfing a broader cultural tsunami. He and the new right-wing radio talkers were the political half of a coin that—on its flip side—featured FM shock jocks riding a wave of loud, potty-mouth "morning zoo" programs (including one who bounced from station to station by the name of Glenn Beck) and the so-called King of All Media, the top-rated Howard Stern, who would say anything to shatter taboos. The common enemy? Something they called "political correctness"—a newish term meant to ridicule the political left's growing obsession with identity politics, and specifically language around race and gender—as the 1980s melted into the 1990s. One survey of a comprehensive database of American newspapers and magazines found that the term, quickly shortened to "PC," had barely existed before 1990, when it was used 700 times, rising by 1991 to a whopping 2,500 references.

The coverage reflected a broader backlash among white male academics who felt that the downgrading of mostly white, mostly male, Western-civilization thought in college learning was driving a dumbing down of America. Most famously, the philosopher Allen Bloom's 1987 book, *The Closing of the American Mind*—which surprised even its publisher by becoming a runaway bestseller—argued that the era's college students and professors had, paradoxically, in pushing for "greater openness" and in questioning authority, instead narrowed their worldview by rejecting the Great Books of the Western canon. The writer Camille Paglia would later credit—if that's the right word—Bloom with launching America's culture wars into a new orbit.

But books like Bloom's served as the intellectual underpinning for taking the new-and-improved culture war to the wider world off campus, sped by this new conservative megaphone of AM talk radio. As the spiral of tuition increases and other obstacles turned the ivory tower of academia into a kind of a Berlin Wall facing out toward a wider swath of America, the notion of college as a bastion of radical indoctrination was an appealing one—and the crazier the example of "political correctness" run amok, the higher the radio ratings.

All this happened at a moment when the conservative political movement in America desperately needed a spark. The "Reagan revolution" was over at the dawn of the 1990s, a victim of both American success—the end of the Cold War, weakening the movement's glue of rabid anti-communism—and failure, as an economic recession in 1991 laid bare the contradictions of "trickle-down economics." The milquetoast, Eastern-elite centrism of Reagan's GOP successor, George Herbert Walker Bush, would be shoved aside dramatically at the 1992 Republican National Convention in Houston; there, the party's unapologetic populist Pat Buchanan delivered a "we-will-fight-them-on-the-beaches" exhortation against feminism and gay rights, declaring, "There is a religious war going on in this country. It is a cultural war, as critical to the kind of nation we shall be as was the Cold War itself, for this war is for the soul of America."

Yet the political left in many ways had forged the ammunition for the Pat Buchanans and Rush Limbaughs of this new American civil war—by turning inward, shunning the great universalistic causes that had galvanized college students in the early and mid-1960s, and embracing narrow spats over language, or the arcane internal politics of academia. Although the onslaught against the "PC culture" on campus was mostly coming from the right flank, some people associated with the 1960s rise of the New Left were dismayed that the Democratic Party now seemed dominated by identity politics. The most vocal such critic was Todd Gitlin, a communications professor and author who'd served as president of the national SDS in the period right after Tom Hayden had published the Port Huron Statement. In a 1995 book titled *The Twilight of Common Dreams: Why America Is Wracked by Culture Wars*, Gitlin bemoans the fact that late-twentieth-century leftists "were marching on the English Department while the Right took the White House."

Gitlin argued that the notions of individualism and personal freedom embedded in the founding of the New Left had fallen apart once it no longer had the unifying causes of civil rights and Vietnam, and that a natural tendency to unite along identity lines began to fill that void in the late 1960s and into the 1970s. On campus, the universalist ideal of a left-wing mass movement, he wrote, "was scorned as nonexistent, hypothetical, nostalgic or, worse, deceptive—a mask assumed by straight white males as they tried to restore their lost dominion." Of course, the early surge of identity politics in the '70s had also brought greater awareness and some major civil rights victories for women, the LGBTQ+ community, and other groups that had long been marginalized.

But by the time that Gitlin was writing in the mid-1990s, some of the most blatant barriers had been knocked down in the broader society while the focus at universities seemed to be narrowing—viewed by puzzled outsiders as not just going too far but borderline ridiculous. During the twelve years from 1981 to 1993 that Republicans controlled the White House and the dominant narrative was that America had turned rightward, battles over issues like faculty hiring or language in school textbooks burned up critical energy on the left. Gitlin pointed out that the structures created in the late '60s and early '70s—departments of racial, ethnic, and gender studies, their conferences, affinity groups, and a plethora of new writings—made it easy to embrace identity politics, while protesting the broader political shifts in post-Reagan America felt overwhelming, so that "university life could come to feel like a consolation prize."

Gitlin noted that the most passionate student protest he had ever seen at Berkeley concerned the hiring of a French sociology professor to teach race and ethnic studies. The man had written extensively on those topics but was not a person of color. During that same era, there'd been a steep spike in California university tuition that would fall most heavily on Black and Brown students yet "there was virtually no public protest from students at Berkeley or at any other California campus." Likewise, Gitlin had lashed out when one of his classes was disrupted by strikers demanding more Black admissions and faculty hiring and one said, "We're dying out here"—a seeming reference to the high murder and drug overdose rates in the African American community. "How," Gitlin, the veteran of '60s civil rights protests asked, "is admitting more Black students and hiring more Black faculty going to stop the dying out there?"

THIS QUESTION MANAGES TO CATCH ALL OF THE UNDERCURRENTS of America's long, strange political trip from the 1960s to the end of the twentieth century. In declaring the New Left, Hayden, Gitlin, and their comrades made college the nexus for political change. In doing so, they accelerated the severing of ties between the Democratic Party and the blue-collar workforce that had given the party a governing majority for close to forty years. Rather than trying to rebuild those ties—and there was plenty of opportunity to do so as Republicans were crushing unions, holding down wages, and making health care and college more expensive—the new Atari Democrats of the "knowledge economy" instead turned inward, indulging campus-based cultural obsessions that all but assured a socially conservative working class that the political left would keep them at arm's length.

The focus on identity politics handed an opportunity for savvy political operatives and their billionaire funders like the oil-rich Koch brothers, the major funders of the pro-higher-tuition economist James Buchanan, and of the new network of far-right media outlets and think tanks that had taken root in the generation following the Powell memo. The wealthy capitalists' umbrella of radio stations waged the new culture war on their AM frequencies across America to help these millionaires and billionaires fulfill a dream that had once been unthinkable: converting the working class that had been the backbone of FDR's New Deal into Republicans.

IN 1994, REPUBLICANS CAPTURED FULL CONTROL OF CONGRESS FOR the first time in forty years. Meanwhile Clinton—although he was easily reelected in 1996 amid a surging U.S. economy—governed even further to the center-right much of the time. Less analyzed at the time was the impact that this new culture-war-on-steroids was having on the American university itself. In his *Unmaking the Public University*, Christopher Newfield argues that the right's assaults on both PC and affirmative action meant both decreased support for state universities and fostering an idea that civil rights on campus existed to hold back the unbridled capitalism of the new "knowledge economy." He noted that "the public might have asked why state leaders had not built a new University of California in thirty years, during a period in which the state population doubled and the state gross product tripled. Instead, their leaders encouraged them to ask why some Chicanos were getting into UC Berkeley without 4.0 grade point averages."

The problem was that—as the Big Sort widened the fault lines across America—the nation was lacking both the tools and the will to have a coherent and reasonable political conversation about the role of college education like the one that took place, however briefly and inconclusively, in the years immediately after World War II. Instead, Americans saw college through the narrowness of their carefully constructed silos.

As rents skyrocketed and the large, cosmopolitan cities on the East and West Coasts became more like island fortresses, both parents and their kids were becoming so caught up in the paper chase of a college credential that few noticed the political decisions behind out-of-control tuition hikes and paltry government aid. They were surely too busy driving their offspring to SAT prep to care much about how decreased college access looked to folks they dismissed as "flyover country," where growing hysteria about Marxist indoctrination on campuses offered cover for resentment that the American Dream of college was slipping away. A new millennium dawned, and with it a new privatized and uber-expensive iteration of the American way of college that made the universalist, pro-democracy visions of the 1940s feel like a distant fever dream.

Indeed, one of the few things that *didn't* change about the American university from the late 1980s through the critical 2020 presidential election was Rush Limbaugh's passion for attacking it. As skyrocketing costs made college look more like either a playground for pampered and hypocritically left-wing elites or else a "risky gamble" for the stressed middle class, Limbaugh upped his attacks on the academy and the science it was producing on life-or-death issues like climate change. As late as 2019—a year that wildfires ravaged California and the Midwest suffered epic flooding—Limbaugh attacked "this entire silly notion that man is destroying the planet . . ."

Whatever would happen on the climate front, the reigning king of talk radio knew he would not live to see it. Limbaugh died from lung cancer on February 17, 2021. It was just over a year after he'd been awarded the Medal of Freedom by then-president Donald Trump, the man who truly "got" how Limbaugh's daily battlefield wins in the culture war paved the road for his march on Washington.

CHAPTER 5

THE "WHOLE COLLEGE THING" AWKWARDLY ENTERS THE 2020S

By the late 1990s, Harvard was only accepting about 11 percent of the thousands of high schoolers who applied there every year. So naturally you'd expect that officials at New Jersey's Frisch School—a small, elite institution in the suburb of Paramus, not far from New York City—would have been at least quietly pleased in 1998 when one of their graduating seniors was admitted into the most selective university in the Ivy League. Instead, they were so baffled and dismayed by this kid's acceptance letter that a few years later one ex-administrator blabbed his doubts to an investigative reporter.

"There was no way anybody in the administrative office of the school thought he would on the merits get into Harvard," the former school official told Daniel Golden, a Pulitzer Prize–winning *Wall Street Journal* reporter and author. "His GPA did not warrant it, his SAT scores did not warrant it. We thought for sure, there was no way this was going to happen." Nevertheless, this young man was accepted. Added the still-stunned official: "It was a little bit disappointing because there were at the time other kids we thought should really get in on the merits, and they did not."

In a system that soaked in its own myth of meritocracy, "the merits" weren't really a factor for this particular son of a billionaire. Golden had started checking into his story in the mid-2000s, when he was earning his Pulitzer for articles on who gets into college—stories that would become a book, *The Price of Admission*. Like most scoops, Golden had worked hard to make his own luck, when a source slipped him an internal Harvard document that revealed many of the school's biggest donors. Golden scanned the list for wealthy folks with no ties to Harvard before their sons or daughters were accepted there. And he was intrigued by one couple who fit that description—a superrich New Jersey real-estate developer and his wife. Their two sons attended Harvard—including that 1998 Frisch grad.

But something else caught Golden's attention: By the time of his reporting in the mid-2000s, the developer had become embroiled in a federal corruption case that had put much of his finances into the public record. Because of that fluke, Golden was able to discover that—while Harvard had never publicly announced any gift from the developer—he had pledged $2.5 million over ten years to the university and even met with Harvard's then-president to discuss funding additional scholarships for lower-income kids. It all happened in 1998, the same year his merit-deficient son was applying to college.

The anecdote might have stayed tucked inside Golden's book and not widely known otherwise—until something that happened in 2016. That's because the former student at the center of the anecdote was Jared Kushner, who was now, also, the son-in-law of Donald Trump, shock winner of that fall's presidential election. Suddenly, the young man whose grades weren't up to snuff but got into Harvard was getting a big office in the West Wing. Trump was promoting Kushner, and his Ivy League credentials, as the man who could finally bring peace to the Middle East after seventy-five years of bloodshed—despite no prior experience in the region. Kushner would also, the president promised, make the federal government run more efficiently, presumably in his spare time. Born on third base, Jared Kushner was trotting for home as if he were the Hank Aaron of American politics.

Now, one could argue that a high-net-worth individual like Charles Kushner greasing the path for his not-so-bright offspring was not the newest thing under the sun. In fact, then-president Trump himself—an icon of the baby boom, born (along with Bill Clinton and George W. Bush) in its first year, 1946—had long been the subject of rumors that his junior year transfer from Fordham University in the Bronx to the University of Pennsylvania wasn't the meritocracy's finest hour, either. The president's own sister, Maryanne Trump Barry, told her niece, Mary Trump, that her brother only got onto the Ivy League campus because someone else took the SATs for him, while at the same time other family members were frantically ringing their contacts in the Penn admissions office. Whatever the real story, Trump carried the validation of his Penn diploma with him through life—producing it, symbolically, like a kind of passport anytime his credentials were attacked. "I went to the best colleges for college," he blurted once to reporters in 2018.

But why would Trump or, a generation later, Jared Kushner, care so much about college anyway? Both men were long destined to take over their fathers' real-estate empires, regardless of credential. Neither seemed burning with intellectual curiosity that needed to be quenched by the world's top professors. Even Trump's friends remembered him as a mediocre student of business at Penn's Wharton School— one professor later called him "the dumbest goddamn student I ever had"—who put more energy into wooing female classmates like the model and future actress Candice Bergen than into his homework. Kushner studied government at Harvard—although it's unclear how much attention he paid, given his performance in the Trump White House—but reportedly spent much of his undergraduate years doing real-estate deals in and around Cambridge.

Yet they both presumably knew that the cachet of an Ivy League degree would offer a short-cut to acceptance and recognition in the elite circles where they hoped to do business deals and socialize—and that lacking one might cause others to question their bona fides, even their intelligence. The meritocracy myth, in fact, demanded that sheepskin—even if merit needed to be purchased in under-the-table cash. The story of college in the twenty-first century must start with cautionary tales like Jared Kushner and Donald Trump. Because they show the length to which American elites pushed the higher-ed system to lock in gross inequality rather than disrupt it—that quaint, outdated postwar egalitarian ideal—and thus created a long tail that affected everyone else.

But in the early 2020s, it's also fun to revisit the Jared Kushner story because the notion of a billionaire buying his son's way into college with large, but legal, donations already seems old-fashioned, even naive. In 2019, the millions of Americans who hadn't really been paying much attention to what's happened with college—because they weren't stressed-out teenagers or their maxed-out parents, or thirty-somethings barely paying down a $90,000 debt—were shocked by news of a higher-ed scandal involving some well-known Hollywood luminaries. Federal prosecutors revealed that TV and movie stars Lori Loughlin and Felicity Huffman were part of a ring of wealthy people whose bending of the rules (and federal bribery laws) went far beyond Charles Kushner's old-school methods.

The U.S. Justice Department probe named Varsity Blues revealed that parents like Loughlin and Huffman were not only paying massive amounts for ringers to take the SATs for their kids—yes, shades of the Donald Trump allegation—but also bribing exam proctors to change wrong answers, faking learning disabilities to get testing accommodations, and—even more craftily sinister—using Photoshop or fake news reports to pretend children were star athletes in sports they didn't even play. Loughlin and her husband Mossimo Giannulli were accused of bribing officials at the University of Southern California a whopping $500,000 to present their daughters as must-have recruits for USC's crew team. (Loughlin eventually spent two months in prison after she and her husband pleaded guilty to conspiracy to commit fraud.) But in the spirit of Donald Trump's coed crushes or Jared Kushner's undergrad real-estate empire, you weren't likely to find Loughlin's daughter, Olivia Jade Giannulli, in the library or a science lab at USC's campus in sun-soaked Los Angeles.

Already a youth celebrity as a "beauty influencer" with a wildly popular YouTube channel, Olivia Jade—as she branded herself—had posted a 2018 video in the weeks before her mom was indicted for what she'd done to get her accepted at USC in which she talked about her life on campus, such as it was. "I don't know how much of school I'm gonna attend but I'm gonna go in and talk to my deans and everyone, and hope that I can try and balance it all." She called this a commentary on "the whole college thing." The notion that Olivia Jade would actually talk to a dean, or even knew where their office was, seemed pretty far-fetched. "But I do want the experience of, like, game days, partying," she explained. "I don't really care about school, as you guys all know."

In her own updated "Valley Girl" style, Olivia Jade managed to ask the question that had vexed America since 1944: What is college really for?

THE MESS THAT IS THE AMERICAN WAY OF COLLEGE IN THE TWENTY-first century was the inevitable outcome from three wrong turns of the latter twentieth century. First came the conservative backlash—fueled by a mix of anti-intellectualism, white panic over rising Black and Brown enrollments, and hatred of government in general—that decided college was not a public good, and instead turned ambitious young people into indentured servants of debt. Then there was the social desire to attach "merit" to who gets into college and how much they should pay, creating a system that screamed out for rigging by the Charles Kushners and Lori Laughlins of the world. And finally came the cementing of the idea that college was less for rigorous learning and more for getting a diploma that would act as your passport—proof of your merit—in a hypercapitalist society. Never mind that the word "credential" meant one thing (social status, self-worth) to the super wealthy who hoarded elite college slots and something else to the daughter of a laid-off factory worker (employability, at least a shot at a future). In such a broken system, a college education started to feel like some crazy Beeple artwork NFT—bid upward to irrational prices, seemingly destined to collapse at any minute.

American higher education by the time of the Varsity Blues scandal was a rotting fish that stunk from the head. The Ivies and other elite schools had enormous power to set the direction of the marketplace. And what they chose—prestige "branding" around exclusivity, luxury perks, and sky-high tuition—unavoidably trickled down through the rest of the system. The race for young people—and, increasingly, the parents who raised them—to prove their merit and to redeem this credential of self-worth for the rest of their career had created a kind of an odd pyramid where almost everyone was crushed by the weight—psychological, emotional, and, of course, financial.

This pyramid started with the narrowest band at the very top—the top 1 Percent of young people who could make it through adulthood just on their trust-fund dividends yet were desperate for the social benefits and validation of an elite-college degree, making families willing to pay top dollar and (as the Varsity Blues scandal showed) sometimes take much crazier shortcuts. Right below them came upper-middle-class families striving earnestly to keep pace—and maybe even move up into that 1 Percent—by showing their academic merit, even if it required years of SAT and essay prep and financial agita to prove it. For the vast middle and lower middle class in the heart of the pyramid, "credential inflation" meant needing a diploma for virtually any worthwhile job, which forced them into the risk pool of ever-rising tuition at public universities being defunded by the politicians even as they built swank dorms and rock walls to compete with the elites. Today, privatization has meant that even what was supposed to be the sturdy base of the pyramid—community college—has become too expensive and less accessible to the communities they serve.

This broken system has managed to survive, barely, on borrowed money—$1.7 trillion of it. This millstone forced millions of Americans under thirty-five to live with their parents or in cramped apartments—using the money that in the past would have gone toward a mortgage to instead pay off their never-shrinking loan balance—and postpone getting married and starting a family. What's stunning about America's college debt crisis is not only how quickly it happened but how quickly it was normalized, as the concept of higher education mostly as a taxpayer-funded public benefit was tossed down the memory hole.

It happened so fast that few even questioned the insanity of this uniquely American system. Imagine celebrating your kid's high school graduation—and telling your party guests it was worth the $30,000 you borrowed to pay for it. That would be crazy, right? And yet we all know young people who now owe $80,000, $100,000, or even $150,000 for the privilege of attending college, even though today a university degree means what a high school diploma meant 80 years ago.

Still, the attention paid stories like Varsity Blues simplified the real crisis of higher education by only dwelling on its upper crust. I came to think of this as Malcolm Gladwell Syndrome, after a college administrator urged me to listen to podcast episodes from the bestselling author that addressed America's college problems. These shows were frustrating. Gladwell's takes weren't totally wrong, but he seemed to miss the big picture of what American college means for the vast middle class. One episode focused on campus food highlighted the differences between one high-end liberal arts college, Bowdoin, that literally catered to rich applicants with gourmet cafeteria fare, and another selective private school, Vassar, that served an unappealing slop because it had redirected dollars into scholarships for lower-income applicants. Gladwell seemed oblivious to the reality that for hundreds of thousands of food-insecure U.S. college students, Vassar's mystery meat might look like a Kobe steak.

ON A GRAY, CHILLY SPRING WEDNESDAY IN THE STILL-CORONAVIRUS spring of 2021, I watched as student volunteers from Pennsylvania's Kutztown University packed up the last of dozens of paper grocery bags. They contained items like blue-corn taco shells, Splits pretzels, Monster Pop! Popcorn, and boxed macaroni and cheese. For about forty or so undergraduates who'd be swinging by the campus Lutheran Center for the twice-weekly KU Student Food Pantry later that day, the bags were meant to get them over the hump for another stressful week of classes and studying.

"It used to be that the food pantry was just this room," Ryan Tuerk, the thirty-one-year-old who manages the program—when he's not working as a handyman or a computer repairman, using the skills he gained from a handful of IT classes at Kutztown—told me. But hungry students just kept coming, and so now the entire first floor of the Lutheran Center—a handsome nineteenth-century redbrick building with a rainbow flag outside, overlooking a historic cemetery near the university's ancient Old Main headquarters—has been taken over by tables with stuffed grocery bags.

A decade ago, none of this existed. With an enrollment of just over eight thousand students—most from a triangle of blue-collar eastern Pennsylvania that stretches from Allentown and Bethlehem, the former steel-producing towns made into Top 40 music by Billy Joel, to Reading, an ex-coal depot with the nation's highest poverty rate—no one at Kutztown back then had any idea how many young people were going to class without enough to eat, or how to best serve them. "We didn't want to put a food pantry right in the middle of the cafeteria—because that would be awkward," Tuerk said, recalling initial discussions among church activists in the mid-2010s, when campus food pantries sprouted everywhere. An initial site that was a mile off campus struggled, but the move to the Lutheran Center, on a busy main street, changed everything. On its busiest Wednesday night, the Kutztown food pantry served 188 students, and another 55 showed up the next day. That's about 3 of every 100 KU students, and yet surveys have shown food insecurity on campus—a concept that wasn't part of the college conversation just a decade ago—is much higher than that.

Sprawling across rolling hillsides in Pennsylvania's Berks County, which went strongly for Trump in 2020 despite the Democratic votes from this college town and a large Latino population in Reading, Kutztown University is a microcosm of the post–World War II college story. The stately Old Main is the carryover from its creation in 1866 as a teachers college called the Keystone Normal School, but the institution changed rapidly in 1960, after the G.I. Bill and just before the baby boom, with a rebranding as Kutztown State University. Its mission was now to be "a center for learning for the best possible education of the youth of Pennsylvania." Built out rapidly with the bland, boxy architecture of the Great Society era, KU's charge took on greater urgency as coal jobs disappeared from the region, factories sputtered to a halt, and farming became less tenable. The Keystone State built up its network of fourteen strategically placed regional public universities like Kutztown, called the Pennsylvania

State System of Higher Education, right at the moment when the sons and daughters of those miners and farmers knew they needed to—in many cases—become the first generation in their family to attend college, to have any shot at a future.

This basic social contract started to fall apart near the end of the 2000s. Bad planning was surely part of the problem—Pennsylvania's regional campuses, desperate to compete for a shrinking demographic of young people, entered the arms race of fancier, more expensive dorms and sleek new gyms—but bad government was a bigger issue. Over the 10-year period after the 2008 fiscal crisis, state government aid—driven by Republicans who controlled the state legislature and, for four critical years, the governor's mansion—plunged by 33.8 percent per student. The fourteen universities like Kutztown made up this gap through tuition. A student now paid for nearly 75 percent of his education through tuition and fees; as recently as the 1980s state taxpayers had picked up 75 percent. The rise in tuition and mandatory fees at Kutztown—just over $11,000 a year for state residents in 2020–21, plus a roughly equal amount to live and eat on campus—meant steep debt for many, and difficult choices around money, housing, and food.

Nykolai Blichar, now twenty-six, came to Kutztown University in 2013 when he realized his family couldn't afford the small private college in Allentown, near his hometown, that he'd really wanted to attend. Blichar ended up staying at Kutztown for grad school and now works as assistant director of the university's student involvement office. He's seen a lot of changes over those eight years, in part because Pennsylvania's public universities pushed to accept more applicants from marginalized communities right at the moment that taxpayers and elected officials decided these youth weren't worth investing in. Today, he said, "a lot of students are in situations that aren't always the best for them." That means children of middle-aged laid-off workers, or those from broken homes, or those whose parents sold their houses and moved into small apartments during the Great Recession. Or those whose parents won't pay for college because they don't support their kid's "lifestyle," particularly in the LGBTQ+ community in a conservative place like Berks County.

"We didn't have a food pantry when I started here, and we didn't have a diversity-related population like the LGBT community and around racial justice—and now we're trying to focus on these things because ultimately what happens on a national and state level really pushes down on our students," Blichar told me. I was sitting with him in Kutztown University's student-life office along with another grad student who worked there, twenty-four-year-old Chloe Marks. Students who enter the small suite of offices will see a Whirlpool refrigerator with a sign taped to it: PLEASE HELP YOURSELF TO FOOD, CLOTHING & SCHOOL SUPPLIES. At Kutztown, student life has become defined by dealing with life's emergencies.

There are three full racks of clothes—including some heavy coats to get through northeastern Pennsylvania's harsh winters—and the walls are lined with shelves containing pasta, canned corn, and quite a bit of peanut butter. The office basically functions as a mini–food pantry, sort of a convenience store for food insecurity. "We have some people who come in here every day," Marks said—sometimes to grab a quick lunch and sometimes to bring back food for their whole apartment. She said she'd also taken to collecting coupons to help students stretch their food budget. "Last week," she noted with a sense of accomplishment, "we had two people come in for coupons."

In 2016, then-University of Wisconsin sociologist and higher-ed analyst Sara Goldrick-Rab convened a national conference and launched a Twitter hashtag, #RealCollege, to publicize problems—food insecurity and homelessness on campus—that virtually no one was talking about. Soon, talking about what day-to-day survival was really like for students seeking the diploma that would at least keep them from dropping out of the middle class altogether became a movement. Its followers promoted statistics that would shock the average American, and which only worsened after COVID-19 ravaged Middle America.

One year into the pandemic, the Goldrick-Rab–led Hope Center for College, Community, and Justice at Temple University published a survey of 195,000 students at 130 community colleges and 72 four-year institutions across America. It found that large numbers not only faced food insecurity around not having enough to eat—nearly a third at the four-year schools and closer to 40 percent at two-year institutions—but that even higher numbers struggled with paying rent or utility bills. Not surprisingly, more than half of 2021's #RealCollege students were challenged by anxiety as well. A good chunk of that was surely about what waited for them on the other side of college: massive debt.

Nykolai Blichar definitely feels that stress at age twenty-six, even after earning his Ph.D. in higher-education management and landing a full-time job at Kutztown. He did everything right—as the first in his family to get a college degree, despite his parents' struggles with health and employment issues. In addition to his studies, Blichar also found his voice as an activist, initially as part of the LGBTQ+ community on campus, then in Democratic Party politics. But to carry out his plan with no family support, while living in Kutztown and earning his advanced degree and working as a graduate assistant, he had no choice but to turn to the government for help. "The biggest thing for me is that I'm $102,000 in debt," he said casually. Marks—who at twenty-four has been living at home with her parents and commuting forty minutes each way from Reading, trying to avoid the same fate—nodded her head.

"Just for going to college," Blichar added softly. "To a state school."

The #RealCollege movement is a not-so-subtle jab at the higher-ed mythology of the twentieth century, as well as the notion perpetuated by today's leaders—from the president of the United States on down—that matriculation at a four-year campus is a pathway out of the problems facing the lower middle class. Instead, for millions saddled with staggering tuition bills and looming debt, it can feel more like a continuation of them. Indeed, the privatization of higher education—and the structural inequality that came with that—proved much more powerful than twenty-first-century governance could overcome, even when the White House had its heart in the right place.

WHEN BARACK OBAMA BECAME AMERICA'S 44TH PRESIDENT IN JANU-ary 2009, he made higher education a priority as he looked to solve the economic problems of a U.S. middle class reeling from the start of the Great Recession. Arguably, the issue was more of a priority than any commander in chief had had since Truman. In his very first State of the Union address, the new president seemed to acknowledge the many cracks in the college dream when he proclaimed, "We will provide the support necessary for you to complete college and meet a new goal: By 2020, America will once again have the highest proportion of college graduates in the world." It was a JFK-style moonshot declaration, and to education watchers it would loom over his eight years in office—especially when he failed to achieve it.

Obama's most ambitious college-related ideas either went nowhere or failed to measure up to the parallel tsunamis of rising tuition and the debt that was mostly paying for American higher ed. During the less than two years at the start of his first term when the 44th president had a House majority and a filibuster-proof Senate, he won a middling increase in the maximum Pell grant and new tax credits for beleaguered parents. Then facing mostly GOP obstruction for six years, Obama's biggest college victories were more bureaucratic—a crackdown on the dodgiest for-profit universities, and tougher rules aimed at preventing sexual assault. The first Black president had risen with the wave of new

nonwhite college enrollment at the end of the 1970s, winning scholarships to attend Occidental College, Columbia, and Harvard Law—
but the priorities of higher education had changed dramatically in the
years since he'd left campus.

Toward the end, the president increasingly complained—in speeches
and closed-door meetings—about the cost of college, and even threatened to create a federal system to rate colleges on how much bang families were getting for their tuition bucks. It was one more idea that Big
College easily swatted away. The bottom line was that when Obama
left office, America's college debt had roughly doubled, from just over
$600 billion to $1.2 trillion, as average tuition at both private and public universities rose in the ballpark of roughly 25 percent. The United
States was still only 13th in the world in college completion rate. Simply put, the college problem in America got worse—arguably, a lot
worse—during Obama's eight years in the Oval Office despite his efforts to deal with it. His administration did achieve some success on
the margins. Overall college attendance did rise—financed, of course,
by that growing mountain of individual debt. But the big decisions of
the 1940s and '50s that centered college around personal responsibility
rather than the public good meant the government now really only had
the ability to tinker.

Ironically, the trend toward skyrocketing tuition started in the late
1970s at elite private universities and colleges in a manner that seemed
to defy the basic laws of supply and demand that freshmen were learning in their Econ 101 classrooms. After the boom years that peaked in
the 1960s, the United States had experienced a "baby bust" that would
reduce the pool of applicants and the demand for admission—and yet
tuition rose anyway. As Roger L. Geiger chronicled in his *American
Higher Education Since World War II: A History*, the institutions at the
top of the college food chain figured out how to compete on prestige
rather than on price—and smartly put their financial resources to work

in selling that idea through sophisticated marketing and recruitment. Geiger quotes an internal memo from Oberlin College in Ohio that noted, presciently, that while making "cost more attractive does have a positive impact on yield (i.e., the number of accepted students who decide to matriculate), turning attention to academic reputation and social life provides a larger return."

He points out that it was Harvard, not surprisingly, that pushed the envelope on what American families were willing to pay for a prestige diploma. In 1978, in a year when the broader U.S. economy was starting to reel from the "stagflation" of higher costs and higher unemployment at the same time, the Ivy League university jacked up tuition by a whopping 18 percent (from $4,450 to $5,265), which was offset for the lowest-income students by boosting their financial aid. The move clearly worked—for Harvard, anyway. When applications that year stayed the same, the university raised tuition by an average $840 every year for the next decade. Thus began both an upward spiral of tuition—and a kind of arms race for campus prestige that would prove devastating for all but the most elite schools, and for the young people who desperately needed a college credential.

What Harvard had invented came to be known as the "high-tuition/high-aid" model. The system would work well for dozens of the most elite institutions, because the chase for their increasingly golden diplomas meant that parents from the wealthiest families—a growing pool, as the American economy boomed again in the 1980s—would pay any price to send their kid to Harvard or Yale. Meanwhile, a new system of so-called discounts allowed middle-class arrivals to pay less—sometimes considerably less—while the disadvantaged would benefit from an admissions-and-financial-aid system advertised as "need-blind." The new college economics proved a boon to the top-flight campuses. The income from the steep tuition hikes on the wealthy helped to underwrite these discounts for lower-income students.

What's more, these name-brand schools could partially underwrite financial aid through their huge endowments, which dwarfed those of both public universities and smaller private colleges. By 2014, one study found that endowments at the fifty wealthiest schools averaged about $3.5 billion, when the average for all accredited four-year colleges was just $113 million. The return on these investments could also be spent on the kinds of things—big-name professors in endowed chairs, or high-rise dorms that look like luxury hotels—that would keep attracting the richest students, who would then graduate and, hopefully, make sizable donations to their beloved alma mater to keep the scheme going.

The chase for prestige that escalated in the 1980s and '90s led to what Geiger and others have called "the selectivity sweepstakes." Influenced both by the consumer movement of the 1970s and the cost pressures as tuition began to rise near the end of that decade, a ranking of colleges and universities first published by the national magazine *U.S. News & World Report* in 1983 quickly became required reading for prospective students and their parents. Supposedly based on the growing availability of hard data, such as the SAT scores of incoming freshmen, the *U.S. News* rankings were arguably a silly self-fulfilling prophecy, tweaked so that the top-ranked schools were the ones already with the most money, and who rejected the most applicants. Put succinctly by Libby Nelson in a 2014 *Vox* article: "The *US News* rankings are a system precisely calibrated to tell us what we already know."

And yet the rankings became so influential that college presidents saw a noticeable drop in applications if their score—subject to various tweaks by the editors at *U.S. News*, more to keep people buying their magazines and books than to reflect anything meaningful—declined in a given year. By the early 2010s, it was mundanely commonplace to learn that a well-known university had skyrocketed in the magazine's ranking using techniques that are hard to describe by any other term than deliberate cheating. Sometimes the methods were blatant—submitting bogus numbers about SAT scores (prestigious Bucknell University did this) or the high-school class rank of incoming freshmen, or about the acceptance rate. Other plots were more intricate; Clemson University "reverse-engineered" some of its academic programs to look better in the magazine, shrinking some class sizes to nineteen (the upper limit of "small" for the *U.S. News* rankers) while raising others, and hiking tuition to better pay professors, another metric. A former institutional researcher for Clemson told a 2009 conference, as later reported by Inside Higher Ed, that "we have walked the fine line between illegal, unethical, and really interesting" to move up on the magazine's list.

The selectivity sweepstakes was in many ways a rigged game from the start. The "high tuition/high aid" model really only worked for schools like its inventor, Harvard, and its elite private peers at the top of the food chain. The model faltered at the wider and supposedly more egalitarian level of America's public universities, which felt enormous pressure to both keep enrollment high despite the "baby bust" but also to cling to the prestige of their institutional heyday of the 1960s. These large state institutions felt compelled to compete for kids by also showcasing modern new dorms for the computer age, or state-of-the-art gyms with doodads like rock-climbing walls. But unlike, say, Yale or Stanford, most public universities lacked the huge endowments to underwrite capital projects or create academic chairs for big-name research, weren't producing many alums who made seven-figure contributions, and weren't getting huge federal research grants like they had in the postwar era, thanks to the retrenchment starting with Reagan. And pushing the envelope on the *U.S. News* rankings like the shenanigans at Clemson (a public university in South Carolina) only helped to a point.

Of course, the golden age of state public universities in the 1960s and '70s was well-financed by a model we might call "high tax/low tuition"—a system that had utterly collapsed in the decades of tax-cutting politics, from conservative state lawmakers who prioritized new penitentiaries over new college dorms. These institutions faced a horrible dilemma around the turn of the millennium: Either face a slow downward spiral of declining admissions and prestige on rusted campuses that would start to resemble the crumbling shopping malls of the American Heartland, or figure out how to raise the cash to compete in the selectivity sweepstakes. Most went for the cash.

The exclamation point on these trends came in a 2018 *New York Times* op-ed from James V. Koch—a former president of the University of Montana and Old Dominion University—with the title "No College Kid Needs a Water Park to Study." He chronicled a race among state universities in warm Sunbelt locales to build "lazy rivers," the floating party zones you'd more expect to find at a Vegas resort—not snaking past the science library. At the time of the article, Louisiana State University had just opened the most grandiose "lazy river" in modern academia (topping archrivals like the Universities of Alabama, Iowa, and Missouri), some 536 feet in length, spelling out "LSU" in warm, chlorinated fashion.

With the word "lazy" right there in the title, these luxury amenities were easy targets for critics to carp that kids today only cared about social life, not sociology. But by the 2010s, luxury amenities at both elite private universities and the state institutions panting to keep up with them were so common that glossy magazines and snarky websites struggled to keep up with all of them. Boston University's "luxury condo" twenty-six-story high-rise offering kids private bathrooms, walk-in closets, and lounges with flat-screen TVs; the Virginia Tech food court where students could get steak or lobster; or the free ski resort at Michigan Tech were all included in a 2014 Thrillest website feature titled "10 College Amenities So Insane You'll Want to Go Back to School."

The author and journalist Ron Lieber, in promoting his 2021 book *The Price You Pay for College*, described this process best, as "an amenities arms race." Lieber profiled a university that had taken stock of the American way of college in the early twenty-first century and decided to take things to the logical end point: High Point University, in North Carolina. If status-conscious parents were eager to see luxury attached to their four-year, $300,000 investment, he wrote, High Point was going to drop any lofty "ivory tower" pretense and put these five-star Four Seasons features front and center. He notes that one of High Point's five open-air swimming pools is directly behind the admissions office where families—greeted with their name and hometown in LED lights on an assigned parking place—start their golf-cart tour of the campus, including its steakhouse. This luxury pitch has tripled enrollment to 4,500 kids since the university reinvented itself in 2005.

IN THEORY, PUBLIC UNIVERSITIES WERE UNABLE TO USE THE "HIGH tuition/high aid" model; their growth in the 1950s, '60s and '70s had been fueled by the opposite approach of low tuition and generous taxpayer support, both from direct subsidies and research. Now the incentives for state campuses—especially the flagship research universities—to spend handsomely to attract students and the best faculty were rising exponentially, and yet support from state governments, which had already been declining for decades, took a steep nosedive after the 2008 financial meltdown and the Tea Party conservative political backlash that followed.

Rather than dramatically downsize their ambitions, state university administrators concocted a state school version of the "high tuition/high aid" model. Tuition and mandatory fees for in-state students, whose training was their core mission, did rise sharply in most jurisdictions—more than doubling from 2000 to 2016. But to keep in-state costs low enough to avoid a political revolution, these schools looked increasingly to more affluent kids from out of state as well as a surge in wealthy foreigners—especially from China—eager for the cachet of a U.S. diploma and willing to pay the considerably higher out-of-state tuition. Universities built in postwar America with ambitious, egalitarian goals of making their home states better educated, more civic-minded, and economically prosperous became instead four-year party pit-stops for millionaire kids. The model looked a little like a police speed trap in a sleepy Southern town on the route to Florida—balancing City Hall's budget with hefty speeding tickets on out-of-towners, to keep local taxes low.

The numbers are dramatic. By 2014–15, out-of-staters comprised 40 percent or more of the incoming freshmen classes at twenty-four flagship state public universities, and more than half at eleven of them. For example, the University of Delaware—which famously during the low-tuition 1960s boosted a middle-class local named Joe Biden on a path toward the White House—saw its freshman class rise to nearly 64 percent out-of-state kids. (The University of Vermont was even higher, at 76.5 percent.) As chronicled in an in-depth 2017 report by UCLA's Ozan Jaquette, these flagship state institutions educate about 11 percent of all U.S. higher-ed students, considerably more than the elite private schools that hog most of the media attention. Historically, Jaquette demonstrates, the top public campuses had once been drivers of upward mobility for working-class and disadvantaged kids—exactly the kind of student squeezed out by the scramble for wealthy out-of-staters.

Few schools dramatized this better than the University of Arizona, an institution blessed by perfect weather, in a state that during the 2010s was under the sway of an ultraconservative, low-tax government. Starting with the 2008 recession, Arizona lawmakers began aggressively cutting state appropriations for higher ed. They didn't stop when the economy began to improve—in 2011, prioritizing a 30 percent corporate tax cut over educating the state's young people. From the 2008 crash through 2019, the drop in Arizona's state subsidies for higher education of more than 54 percent was the worst in the nation, by a big margin. During that same period, in-state tuition rose by 78 percent to help make up for the deficit—despite specific language in the state constitution that higher education "shall be as nearly free as possible." And the number of out-of-state kids at the flagship Tucson campus rose steadily.

In 2013, the future *New York Times* columnist Michelle Goldberg visited the campus for *The Nation* and described a Dickensian contrast between the luxury she saw in and around the campus—from Arizona's only outlet of the upscale Pinkberry frozen yogurt chain in the swank food court and the private, students-only luxury apartments with rooftop infinity pools that ringed their edges—and the struggles of Arizona working-class students. She spoke with several—a returned veteran, a single mom—who worked multiple jobs or faced mounting debt to pay the rising tuition and whose complaints to GOP lawmakers for higher state funding were met with angry lectures about personal responsibility. "What the Capitol is doing right now," a law student named Mark Ryan who was on the board of the food pantry told Goldberg, "is they are making this divide even larger between the middle-class and the lower-income students and the ones who can actually afford to come here and pay full freight."

As the 2010s unfolded and as flagship state universities competed for these high-wealth, low-motivation, lazy-river floaters, there were a limited number of American high school grads who fit the description. However, the pool of foreign families who wanted the prestige of a U.S. diploma, wanted to break free of the sometimes stilted and test-driven college environments in their home countries, and could pay full tuition was rising dramatically. And no country fit the bill better than China.

From 2006—a year that coincided with a loosening of entry requirements for foreign students—through 2012, the number of Chinese students attending American universities nearly quadrupled, from about 67,000 to roughly 235,000, and the tally continued to rise during the rest of the 2010s. In one sense, the growing internationalism on American campuses arguably fulfilled one of the idealistic ambitions of the post–World War II boosters of universal college—to promote understanding of different cultures. But, as Eric Fish, who authored a book on Chinese millennials, wrote, "American universities became addicted to these students for the wrong reasons"—making up for the steep loss of taxpayer dollars amid the Great Recession.

Inevitably, there were allegations of admissions fraud as the influx happened so quickly, and some students arrived from China with underdeveloped skills in speaking or writing English, or more broadly weren't prepared for the American college experience. In 2016, the *Wall Street Journal* profiled a twenty-two-year-old Chinese student attending the University of Illinois main campus who lived and studied with his Chinese friends and had uttered only two fragments of English during his entire day, including a stop at Chipotle where he said, "Double chicken, black beans, lettuce, and hot sauce."

Ironically, some of the most aggressive recruiting of Chinese students—to offset both budget cuts and otherwise declining enrollments—occurred in the so-called "red states" with traditionally small immigrant populations. Scandal erupted in 2012 at Dickinson State in North Dakota—where a fracking boom had local youth spurning college to join the workforce—after an audit showed that 400 of the 410 Chinese students awarded diplomas there hadn't actually met the graduation requirements. The news conference announcing the audit findings was interrupted by news that a business-school dean had publicly died by suicide a few blocks from campus.

These macro trends on campus not only violated the mission statements of public universities to prioritize educating the young people of their home state, but had other unintended consequences that dragged down campus life. Academics who studied the accelerating trend of students crossing state lines for a college diploma found that a certain kind of student was most prone to seeking this experience: kids from affluent families who had underperformed in high school or on standardized tests like the SAT or ACT. With flagship state universities in some states rejecting thousands of applicants (Ohio State turns away 46 percent of applicants, and Michigan a whopping 77 percent), this growing pool of full-tuition students seeking status in other states might never find the campus library but seemed to know the location of every frat party—a small army of Olivia Jades.

In the groundbreaking sociological study *Paying for the Party: How College Maintains Inequality*, the professors Elizabeth A. Armstrong and Laura T. Hamilton looked at fifty female students at a top Midwestern research university to argue that modern college is supported largely by students on "the party track." These youths come from affluent homes, are drawn like fireflies to the Greek life on campus, and do the bare minimum to earn a diploma—yet find success after college, perhaps because of social connections or because they, in the spirit of Jared Kushner, are teed up to take over the family business. Life isn't as easy for students on the harder-studying "professional track," because of intense competition for grad school and good jobs. It's even rougher for the so-called mobility track of middle-class kids who—if they're not chewed up and spit out by the party culture—graduate with steep debt and may not be able to afford places like New York or Silicon Valley where the jobs are.

In their 2013 book, the academics offered the example of two girls from a floor in a dorm with a "party" reputation—where the two professors and their assistants focused their extensive research—who'd arrived on campus with similar high school grades and test scores. But one, Taylor, came from an upper-middle-class family with extensive parental support and preparation, which propelled her after graduation to a top dental school (with her folks paying the tuition). Middle-class Emma—dragged down by troubles at home, keeping up her relationship with her working-class boyfriend, and the distractions of "the party track"—finished with a 3.0 average that didn't get her into dental school, as she ended up living at home with her parents and working at an $11-an-hour job as a dental assistant. She told the authors she felt ridiculous and that "I felt like I was wasting all of my schooling and I felt that I didn't belong there with those people (at her dental job) because I should be doing something else with people who have college degrees."

Emma's postcollege resentments were not unusual among her generation.

Meanwhile, as you might guess, the fact that these big research universities like Michigan (where the median family income of students is $146,000, in a state that's spent decades coping with the collapse of the auto industry), which once thrived on moon research for NASA in the 1960s, are now hoping to balance the books with checks from the parents of keg-toting dude-bros has had a negative impact upon campus learning. Armstrong and Hamilton are brutal in acknowledging what outsiders have long suspected, which is that to some extent college today is a devil's bargain. They write that neither the school administration nor prospective students—in this buyer's market—have much incentive for rigorous academics, when college is "built around an implicit agreement between the university and students to demand little of one another."

The author Murray Sperber coined the phrase "beer and circus" to define a system in which kids from tuition-paying families were lured to attend universities where they'd have minimal contact with the faculty, and where the excitement of big-time college football or basketball, along with posh fitness centers, would trump low-grade academic demands. Armstrong and Hamilton argue this made the task of university administrators "solving the puzzle of how to systematically, and in large-scale fashion, generate 'fun.'" Arguably, this built on a long-term trendline. A 2010 report from the National Bureau for Economic Research found the amount of time that undergraduates devoted each week to class and studying had already plunged from forty hours in 1961 to twenty-seven hours by 2003—and that was before "the party track" really hit the dance floor.

At the dawn of the 2020s, there was a new urgency to questions about the ultimate purpose of higher education that had been echoing since the Truman Commission seventy-five years earlier. Increasingly, it felt like the life-changing decisions that really mattered for young people were made before they even arrived on campus, with the stamp of an admissions officer at these increasingly selective universities. That was in part the fault of job recruiters who cared more about the name of the school on their diploma—in other words, the credential—than what the applicant had actually learned there.

Scott Galloway, a New York University business professor, said in 2021—after most elite private universities set new records for rejecting applicants, with Harvard's acceptance rate at a rock-bottom 3.4 percent—that a big part of the problem lies with corporate recruiters for Wall Street or Silicon Valley. Said Galloway in a radio interview, "The incendiary here—the thing that fuels this inequality—is American corporations' fetishization of only recruiting from elite universities." He applauded a handful of large employers such as Tesla and Google that were looking to create on-ramps for young career-seekers who didn't attend an elite institution or who perhaps didn't attend college at all—which would surely be a high-tech-led disruption of the American way of college.

But that disruption was still mostly theoretical at the dawn of the decade. Most upper-middle-class parents—at least the ones who weren't Hollywood stars willing to pay hefty bribes or Photoshop fake superstardom in squash or rowing—struggled with the cost and anxieties of gaming the system the old-fashioned, legal way. Many of the tricks they had at their disposal centered on a single admissions data point: the SAT.

THE ORIGINAL IMPETUS FOR THE SCHOLASTIC ACHIEVEMENT TEST (originally called the Scholastic Aptitude Test) may sound familiar: create a meritocratic system for high school students to disrupt elitism and bring greater social mobility. Like so many key developments in the American way of college, the influence of the SAT really took off at Harvard—in the early 1930s, when the wealthy classes were under attack over the Great Depression, and when the Ivy League icon was facing criticism for clearly blackballing the high-achieving kids of Jewish immigrants. According to Nicholas Lemann's *The Big Test: The Secret History of the American Meritocracy*, Harvard leader James Bryant Conant believed the SAT—invented in 1926—could be the perfect tool to create a scholarship program for Harvard to implement his lofty ideas, borrowed from Thomas Jefferson, for what both men called "a natural aristocracy" but that we today would call a meritocracy.

The SAT took off during World War II—which had wreaked havoc with the normal admissions process—and with the astronomical growth of enrollment in the G.I. Bill era that immediately followed. The idea of a uniform, unbiased test that would shatter favoritism toward snobby Eastern prep schools surely matched the egalitarian spirit of those postwar years, but with the dog-eat-dog environment around college admissions that began in the 1970s came the predictable scheming. By 2019, MarketWatch reported that while many upper-middle-class families were enrolling children in prep classes like a Princeton Review summer session that cost $1,699, the wealthy were often going further—hiring private tutors who claimed they could raise a teen's SAT scores by as many as 215 points, and did so through hourly one-on-one sessions that could cumulatively run to $10,000. At the dawn of the 2020s—and then accelerated by the COVID-19 pandemic—a growing number of colleges and universities were dropping the SAT, citing studies proving the test promoted inequality in admissions, the exact opposite outcome of why it had been created. In 2021, admissions officers credited the reduced reliance on the SAT for a surge in Black and Brown applicants.

The twisted history of standardized admissions tests is just the most clear-cut example of how wealth could be used to purchase not-fully-earned merit. The richest families—but also, millions in the next tier of upper-middle-class families dipping into their savings to keep pace—have also spent handsomely on essay coaches, who helped applicants game another key aspect of the college admissions process. The college-entry racket had never been a truly egalitarian affair; the practice of preference for the children of alumni grew to the level where a whopping 36 percent of Harvard's arriving freshmen in the fall of 2018 were legacy admissions. And children from more affluent households, where both parents were likely college graduates themselves, benefited in many other ways that were sometimes obvious and sometimes intangible—opportunities for enriching youth experiences like world travel, attending private, elite-college-track high schools, or the freedom to study without working after-school jobs for extra cash.

These pressures affect every social class, but with a law of gravity that increases pressure as you go down. Let's look at the top two levels. Of course, the stakes of a college fail for the superrich would seem to be the lowest, even if the Varsity Blues scandal proved that they don't see it that way. But for the wider band of upper-middle-class families, the belief that a college admissions decision at age eighteen could decide whether a kid is on track for the Starbucks C-suite or a gig as a Starbucks barista is terrifying. That's what happens when you decide the American Dream depends on your child doing better than you did, and then you see that getting there looks like a jungle obstacle course on a cruel TV reality show.

I've seen this firsthand in the upscale Philadelphia suburb where my own two kids grew up—where pushing children toward the right college and, perhaps more important, somehow paying for it, often drives parents' life decisions, like not changing careers, or staying in an unhappy marriage. Indeed, the weight of college ambition—always present, yet rarely spoken about openly and honestly—became such that it took an anthropologist, New York University's Caitlin Zaloom, to dig deeply into what it all means. In seven years of research interviewing scores of middle-class families, published in a 2019 book, *Indebted: How Families Make College Work at Any Cost*, Zaloom documents how decades of steep tuition increases "fundamentally changed the experience of being middle class in this country."

Zaloom argues that—with getting into college, and typically "the right college," viewed as a statement about a family's fundamental values—parents see paying for higher education as both a moral obligation and a moral lesson for their kids about what is important in life. But meeting such an obligation in the high-tuition era is easier said than done: Middle-class parents often spend handsomely on their kids when they're young—making it hard to begin saving for college—and then idealize going to the "best" school, regardless of cost. The result is either parents not saving for their retirement—risking their own place in the middle class in order to keep their children from falling out of it—or taking on high levels of debt, in a kind of a roll of the dice that only that "right college" will result in a career that can pay the money back.

The research by Zaloom felt spot-on, but like so much of the media coverage and even academic research, it focused heavily on students vying for the fairly narrow band of private four-year colleges or flagship state universities. In 2014–15, when Zaloom and some of the others cited in this chapter were conducting their research, more than 23.5 million Americans were enrolled in higher education. Yet just 626,000 of them were at elite private campuses, and just 2.6 million attended flagship public schools. Those totals were dwarfed by the 9.2 million young people and adults in community college, let alone the 5.5 million in regionally oriented state universities, like Kutztown.

The Malcolm Gladwell Syndrome of focusing on the elite schools—the type attended by top journalists and academics—has kept its magnetic pull. In April 2021, as schools revealed their stunning at-or-near-all-time-low acceptance rates—not just Harvard's 3.4 percent but even just 18.3 percent at Berkeley, so far removed from the Clark Kerr multiversity era—an idea gained traction. Why didn't Harvard, the other Ivies, and comparable elite schools follow the normal law of supply and demand and dramatically increase the size of their freshman class? Jeffrey J. Selingo, an Arizona State University professor with a focus on college admissions, wrote of 2021's low acceptance rate in the *Washington Post* that "these numbers are signs of institutional failure." There's no reason, he argued, that the Ivies with their massive endowments and tax breaks couldn't expand considerably to admit more low-income kids and thus give social mobility a shot in the arm, without any drop in academic quality.

He's right, of course. But while bad ideas from Harvard and other elite schools played a disproportionate role in causing the college problem in America, sending another ten to twenty thousand people to the Ivy League would be just a blip in solving it. If nothing else changed, this "we need to build a bigger Brown" strategy still wouldn't lower tuition for the millions at overpriced and undersupported state schools, wouldn't alleviate these students' need to go deep into debt, and wouldn't slow the traffic at the busy free-food pantries on so many college campuses.

No wonder the arrival of the Trump era coincided with a surge of campus activism more intense than anything seen since the chaos of the 1960s. In Kutztown, Nykolai Blichar's $102,000 in student debt didn't stop him from launching a political career. He won a seat on the borough planning commission in Kutztown—a progressive college town surrounded by a sea of Trumpian red—and even ran twice for a state House seat, a political suicide mission in a heavily Republican district. During that time, many students embraced more radical politics, with nearly half of all young adults nationwide voicing support for socialism.

Indeed, when you step beyond the Malcolm Gladwell Syndrome of elite-college fixation and look at the #RealCollege picture—how the idea of higher ed as a public good got warped into a privatized dog-eat-dog inequality machine jokingly called "a meritocracy," the mismatch between young people's degrees and the actual job market, the soaring debt for those who gambled on college, and the rising despair among young people left out—you start to get a sense of how America's college problem doesn't just affect people applying to college. In one way or another, it affects all of us. To ponder where we've been these nearly eight decades since the G.I. Bill, and where we're going, I spent some time with four people who symbolized the way that college has so starkly divided America.

Gap Year

THE QUAD:
The Four People You Meet in Today's America

There are four people you meet in the less-than-heaven that is our bitterly divided America in the 2020s.

OK, sure—that's a gross overgeneralization about one of the most diverse nations on Planet Earth. What I really mean is this: In the great and heated political conversation that increasingly saps our mental energy, the conversation is no longer a simple bipolar one. Instead, I see people gravitating toward four different magnetic poles—their location in the great American debate determined heavily by two factors, age and education. Either way, a person's attitude toward college is critical to shaping this. If you turned eighteen in the United States before 1990 (today, age fifty or older), the odds are that you either (a) attended a university when college was affordable and popular . . . the imperfect embodiment of the American Dream or (b) believed that anyone, regardless of education, could succeed in this nation . . . right up to the moment that was no longer true. If you turned eighteen after 1990, it's likely that (c) despite high pressure, high tuition, and—for most families—high debt, college remained the only roll of the dice to get somewhere in life or (d) you were increasingly disconnected from middle-class dreams or civic life, in a world of low-paying McJobs fueled by various opiates of the masses, from YouTube radicalization to actual opioids.

I think back to my original notion of the cheesy American pie of politics and a large, very sharp pizza cutter. Somewhere around the 1960s or '70s, in a time of mass college education, campus unrest, reactionary backlash and the first shots of an endless "culture war," the blade came down and split the United States in two. But around the early twenty-first century, in a moment of generational change, the cutter was rotated 90 degrees before whacking us again, into these four distinct slices. In reporting on the state of discord and division that exists today, I came to see these groups as defined not only by what they had but by what they felt they had lost, in a nation of broken promises. And in the spirit of the college campuses that played a role in shaping it, I came to call these groups The Quad.

Here's how they break down:

The Left Perplexed are the generations advantaged by the changes in American society in the quarter century after the end of World War II. Millions reaped the benefits of expanding lower-cost college options. But as a voting bloc, this cohort also includes older, home-owning people of color and women, as folks who benefited—albeit in wildly uneven ways—from the wider ethos of new opportunity that accompanied the postwar college boom. Consumed with protecting their gains in both economic and social status, baby boomers and to some degree Gen Xers have been left bewildered both by the resentments of the non-college-educated Trump voters in what was once brushed off as "flyover country," but also to some extent by the radicalism of today's rising youth, as many embrace socialism.

The Left Broke are, for the most part, the children of the Left Perplexed. They were raised with the idea that going to the right college was a defining moral value for their family and for themselves—even when confronted with the high hurdles of SAT-and-essay pressure and astronomical tuition and fees that should have challenged all of their fundamental assumptions. For those who earned their degree and even for some who fell short, college was a formative political experience, because it would meld the identity politics that dominated on campus with the debt crisis that so many faced after graduation. The new ideas and new reality for America's under-forty college-educateds would lead to the rise of a New New Left that would march in the streets for racial justice, strike for debt cancellation, and become highly receptive to the democratic socialism of leaders like Senator Bernie Sanders—often perplexing their parents, who hewed to more traditional liberalism.

The Left Behind are the baby boomers and Gen Xers who were raised in a bygone world in which they could go directly from high school to a job that provided a middle-class lifestyle. For the Left Behind, it was during their lifetime that America's growing numbers of college grads came to be perceived as a threat to their standing—primarily in the job market, as their assembly-line regime was toppled by "the knowledge economy," but also from their identity politics against entrenched racism and sexism in Middle America. In Donald Trump, these older, blue-collar voters found a champion—not so much because he embraced their concerns, but because he tormented their enemies in the professional and managerial classes.

The Left Out are the forgotten young people born into shrinking factory towns, or isolated communities—or urban poverty—who were never on a college track and then, adding insult to social injury, were judged as lacking merit, or worth, for not getting their degree. These Left Out young people are increasingly atomized—living online, disconnected from any kind of community fabric. They had little job prospects beyond the massive new warehouses that lined the interstates, and the dim neon worlds of fast food and retail. Increasingly, they were lowering the nation's life expectancy thanks to booze, or opioids, or suicide.

The Quad shines light on some recent developments that don't easily fit into the round "red state/blue state" pegs that so much of the media has been stuck on since the turn of the millennium. It explains, for example, how Sanders and Hillary Clinton—an icon to that first-generation of female-college-would-be-glass-ceiling-breakers, but not so much for their children—divided the Democratic Party, or why not holding a college degree is linked to the growing rate of "deaths of despair" from drug overdoses or suicide among increasingly disconnected youth. But the four-way divide also helps explain why "the college problem" has come to define modern politics, even for the sizable majority without a bachelor's degree. What follows are portraits of four different pillars of the Quad. These are Americans with very different experiences, resulting in their different ideas about where our nation should go next.

Roz Holtzman, Left Perplexed

Roz Holtzman never would have predicted some of the twists and turns her life has taken since she stepped onto the University of Pennsylvania campus in the fall of 1976—as the first in her family, which so valued education, to attend an Ivy League college, and right at the magical moment when more women in America were enrolling for a university education than men, when the dorms were buzzing with talk of a new wave of feminism.

Today, at age sixty-three, she still can't explain—to herself, let alone others—why her studies at Penn, which had started in physical anthropology, took an abrupt turn into the school of nursing. Her spontaneous career path saw her become a pediatric nurse, a childbirth educator, and finally a religious-school instructor at her synagogue in Elkins Park, Pennsylvania, an older upscale suburb just north of her native Philadelphia. She definitely never could have predicted that she would be arrested five times beginning in her late fifties—all for civil disobedience.

And she surely could have never pictured the way she looks on this particular Tuesday—wearing a cartoon-purple wig and glittery owl sunglasses, tightly wrapped in black knee-high boots and black blouse. Her outfit is truly completed, though, by the subtle pattern of her skirt that features bees, as well as a couple more of the stinging creatures temporarily tattooed on her arm. The drones are there to needle her *bête noire* for the last four and a half years, Pennsylvania Republican U.S. senator Pat Toomey, whose two main hobbies are beekeeping and kowtowing to his billionaire donors like Charles Koch. For nearly an hour on the sidewalk outside Toomey's Philadelphia office in the heart of the Old City neighborhood, three blocks from Independence Hall, she is no longer Roz Holtzman but Dame Edna VotingAge, her campy protest persona—modeled directly after the baby boomer fringe over-the-top character Dame Edna Everage.

This protest is called Tuesdays with Toomey (although sometimes now called Tuesdays Without Toomey, given the voter-shy senator's reluctance to meet with them—or to hold public town halls). It's a weekly extravaganza born out of spontaneous rage in the first fretful days after Donald Trump's 2016 election and now a weekly labor of love that somehow survived the pandemic—on Zoom, of course—and is holding its first outdoor rally of 2021 on this sun-drenched May afternoon. The crowd isn't monochromatic, but it is more white than Black, more women than men, and definitely more old than young. It's a snapshot of what folks for four Trumped-up years called "the Resistance." What emerged from anger and sorrow in those stunned hours after Trump's victory had morphed into a sisterhood that offered sustenance through rituals—wild get-ups, and goofy eruptions of song.

Joining Roz's Dame Edna VotingAge among the twenty-five or so protesters were a middle-aged man in black top hat and tails who looked like he'd jumped off a Monopoly board, calling himself "Mr. SOB, of the Society of Oligarchs and Billionaires," and standing on a soap box with a sign proclaiming that Toomey is "the billionaire's best friend"; the weekly protest's long-time MC Vashti Bandy, who wore a long, bright-green boa and psychedelic yoga pants; and more serious types like Kadida Kenner, a midlife convert to activism who'd just founded a Stacey Abrams–inspired voter drive for Pennsylvania and who carried a placard with the visage of '60s civil rights activist and Philly-area local hero Bayard Rustin. The attendees took turns grabbing the mic, for moments as serious as an update on the city's new civilian police-review board and as frivolous as a mass outbreak of the Chicken Dance, directed at the senator avoiding them 150 miles away in D.C.

Roz Holtzman, as Dame Edna VotingAge, tried very hard to veer toward the silly side of things, oddly leading the group in a cheer of the Benjamin Franklin aphorism "A pound of prevention! Is worth a pound of cure!" But her main contribution to Tuesdays with Toomey was as songstress, serenading Toomey in a kind of musical-review karaoke while a helper flipped cue cards in the mode of Dylan's video for "Subterranean Homesick Blues."

"Lie, Toomey, Lie!" Edna/Roz belted out, to the tune of Philadelphia's civic anthem "Fly, Eagles, Fly," fight song of the beloved NFL Eagles, "Because we know that's what you do! Why, Toomey, why? . . . would we ever believe you? We deserve so much more, and now we're keeping score! When you lie, Toomey, lie, you can't fool us anymore. T-O-O-M-E-Y! Liar!! . . . Thank you, thank you."

For all their rehearsed goofiness, the diehards of Tuesdays with Toomey believed they had made a real difference, and most of us who kept an eye on Pennsylvania politics were inclined to agree. The influential senator—former Wall Street trader and ex-head of the zealously pro-business Club for Growth—should have been riding high when he won a second term on the same night as Trump's shock victory. Instead, Toomey was constantly on his back heel, anxiously trying to explain his lack of town halls or his votes that aligned with Trump's agenda. In late 2020, he shocked everyone by announcing he'd retire from politics when his term expired in 2022, and then he became one of just seven GOP senators to vote to convict Trump for inciting the January 6 insurrection. By then, Joe Biden was the 46th president, helped by a shift of white suburbanites and college-educated women, also the very spine of the Tuesdays with Toomey movement.

Roz Holtzman and the other leaders of Tuesdays with Toomey were exemplars of an American cohort that had been shaped by its own college experiences and then the twists and turns of U.S. politics in the decades that followed. They clung to values forged in an era when knowledge was accessible, affordable, and almost universally sought. Among those with children, their parenting had become deeply intertwined with achieving those same things for their kids, despite the ever-rising bar of absurd college costs and tight admission standards.

Any resentment of their lifestyle or their status in society by working-class folks in "flyover country" was something they mostly weren't even aware of—until the people of "flyover country" imposed their own president on the rest of the United States in Donald Trump. Trump's election was a direct affront to the values that mattered most to this cohort. The 2016 Republican nominee had mocked their education, played dumb on the science about climate change, campaigned as if the notion of provable facts didn't matter—and won the Electoral College in spite of that, or maybe because of it. But Trump's ascension fell especially hard on women from the baby boom or Gen X who'd been on campus in the heyday of second-wave feminism. That America had rejected a qualified and overprepared career woman in favor of a crude developer credibly accused in more than two dozen cases of sexual misconduct made these perplexed women beyond furious.

And so they did something that was every bit as unlikely as donning a purple wig and belting out karaoke at 2nd and Chestnut Streets during lunch hour. They resisted—starting with the massive January 21, 2017, Women's March that drew 3 million people all over the world, and then with endless meetings and all the door-knocking and finally electing a Democratic House in 2018 and Biden two years after that. But the so-called "Resistance" of the late 2010s was also a reaction to a bewildering America that wasn't what they'd been promised on Graduation Day. They hadn't foreseen how hard it would be for their children to do better, or how those young people would reject their pragmatic politics for the socialism of firebrands like Bernie Sanders or Alexandria Ocasio-Cortez, or how people proudly calling themselves "deplorables" would overrun the White House.

Holtzman was raised in the suburbs outside Philadelphia—first in Cherry Hill, New Jersey, in a heavily Jewish enclave, and later in Delaware, where her dad was a top researcher for DuPont chemicals. Like so many other people from my own generational cohort of second-half baby boomers who went to high school and entered college in the 1970s, the idea that she and her younger sister would eventually earn at least a bachelor's degree was so deeply ingrained it was rarely even discussed.

Her family's views on learning and self-betterment were heavily shaped by her maternal grandparents, who fled Ukraine during the awful years there following the Russian Revolution. Holtzman's grandmother was drawn to knowledge—a classical pianist, fluent in five languages—in a way that the man she'd married in coming to America, a barber, was not, and it was the grandmother's values that were passed down. Holtzman's mother got her degree at Temple and a teaching certificate, only to be told she could no longer teach third-graders once her first pregnancy began showing. When Holtzman reflects back on her own childhood, she doesn't remember her parents talking much about politics, but that they insisted on strong moral values.

Growing up Jewish also shaped Holtzman's worldview, both then and now. When she moved from Cherry Hill to Delaware, she suddenly found herself one of the few Jewish students in her new public school system, struggling to explain to her classmates why she had to make up the tests given on Yom Kippur. She felt like an outsider, and she started to empathize with others she perceived as in the same boat. On top of that, "my family had a contrarian streak," she recalled. " 'Think for yourself.' "

Arriving at Penn in the fall of the Bicentennial year of 1976, Holtzman hit that moment on American campuses when traditional politics had been numbed by the end of the Vietnam War and Watergate, but social movements like environmentalism and feminism were in the air. She recalled that "I lived with this woman who was very strident about feminism, and another roommate was very strident about vegetarianism—and I learned to be wary of zealots. It's not that zealots are wrong, but because their thinking is so black and white."

Listening to Holtzman's saga as someone who arrived on an Ivy League campus just one year behind her in the late 1970s, her personal story rang true for our broader generation of college-bound, tail-end baby boomers—liberal-minded but not radical, not after the painful fires of the 1960s had just been extinguished. Still imbued with the eternal desire to change the world, but after a failed revolution, no longer sure how.

For Holtzman, her contrarian streak led her in that series of unexpected career choices after she dated and eventually married a Penn classmate and then raised two daughters. Jumping from nursing to religious educator at a reform synagogue, she also dabbled in writing and wanted to focus on "big picture" questions, but not politics—not at first. Nothing in the public square in the late twentieth or early twenty-first century really rose to that high bar—until that night in November 2016 that Donald Trump was elected president of the United States. Suddenly, in her late fifties and with her children grown, the seeds that had been planted when her grandmother fled the pogroms in Ukraine rose to the surface.

"Again, being Jewish really shaped my experience, because I grew up with a very acute sense of what I would call 'Jewish paranoia,'" Holtzman said. Like many Jewish Americans, she didn't lose any close family members in the Holocaust but heard grim tales of more distant relatives, and read other horror stories from the war years. Those feelings were triggered as she watched Trump on the 2016 campaign trail, lashing out against Mexicans and other immigrants and stoking violence at his rallies. That was the prism through which she saw the white working-class resentments that bubbled up from those crowds—that Trump and his aides like Steve Bannon were invoking Nazi-style tropes in calling refugees "litter." "I thought, 'We have seen this before.'" Holtzman's rage and her fears over these scenes became the lens, albeit from a distance, through which she viewed Trump's ascent.

On the morning of November 9, 2016, Holtzman struggled to get out of bed, and when she saw the newspaper on her front doorstep, she literally ripped off the front page. She was hardly alone in despair—after all, Hillary Clinton had won the popular vote by roughly 3 million. But college-educated women from the baby boom or Gen X—those roughly thirty-five and over—took Trump's win particularly hard. While many factions within the Democratic Party had never warmed to Clinton, these voters—from the generation when college enrollment by women surpassed men—saw their own struggles in the workplace, or simply for respect, reflected back in the first female major-party nominee. Now America's crazy political system had rejected her for a guy who acted like their last boss or their first husband, crudely boasting of grabbing women by their private parts.

Before that dreary November day was over, a Clinton voter in Hawaii had posted on a pro-Hillary site called Pantsuit Nation that women should flood the nation's capital for a protest march on Trump's inaugural weekend, that the president-elect was such an existential threat he should be resisted before he even did anything in office. Not only did the idea for what would become 2017 Women's March—with as many as 3 million attendees coast to coast—instantly catch fire, but activists looked for other outlets for this new "Resistance." In Philadelphia, Holtzman saw a conversation on Pantsuit Nation about targeting just-reelected Pennsylvania GOP senator Toomey, who'd waited until fifteen minutes before the polls closed on Election Night to reveal that he'd voted for Trump. What if they showed up at his office to pressure him to check the new president's worst instincts? What if they went every Tuesday, and called it Tuesdays with Toomey?

The Tuesdays with Toomey movement shook Holtzman out of her postelection despair. She organized rallies that centered on issues like immigration or the environment, fired off impassioned letters to Toomey, and made a new gaggle of friends. The weekly format encouraged the group to get wilder and weirder to keep things interesting, to write wacky songs and adopt improv-comedy personas. Yet for all her Dame Edna–inspired outlandishness, Holtzman was deadly serious about the threat posed by Trump and an American slide into authoritarianism. She told me she thought often about Sophie Scholl, the German college student who resisted Hitler and was executed by the Nazis. "What is my responsibility? What am I willing to risk? How can I be brave?"

In 2017, with a GOP-led Congress seemingly on the brink of repealing Obama's signature Affordable Care Act, Holtzman and other protesters descended on Capitol Hill with what at first felt like a desperate—but an ultimately successful—effort to stop them. She and her allies sat down in front of Toomey's Senate office, and when the Capitol Police ordered them to leave, she refused to move. Nearing sixty, it was her first act of civil disobedience. Once wary of extremes, Holtzman suddenly found there was no limit in what she would do in opposing Donald Trump and the prejudice he stood for.

"I feel like I was using my privilege," Holtzman added, meaning the fact that she's a white, upper-middle-class suburban woman meant she could make a political statement with her arrest, but not be ruined by the consequences. Even though it was in many ways a miserable experience—so many protesters were arrested that day they detained Holtzman and some others in a parking garage, finally releasing her at 12:30 a.m.—taking action was also exhilarating.

And so Holtzman got herself arrested four more times during Trump's presidency. She gained entry to the confirmation hearings for controversial Supreme Court nominee Brett Kavanaugh—a hot ticket—only to be led away from her seat by police when, during a monologue by Judiciary Committee chair Senator Chuck Grassley, she yelled out the name of Obama's 2016 nominee who'd been denied a hearing: "Merrick Garland!"

After her first arrest, Holtzman had called one of her daughters from D.C. to tell her the news. "'It finally happened!'" she replied. "She was so proud of me."

Ewan Johnson, Left Broke

Ewan Johnson's college dreams nearly crashed down on him after just four days. The saga had started in the mid-2010s near the end of what by his own admission had been an unambitious high school tenure. Then, most unexpectedly, his dreams and his notions about how to get there were abruptly transformed by an unplanned trip across the Delaware River from working-class South Jersey to see Temple University in Philadelphia. It was as if someone had flipped on a light switch.

"This was my junior year of high school, and it was my first time on a college campus," Johnson told me when I met him on an unseasonably warm afternoon late in the coronavirus winter of 2021. "I remember driving down the main road and looking to the left and seeing all the college students sitting on the grass." The then-teenager was blown away by the curvaceous, modernist design of Temple's student-activities center—so much so that it made him want to learn more about architecture.

When I met Johnson in the center of Rittenhouse Square, a bustling jumble of green grass and concrete fountains surrounded by Philadelphia's most expensive high-rise condos, he was twenty-four. But he spoke, in a high-pitched voice, with the worldliness and brio of someone much older. His generational marker of blue jeans with a massive hole over his left knee was offset by a gold-plated wristwatch and his leather bag with the monogram EWJ.

When he decided he wanted to go to Temple, Johnson's immediate problem wasn't that he lacked the money as much as that he lacked the grades. What's more, he became so removed from the college guidance world that he'd never even taken the SAT or ACT. So after graduating from Rancocas Valley Regional High School in his hometown of Mount Holly, New Jersey, he spent a semester at a local community college. There he became the student he'd never been in high school. He aced all of his classes, including the sociology course at 6 a.m., as well as medical transcription. Thinking back on everything that's happened to him, he said, "If I knew what I knew now, I would have stayed in community college. Instead, one semester and I went to Temple, because my ambition was on Temple."

Johnson filled out his Federal Student Aid form—the FAFSA—and qualified for the maximum federal Pell Grant as well as loan packages, on top of a merit scholarship that discounted his higher out-of-state tuition rate. He described his mindset as, "My mother was making fifty thousand dollars a year, so I'm going to make the financial aid I need to stay in Temple." When he arrived on campus in the middle of the academic year, Temple placed Johnson where they had a residential spot—in Morgan Hall, a $215 million complex anchored by a 27-story high-rise with majestic skyline views of Center City Philadelphia, 42-inch flat-screen TVs in every suite, and a sleek, cosmopolitan facade.

The Temple freshman must have thought he was literally on top of the world—until that moment four days into the semester when he was contacted by the university financial office. Even when the Pell grant and his other financial aid was subtracted from his out-of-state tuition (at that time, more than $27,000 for a full academic year) and the cost of living in Temple's most expensive dorm, Johnson was told that he owed $12,000—money that neither he nor his mom, a single parent of two, had. He moved back home to Mount Holly, changed his status to part-time, and—when he wasn't getting up at 4:30 a.m. to make his trains for an 8 a.m. class—started working on a plan B.

His mom, who worked for the state of New Jersey in disability services, was on board and went with him to meet with Temple officials. "I remember my mom started crying," Johnson recalled, "and she was telling them, 'He worked very hard to get here. I've never seen him work so hard for something. If he's not here, I see him feeling diminished and not feeling the urge to come back, so what can we do to keep him here?'"

There *was* a way for Ewan to attend Temple full-time on campus, as it turned out. He and his mom learned about a federal loan program that has been increasingly used by families determined to propel their kids toward the school and the life they desired, even in the era of skyrocketing tuition. In 1980—roughly the same time that costs at private universities began to skyrocket—the federal government reauthorized the Higher Education Act with a program that hoped to address changing times, called the PLUS loan for parents. As the *New York Times* would later note in a 2021 exposé, the U.S. Education Department views Parent PLUS loans as "'instruments of social insurance policy and not traditional debt,' which is why they are not subject to traditional underwriting norms." That means a credit check is fairly minimal, only seeking major "adverse events." These loans have never capped, though living costs and tuition have soared, even at state-supported schools like Temple. The government essentially acts as a casino for parents like Ewan Johnson's mom to reward their boundless faith that their child's dreams will work out. But they don't always work out. The *Times* offered the example of a middle-class family from the New York suburbs who borrowed freely in the mid-2000s to send their daughters to NYU and Manhattanville College, and who—after bankruptcy and selling their home to move into a small rental apartment—still owe about $500,000. Ewan Johnson's mother likely knew none of this when she enrolled in the program.

With his mom's signature drying on the bottom line, Johnson was on his way at Temple. He truly got the full college experience, including a semester in Italy where he geeked out on the architecture and became close to fluent in the language as he moved with gusto toward his goal of becoming the first in his family to earn a bachelor's degree. But he also would come to realize that his success had a price.

"It wasn't until my second semester of my first school year that I realized I was incurring a lot of debt and . . . I think what's real, and what I can name is that in that moment I felt I was in between a rock and a hard place because there was no way out," Johnson recalled. In other words, even as his debt was accumulating, and accumulating rapidly, he knew that his only hope to ever repay the money was to complete his studies, get a diploma, and then get a job that paid well enough to make his loan payments. If he dropped out now, he already had a large debt—but would have no hope of paying it back.

As he entered his senior year in the fall of 2019, there was reason for Johnson to believe he'd land on solid footing to repay his loans, even as they ballooned. Johnson is—in the words of a long-ago play—young, gifted, and Black, not to mention openly gay, and coming of age when the job market and the broader economy seemed to be booming and recruiters were seeking more diverse hires. Then came 2020, and the coronavirus. Like many students, Johnson had changed his major—deciding that biology, in which he'd excelled at community college, wasn't for him. Friends and mentors urged him to switch to communications—"I know I have a lot of personality, so why don't I go somewhere where it would be best suited?"—and he'd ultimately study that, as well as political science and Italian.

Nearing graduation, Johnson thought his strong academic background might be teed up for a career in international communications. Maybe it was the newfangled virus, or maybe it was old-fashioned prejudice against a bright young man who challenged the stereotypes of what a global communications specialist should look like, but the job offers were not immediately forthcoming. A scheme to head to New Zealand for an innovative work-study program—maybe the beginning of a plan to work toward becoming a lawyer specializing in refugee assistance—was quashed by pandemic travel restrictions.

And then the problem of the debt—his own, his mother's—came into sharper focus.

Rittenhouse Square was packed with other people enjoying a March thaw on the night that we met. Johnson and I spoke over the distant sound of a drummer pounding out a nonstop rhythm, broken up by the occasional bleat of a toddler out for the evening in a stroller. He was planning to meet up after our interview with some Philly friends after a day of working from home in South Jersey. If his family's college debt—now, according to Johnson, about $30,000 in his own name, but an astronomical $150,000 or so owed by his mom as the Parent PLUS loans accumulated—weighed on him or made him anxious, he didn't show it. His sense of calm was almost unnatural, because he had a new plan. He was on a debt strike—not paying—and he'd convinced his mother to join him. Meanwhile, he and his peers in a group called The Debt Collective would continue protesting. They would convince the government and particularly the new president, Joe Biden, to cancel all of America's $1.7 trillion student debt, including the $180,000 owed by Ewan Johnson's family.

Indeed, he told me he'd learned something valuable the summer that he'd graduated, when—idled by COVID-19 and his struggles in entering the job market postgraduation from Temple—he joined so many others who marched in protest after watching the video of a Minneapolis police officer murdering George Floyd. In talking to other students and recent grads, he learned he was not alone. "I realized," he told me, "that I'm not the only one who was in this hole."

Johnson and The Debt Collective were demanding that Biden not only cancel all student debt but make public universities free. Johnson was joined by other protesters like Lauren Horner, a twenty-six-year-old who'd borrowed $80,000 to earn a master's degree in international relations from Penn State and now didn't earn enough as a community organizer in South Philly to pay down any of her loan's principal. In Pennsylvania, high public-college tuition caused largely by lack of political support meant that student borrowers had the second-highest average debt of any state, some $39,027 in 2019. But I'd met other young people who—like Johnson—owed six-figure sums.

The protests of the seven or so months between Floyd's murder and Biden's inauguration were practically a graduate school in activism for Johnson, as he found a way to use those communications skills after all. He launched his own group, called the Black and Brown Coalition of Philadelphia, that joined the marches for racial justice. Then he spent days working with an encampment of those living with homelessness near the Philadelphia Museum of Art until city officials agreed to find shelter for its residents. That latter work also paid an expected dividend, when a rising progressive not-for-profit group called Reclaim Philadelphia hired Johnson for a full-time job as its lead housing organizer.

Americans who seemed taken aback at the several million people who marched in all fifty states for racial justice after Floyd's death shouldn't have been so surprised. The mass protests of 2020 were the igniting of a fuse that was lit more than a decade earlier, when a Great Recession meant that a generation's debt-soaked gamble on the job market wasn't paying off, and which gained intensity in the chilly autumn camps of 2011's Occupy Movement and in the shutting down of freeways after Michael Brown was killed in Ferguson, Missouri, three years later. Ewan Johnson's personal debt crisis may have been a tad extreme, but in many ways he was an avatar of America's under-thirty-five generation: ready to take on the world, but forced to still live with his mom in the suburbs.

Debt has always worked as an instrument of fear—tethering people to jobs, or places, or situations that they wouldn't tolerate without the millstone of financial obligation hanging around their necks. Yet Ewan Johnson struck me as utterly fearless—living his best life and confident all of this will work out, if not because of his personal college diploma then because of a generational political revolution that he'd help lead.

"I think a lot of people are being radicalized, and you know our government hates it when people are radicalized—but it's necessary change," he told me of his political philosophy. "For a long time, we've felt so distant from other people and I think this is where the coronavirus comes in, because it shows us how connected we are. This is a collective fight, and we will achieve some tangible wins along the way. It's interconnected. The common thread is liberation. Nobody is free until we're all free and everybody recognizes that."

The late winter sun was starting to set, and Johnson's friends were waiting for him at the bar down the street. We walked to the edge of Rittenhouse Park and then turned in opposite directions. Back in the park, the drumbeat echoed even louder off the steel towers that ringed the heart of Philadelphia.

Dave Mitchko, Left Behind

After a two-hour trip up the Northeast Extension of the Pennsylvania Turnpike and I-81, past the Scranton International Airport where candidate Donald Trump had landed so many times and then down a stretch where Lowe's and Wendy's give way to squat front porches, and finally a hard right turn at the faded Convenient Food Mart in the little borough of Olyphant, Pennsylvania, there was little doubt that I'd finally found Dave Mitchko.

Halfway up the hill on his otherwise quiet residential street, it was impossible to miss the front yard sign, HONK FOR TRUMP, now taped on the base of the giant TRUMP 2024 flag that sat limp on a hot, sun-baked June morning. But the biggest clue was seeing Dave Mitchko himself, manspreading in his shiny black gym shorts on the simple paint-splattered wood bench in front of the small one-car garage that made Mitchko internationally famous for its bounty of tens of thousands of Trump yard signs that he gave away in 2020.

Mitchko's hair and his Mike Ditka–style mustache are cropped very short, and a blue tank top barely contains his interior-lineman frame, During the hour and a half that we spoke, the fifty-four-year-old occasionally picked up and brandished a small paintbrush intended for some eventual chores around his modest ranch house, because

Mitchko wants more than anything to make himself useful.

His sharp right turn to become a Donald Trump superfan—interviewed by the *New York Times*, CBS News, and Agence France-Presse, even summoned by Team Trump to drive in a motorcade with the 45th president from the Scranton airport—was a midlife audible from a man who used to think when he was growing up in this small working-class borough that he had it all figured out, until suddenly he didn't.

An indifferent student at Mid-Valley High School who was shunted into the shop classes called "the practical arts" and who passed on the baseball team because he'd have to wear a sweater and a tie on game days ("You weren't hip if you did that, with the guys I hung out with . . . you know what I mean?"), Mitchko never thought once about college. That's because he knew, back in the 1980s, he was headed like most of his friends and even his future wife to work at Olyphant's biggest employer, the massive Specialty Records factory just up the hill that made vinyl records, then CDs, then video games.

"That was the golden ticket in this area," Mitchko recalled. And for more than twenty years it was, as Mitchko made more than $20 an hour and worked the plant's quirky scheduling to rack up tons of overtime while scoring enough days off to start a lawn-care business on the side. Until that golden ticket grew tarnished, as Specialty Records became Canadian-owned Cinram and then French-owned Technicolor and as more and more CDs were made in Mexico and then folks started just streaming music instead of buying CDs. When Mitchko was finally laid off in the late 2000s—followed by his wife about four years later—he still had his lawn business, until he had a heart attack right there in his driveway, then suffered a stroke three weeks later. Somewhere between the doctor visits and his constant struggles with an ear disorder called Ménièr's disease, Mitchko discovered Donald Trump.

Mitchko had been largely apolitical. He had always voted for Democrats because, he said, that's how his dad had told him to vote, and twice pulled the lever for Barack Obama. He relished his fifty-dollar bet with a friend in 2008 that America would elect a Black president. Mitchko initially dismissed Trump in the 2016 campaign as a playboy. "He had the 'Lifestyles of the Rich and Famous,' and you know what comes with it—I don't have to say it out loud." But as the GOP winnowed its field, Mitchko liked what Trump had to say about "America First," tightening things on the border, and stopping other countries from taking advantage of the United States. But nothing pushed Mitchko toward Trump more than the way that he drove big-time Democrats batty. "Then the hate started coming," he recalled. "The Democrats started saying this and that, and that's when I started listening"—to the man who was driving these obnoxious cosmopolitans so crazy.

The reason I drove two hours into the heart of Pennsylvania to find Dave Mitchko wasn't because he gave away so many Trump signs from his tiny garage—he says 50,000 and the papers said 14,000 or maybe 25,000 . . . who knows?—or even because Lackawanna County was a 2016 epicenter of white lifelong blue-collar Democrats abandoning the party to vote for Trump, which became a huge selling point for the Democrats turning to a native son of Scranton in Joe Biden. No, I wanted to meet Mitchko because of his longer journey—the epitome of the twenty-first-century Americans I came to see as the Left Behind. These were middle-class and now middle-aged folks who thought they'd signed a social contract—that you didn't need a fancy college education to have a nice life in the United States—only to see it get ripped up right in front of them. Struggling when they should have been slowing down, trying to make sense of it all, the Left Behind were looking for someone to blame. Then the pied piper behind Trump University and Trump Vodka showed up to lead them.

Mitchko was hardly alone in the mountainside boroughs containing descendants of coal miners and factory workers across northeastern Pennsylvania—the east edge of the American Rust Belt—in abandoning his lifelong affiliation with the Democratic Party to support Trump's nationalist message in 2016. The white working-class embrace of Trumpism was so swift that the region's Democratic state senator, John Yudichak, decided to bolt the party and become an independent who caucused with Republicans. He told the *New York Times* podcast *The Daily* in 2020 what he thought had changed: The 80 to 90 percent of voters in his district who lacked college degrees now bitterly resented cosmopolitan elites.

Trying to understand why his constituents went gaga for a rich New Yorker, Yudichak said that in 2016 he went up to a man in a red MAGA hat who told him: "Hillary Clinton and the Democratic Party make me feel bad about myself . . . Donald Trump makes me feel good about who I am. I only have a high school education. But I got a good union job. I go to work every day, go to church on Sunday. I hunt. I fish. I'm pro-gun. Why am I a bad guy?"

Ironically, Yudichak left the Democratic Party a few months before Trump superfan Dave Mitchko, who insists he didn't change his registration to Republican until the winter of 2020—after he watched House Speaker Nancy Pelosi rip up her copy of Trump's final State of the Union address on live national television. That move infuriated Mitchko. "The hate was just like . . ." He struggled for the words—a rarity for him. "I don't know. I could say some things." Every time they called Trump deplorable, they were calling Dave deplorable, at least in his mind. When they ripped up Trump's speech, they were really ripping up him and his life. Every time they hated Trump, they were hating him, and he hated them for that.

In some ways, Mitchko was different than the average Trump supporter. He was both an open book—willing to hold court on that splattered bench with anybody, all day and deep into the night—and also irrepressible once he had an idea. When he asked in 2020 for a Trump yard sign after a chance parking-lot encounter with a local campaign staffer, and he gave a few extras away to his friends and neighbors, he went back and asked for more, and then more, until they connected Mitchko to the national campaign and a warehouse near Harrisburg, and a friend shipped them to his garage by the thousands, on a flatbed truck. After his post on Facebook about the massive haul, the scene soon looked like the end of *Field of Dreams*, with lines of Trumpists' cars snaking through Olyphant's narrow streets.

And yet in many ways Mitchko was the picture-in-the-dictionary version of the voter that Trump had called "the forgotten American," the epitome of the nation's Left Behind. It so often started roughly the same way—the great bait and switch of the late twentieth century in Heartland America, as the industrial age ground to a halt. Mitchko's dad (now eighty-four, suffering from throat cancer) had worked for decades in Scranton's large Trane air conditioner plant, and with the promise of a good life and lots of overtime, the classroom-adverse junior Mitchko had no reason to prepare for college.

"We were, like, the street smart," Mitchko recalls of his days at Mid-Valley High. "Our [shop] teacher would tell us, 'I could drop you guys off in New York City and pick you up there tomorrow morning. That class across the hallway'—the advanced math and science nerds—'I could drop them off at six—and by seven they'd all be dead.'"

Mitchko insists that his classmates "who went off to all those big schools, they're doing no better than anyone else." For about twenty years or so, they probably weren't doing better than Dave. Today, he's at a loss to explain the years of layoffs at the Specialty/Cinram/Technicolor record-and-CD plant that slowly took his job, his wife's, and his relatives', until finally the plant closed in 2018. News accounts suggest that in the era of free trade with Mexico, more and more CDs were manufactured south of the border. Mitchko vaguely mentioned "the Obama thing, waving off jobs to Canada or Mexico"—although the North American Free Trade Agreement, or NAFTA, had happened more than a decade before Obama assumed the presidency.

Dave might not know all the details, but he knows this: Things in Olyphant have gone downhill since he was growing up in the '70s and '80s, when the older guys would occasionally slip him a beer at youth baseball games. "It's definitely changed," he said. "You can't leave anything out. I got cameras all over the place." He gestured up at the Ring-style camera right over the garage. "A lot of things happen. I'm not prejudiced or nothing"—his voice trailed off, and he head-nodded toward some houses down the street—"but the police are over here every night, then over there."

This was one of several times that Mitchko made sure to tell me he's not prejudiced. It really eats at him when people call him a racist for supporting Trump. For Mitchko, a willingness to lend a helping hand to someone who's Black or Brown is his proof that he doesn't see color in people. He told me about "the colored kid" who got a flat tire bicycling up the hill, so Dave fixed the flat and drove him to his bus stop, and he also showed me a photo on his phone with the Black family who came all the way from Philly to get a Trump sign. But the bigger picture gets fuzzier as the lens widens. He thinks that the cop who was convicted of murdering George Floyd got a bum deal—"It's just my opinion, the guy was clearly resisting arrest."

I asked Mitchko where he gets his news, and he told me, "from AOL"—partly because his Ménièr's disease causes him to nod off when he watches TV for more than a couple minutes. Mitchko didn't wear a mask at the height of the pandemic or really believe that COVID-19 was a thing, that "the Left was using it as an excuse to fire along their agenda, get rid of Trump." He told me he would "absolutely not" get the vaccine—even with his underlying health problems. I asked him why Biden defeated Trump in 2020, and he answered, quickly and flatly, "fraud," before spinning a vague story of switched mailbags and ballots for seventeen dead former residents of a local nursing home whom he believes cast ballots. "I gave it to Rudy Giuliani" as a tip for his voter-fraud investigations, Mitchko said.

Mitchko seems fatalistic about his future. His mother died at age fifty-four, the same age he is now. His two kids are nearly grown. His daughter did actually go away to college for a couple of years, on a softball scholarship to Concordia in downstate New York—although she had to borrow for her $17,000-a-year living expenses—but after the chaos of the coronavirus she's back home seeking a two-year degree as a dental hygienist. Like his dad, Mitchko's seventeen-year-old son has no interest in college. One post-2016 survey found that Trump's white working-class voters see college as "a risky gamble"—the perfect description of Mitchko's attitude.

Three years out, and despite the giant flag in his front yard, Mitchko said he has no idea whether Trump will be running for the White House again in 2024, or what Mitchko himself will be doing then. He is candid about his life and his health—about how his conditions mean he's now collecting disability payments from SSI, and that in recent years he's been treated for depression. He said he hates "not being able to do what I used to do." It's little wonder that he revels in his visits from foreign reporters or his dealings with the Secret Service while driving in Trump's motorcade. But he also has reverence for his past—when life was simpler, and the way he was promised when he was growing up in Olyphant.

"They took care of us," he said of the Specialty Records heyday, as a freight train blared off in the distance. "Thanksgiving they gave us turkeys, hams, big goodies baskets. Christmas, they used to put us up at a local wedding hall, Genetti's in Wilkes-Barre. A big Christmas party, all catered." At the local AAA minor league ballpark, he added, "they had a whole section of box seats—whenever you wanted to go to a game, just put your name in, and get hot dogs, soda . . . Everybody in this town probably worked there [at Specialty Records] at one time or another. That was the place to work!"

Suddenly a car rolled slowly by and honked at his Trump sign. "There's a priest, right there!" A few minutes later, I was in my car for the drive back to the Philadelphia suburbs, and I looked back one last time. Dave Mitchko was walking toward his backyard. His paintbrush was dangling from his right hand.

Georgie and Josh Redner, Left Out

A couple years after the morning when Jacqui Redner's oldest son, Georgie—a twenty-seven-year-old firefighter and paramedic—threw himself in front of a speeding Acela train on the busy line between New York and Philadelphia, and a short time after she and her husband found their next oldest son, Josh, also twenty-seven at the time, dead in a local motel room, Redner started going through a mental list of Josh's friends and classmates from Pennsbury High School just north of Philly.

Redner thought about a girl named Julie who was the first classmate to succumb to the opioid crisis, and then she remembered Josh's wrestling teammate who also died of a drug overdose—as had the wrestler's younger brother. Pennsbury is a sprawling school district across the densely populated suburbs of Bucks County, Pennsylvania, but as a mother of five boys, and wrapping up a six-year stint as president of the Pennsbury school board, Redner knew most of the twentysomething kids and the teens in the community.

She tallied up the many, many overdoses. There were also multiple suicides. Her list kept growing until one day she realized she'd counted more than one hundred young people from Pennsbury who hadn't lived to see thirty.

"It's just so many," Redner finally realized. She finally asked herself, "What is going on down here?"

From her dining room, the fiftyish Redner talked for more than two hours, often laughing and almost simultaneously wiping away a stray tear as she told me about Georgie's goofball sense of humor or how she and her husband joke that Josh—obsessed with conspiracy theories—might have joined QAnon if he was still alive. Redner moved a couple of years ago to a large house near Doylestown, Pennsylvania, away from the iconic baby boomer suburb of Levittown where she'd lived her entire life.

"We came here to get away from that area because of too many bad memories—the train station where Georgie took his life, the motel where we found Josh—and there was just too much insanity," Redner said. But her new house is filled with pictures of her family, including Georgie and Josh, in happier times, and inspirational sayings, with two tiny stone plaques honoring her deceased sons at the front door.

Like so many other parents in the same situation, Redner still struggles for answers. "I never would have thought Georgie . . . he was the life of the party. He made everybody laugh. And he jumped in front of a train," she said, her voice soaked with bewilderment. "What possessed him to do that?"

What we do know is this: Statistically, more and more Americans like Georgie and Josh Redner are dying at a young age from unnatural causes such as drug overdoses, suicide, and alcohol addiction—so many that life expectancy in the United States, the richest nation on the planet, actually declined for four of the six years from 2015 through 2020.

In 2015, the year that Georgie Redner took his life, two highly renowned Princeton economists, Anne Case and Angus Deaton, published a paper that chronicled a sharp increase in deaths from those three causes among working-age white men and women without college degrees, especially in rural areas and in blue-collar Rust Belt communities. They coined these "deaths of despair." Two years later, the researchers tallied 158,000 such deaths annually, the equivalent of "three fully loaded Boeing 737 MAX jets falling out of the sky every day for a year." A United States that had been a global pioneer in extending human life in the post–World War II era now ranks just 35th in the world in life expectancy.

The primary reason for "deaths of despair," according to Case and Deaton, is education—or, more accurately, a lack of it. The researchers told Vox in a 2020 interview that as recently as the mid-1990s just 59,000 working-age Americans died from drugs, alcohol, or suicide, and the near-tripling in the generation since then was almost completely attributable to white, non-Hispanic males without a college degree.

The findings by Case and Deaton dovetail with research showing that rates of happiness among Americans with college degrees were similar to those without a diploma until the 1970s, when the results began to diverge. But pinpointing the exact causes is not easy. There's considerable economic evidence that life has gotten harder for the blue-collar working class since the 1980s. Wage growth in that sector has been flat, labor-market participation rates have fallen, and many former factory workers have accepted lower-paying jobs in the service economy. But there is also the complicated dance between deindustrialization and social problems like a rising divorce rate, or the decline in unions and other purpose-giving community organizations—a trend we discussed earlier. What's more, Black or Latino workers facing the same obstacles yet for a variety of reasons—from familial or church ties to differing expectations or coping mechanisms—didn't see the same increase in "deaths of despair" as white households.

"One thing we very strongly resist is that short-term destruction of economic opportunities is what drove deaths of despair," Deaton said in the 2020 interview. "We know that's not true. It has to be this long-term drip of losing opportunities and losing meaning and structure in life." That same year, the Princeton academics published a book that updated their original research, with an alarming new finding. While their first accounts focused more on men in their forties or fifties, new data suggested that "deaths of despair" were also surging for younger people without college diplomas—a cohort that looked very much like the twentysomethings of Jacqui Redner's Pennsbury.

At the dawn of the 2020s, there was considerable anecdotal evidence that went beyond Case and Deaton's research, suggesting that young adults and teens—especially those lacking college degrees or prospects—were adrift, exacerbated by a year of lockdowns caused by COVID-19. And the problems weren't confined solely to young white males, as a 2020–21 homicide spike in America's cities saw troubling numbers of Black youth either getting shot or doing the shooting. The news media tended to focus more on a spate of mass shootings, but there, too, the culprits were often directionless young men—like the twenty-one-year-old Atlanta gunman who killed six women of Asian descent and two others at spas after struggling with what he called an addiction to pornography, or the murderer of ten people in a Boulder, Colorado, supermarket—also twenty-one, also seemingly invisible after high school. These extreme cases arguably weren't typical of the day-to-day struggles of a generation that was spending less time socializing or even having sex and more time playing video games or on the internet.

The broader profile of this new, lost generation of America's undereducated is not an especially political one. In looking at how "the college problem" has sliced and diced America into different social groups, I came to consider these noncollege young adults as The Left Out. Despite the growing crises they face, no one is really advocating for political action on their behalf, even as some leaders focus on student debt and the problems of those who'd gotten further along in their schooling. Of course, politicians feel fairly free to ignore this cohort because these young people tend to vote in relatively small numbers. Atomized and increasingly antisocial, millions of The Left Out are essentially off the grid.

Yet professors like Case and Deaton are using bulk data to look at a problem like deaths of despair from 37,000 feet. Closer to the surface, examining individual lives that somehow went astray—like Georgie and Josh Redner—it gets harder to generalize. The loss of Jacqui Redner's two oldest sons, both at age twenty-seven, follows the pattern of deaths of despair—and defies it.

In many ways, their home community of Levittown surely fits the pattern of Rust Belt decline. One of the first and more famous of the cookie-cutter, auto-based suburbs that William Levitt began developing in 1952—Jacqui Redner's bricklayer father was, according to family legend, the fifth homebuyer—Levittown has fallen into a state of decline since its largest employer, a U.S. Steel plant on the Delaware River, closed in 2001. But the sprawling Pennsbury district also stretches north to include former farmlands turned into upscale suburbs with large McMansions—home to many of Georgie and Josh's school friends, and also a number of drug overdoses and addiction dramas.

What's more, while studies show a correlation between rising deaths of despair and counties that voted for Donald Trump, the Redners—a third-generation union family, with George working heavy equipment for the Operating Engineers—are old-school pro-labor liberal Democrats. Their five kids were put on a path to steer them to good-paying union jobs—aided, at times, by George's web of connections—but not necessarily college, especially as they watched other Pennsbury grads get saddled with debt.

Josh Redner had a different plan. A top-flight wrestler, the second Redner son had, according to Jacqui, been promised by recruiters for the U.S. Coast Guard Academy a full scholarship—only to see his dream collapse when he blew out his knee during a match his senior year. During his rehab, Josh's doctors prescribed him the painkiller Percocet. He would struggle with drugs for the next decade, until the night he died.

"When that"—the Percocet—"wasn't enough, the OxyContin starts getting passed around, and when you can't afford $80 a pill, you go to the next best thing"—which turned out to be street drugs like heroin, his mom said.

But she concedes that Josh lost something else when he lost his wrestling career—his focus. "Wrestling defined him from a young age," Redner said, adding: "I think when he couldn't do it, there was a disconnect, like, 'Now what am I going to do?'" Without athletics, he lost interest in school, even though his mother is convinced that with his love of sports and a head for statistics he could have worked for ESPN. Like his brothers, he did eventually land in a union job—with a Laborers local over in South Jersey—that paid a living wage, but by then the drugs were more powerful than work, or any other mile markers of stability.

Indeed, one of the few things that kept Josh from going completely off the deep end during those ten years spent in and out of drug rehab was his close relationship with his older brother Georgie, the one person he felt comfortable in calling whenever he'd hit rock bottom. "Georgie knew where to take him, so Georgie would come at three in the morning to get him," Redner recalled. "Of course, Georgie would yell at him the whole way."

But Georgie was battling his own, different demons—the stress of frontline work in modern America. The Redners' oldest son—"Reds," his friends and coworkers called him, a mash-up of his name and curly auburn hair—Georgie rejected his dad's Operating Engineers after two months, insisting he wanted a career as a full-time firefighter and paramedic. His dream would become an uphill climb of low-paying rescue jobs working long and often multiple shifts, as well as something no one in the Redner family was equipped to deal with—bouts of post-traumatic stress disorder, or PTSD.

It started when Georgie moved to Goose Creek, South Carolina, where he was able to get on with the fire department, working twenty-four-hour shifts for low pay. One of those long shifts would change him forever. He called his father up late that night and said, "Dad, I think I want to come home." He related the horror of scooping a lifeless two-year-old girl from a swimming pool and the frantic, unsuccessful efforts to revive her. He was haunted by the juxtaposition of that death and saving a drug-overdose victim later that shift.

Georgie did come home two months later, and Jacqui said, "he was more serious and then he started saying he didn't believe in God anymore"—tough words for a traditional, Mass-going Irish Catholic family. "He would say, 'What kind of God lets a two-year-old die and'—not yet knowing about his brother's struggles—'lets a drug addict survive?'" Georgie's parents came to understand he was struggling with depression—including time at a psychiatric hospital, although only years later did they learn he'd tried to hang himself there—but didn't immediately grasp the full extent.

When his demons finally got the better of him in 2015, after a fifteen-dollar-an-hour gig as a firefighter at New Jersey's Six Flags Amusement Park and assorted lower-paying paramedic posts, Georgie was on the brink of his dream job with the Philadelphia Fire Department. His framed acceptance letter wasn't as strong as his PTSD and depression, exacerbated by a bitter breakup with a girlfriend that included a custody fight over their dog, Lucky. When a Bucks County mental health clinic refused to admit him, Georgie went to the nearby Levittown train station, where he jumped in front of a speeding Acela at 10:15 on a Saturday morning.

Josh Redner lived on for two more years, lacking the emotional support he'd always received from his older brother. Just like Georgie, near the end there was a difficult breakup with a girlfriend. He told his parents to pick him up at the motel where he was staying on US 13, not far from where his brother died and at roughly the same time of day, 10 a.m. When Jacqui and George found Josh, he'd stuck a knife in the wall of the motel room and hung his crosses from it. A picture of Georgie was next to his bedside. The coroner ruled it a heroin overdose, but Jacqui tends to side with her lawyer, who thinks it was intentional. "I don't think he could handle the stress," Jacqui said.

How did Josh and Georgie fit into the Princeton-bred theory about "deaths of despair"? Without college, the two union heirs saw mixed results in the blue-collar marketplace—but the problems of being a young adult in America today run deeper than just a paycheck. Both Redner boys searched for what Case and Deaton describe as "purpose and meaning" in life, much harder in a world where twentysomethings postpone marriage and home-buying and increasingly question their parents' God. While it was once the case that entering adulthood meant finding structure, young people in today's America—college-bound or not—feel enormous pressure to find themselves, and struggle when a knee injury or a harrowing memory holds them back.

As school board president in Pennsbury, Jacqui Redner saw the pressure on blue-collar kids and white-collar kids alike—to get into the right school or get the perfect job. "At what point," she asked, "do we let go? And it's going to kill these kids. I get so angry that it was my two kids I lost, because I did all the right things . . ."

CHAPTER 6

A COLLEGE DEBT CRISIS, OCCUPY WALL STREET, AND THE RISE OF A NEW NEW LEFT

The ghosts of American college, past, didn't matter much to Sean Kitchen as he grew up in Philadelphia's working-class, abandoned-factory neighborhood of Juniata Park—watching his dad become increasingly embittered as he lost his good-paying union job when the Acme supermarket chain closed an outdated Philly warehouse in 1999, only to see his next factory job after that outsourced to Mexico.

It was a future without college that haunted him. There was an idea that stayed with Sean for his first twenty-one years, even after he got a weak score on the SAT, even as only one college—Kutztown University—offered him acceptance for the fall after he graduated from his Catholic high school, even after his family's college debt started rising toward the $40,000 mark, and even after he ate nothing but pasta with butter and garlic for a couple of weeks when his money supply ended before one semester did.

"I feel like college was forced on us," Kitchen, now in his early thirties, told me in 2021. Nonstop through high school, he recalled, "they said you have to go to college to be a success, or else you'll be a construction worker or a tradesman"—ironic, since the couple of class-mates Kitchen knows who got into a trade union are actually doing pretty well these days.

Until one day in 2011 when Kitchen—who was doing okay at Kutztown but struggling to get enough credits after switching majors—finally decided he'd had enough.

Drawn to progressive politics after a grade-school teacher's lecture against the Iraq War, Kitchen spent much of the year watching videos of the Arab Spring uprisings and the state-worker revolt in Wisconsin—and then the world's political turmoil came to Kutztown. When Pennsylvania's Republican governor Tom Corbett proposed a 50 percent cut in state aid to universities, Kitchen placed flyers in support of a campus protest on any door he could find.

Kitchen saw connections between the globalization that took away his dad's latest job and the privatization of his own college education—and then he started noticing something else: A Twitter hashtag for a big open-ended protest against the abuses of capitalism that would be called #OccupyWallStreet. Hooked now on the live streams coming from Zuccotti Park—the protest's epicenter—in lower Manhattan, Kitchen was watching on October 1, 2011, when New York cops trapped and busted hundreds of protesters on the Brooklyn Bridge. "I was watching that Saturday," he said, and I said, 'Screw it, I'm making a Facebook page.'"

In just twenty-four hours, Kitchen had signed up about two thousand people for his idea—an Occupy protest encampment in the heart of his native city, Philadelphia. He was far from alone. Before the end of that October, tens of thousands of progressive protesters—in roughly 2,300 cities and towns around the world—had left the comforts of their home to sleep by night in chilly tents, often on hard concrete, and march by day against the banks who'd crashed the global economy or the cops who'd attacked them with pepper spray and tear gas.

The Occupy Wall Street protests of 2011 were arguably one of the important political moments in modern U.S. history—and also wildly misinterpreted. Because the uprising had melted away by Thanksgiving—thanks to both harsh policing and internal squabbles—and because of confusion in the mainstream media over who was leading the encampments and what the occupiers were demanding, too many pundits for too long have too easily dismissed Occupy Wall Street.

The Occupy protests gave Americans a new brand vocabulary to talk about the important things that had happened since 1980: "income inequality," the obscene wealth of "The 1 Percent," and the utter stagnation of "The Other 99 Percent," including families like Kitchen's. Much like the Greensboro lunch counter sit-in that, just one month into that decade, initiated the 1960s as an era of unprecedented upheaval and protest, Occupy Wall Street signaled that the 2010s were a new era in which Americans were no longer going to take it, from the fires of Ferguson to the pink-hatted millions of the Women's March to school walkouts for gun control. The Occupy movement didn't so much fade out as segue into the 2016 Bernie Sanders presidential campaign, which unified a new, young progressive movement that couldn't elect its own president but nonetheless succeeded in pushing an eventual White House occupant, Joe Biden, further left than anyone could have imagined. But we're getting ahead of our story here.

There was something else about Occupy Wall Street. The causes of this seemingly out-of-nowhere political revolution are deeply intertwined with the growing failures of the American way of college in the twenty-first century. To be sure, the 2011 protests attracted a range of characters—disgruntled Iraq war vets, gray-bearded survivors from the anti-war '60s, a few union hardhats. But the heart and soul of Occupy were thousands of young people like Sean Kitchen—drowning in debt, struggling to find a meaningful career, feeling the pressure and frustration of getting pushed into a college education, and wondering what the hell it was all for.

Few people had seen this political tidal wave coming. It had been three years since Wall Street's reckless, speculative practices had caused the greatest financial crash since 1929, and since America's young voters had seemingly celebrated "HOPE" with the election of America's first Black president in Barack Obama. Seeking an understanding of the 2011 protests, some turned to a wildly popular Tumblr account titled "We Are the 99 Percent," where Occupy participants with their hand-written signs tried to explain why they were there.

Massive student loans, and lack of meaningful job opportunities, predominated. One sign read I HAVE $50,000 IN STUDENT LOAN DEBT AND MY B.A. IS USELESS. Another: GRADUATED COLLEGE: MAY 2010. DEBT: $35,000. JOBS IN THE U.S.: NONE. A third read plaintively: I AM 24 YEARS OLD AND AM $90,000 IN DEBT FROM GETTING A COLLEGE EDUCATION. WHY ARE WE BEING PUNISHED WITH DEBT FOR GETTING A HIGHER EDUCATION?

The narrative of the early twenty-first century embraced by politicians and pundits centered around a housing bubble, and the trillions of dollars in bad mortgages nurtured by Wall Street which then crashed the financial markets. Few had paid much attention to the college debt bubble—except the twentysomethings getting those never-shrinking loan statements every month down in their parents' basement.

In 1999 as the last millennium ended, America's overall college debt burden was a seemingly manageable $90 billion. By the middle of 2011—right around the time an obscure magazine called *Adbusters* posted a meme of a ballerina atop the Wall Street bull statue amidst a tear-gas-shrouded protest, the first hint that Occupy was coming—the negative balance sheet had soared 511 percent to $550 billion. And it would soon rise much, much higher. The unemployment rate of the young people in their early twenties who'd gambled by taking on the debt for a diploma was a stunning 9.9 percent (still just half of their contemporaries without college degrees)—and that didn't count the millions of graduates underemployed as baristas or restaurant servers, not earning enough to pay down the principal.

The college debt crisis was a ticking political time bomb, set somewhere near the end of the twentieth century. The ammunition was provided by Wall Street greedsters, including so many of the finance majors arriving fresh from their pricy Ivy League education, who saw profits in the privatization of higher ed. The device would be ignited in 2011, as more and more twentysomething degree holders owed more and more money every month, and as the jobs to pay the money back evaporated.

Ironically, a very different kind of debt crisis—involving not beleaguered sociology grads but the creditworthiness of the entire American government—may have finally convinced the growing cadre of young leftists that all the color had faded from those 2008 HOPE posters. The summer 2011 debt impasse between the Obama administration and the new generation of Tea Party Republicans who'd just seized control of the U.S. House brought the federal government to the brink of default, and showed some activists that it was going to take a lot more than just electing a Black president for America to change course.

"I think there was a tipping point," said Astra Taylor, who took part in the Occupy Wall Street protests from day one that fall and went on with other activists (including, eventually, Ewan Johnson) to co-found the advocacy group The Debt Collective. She came to realize a key reason that other political issues that had angered young people—most notably the Iraq War in the early 2000s—hadn't triggered 1960s-style demonstrations because America's twentysomethings needed to keep their jobs to pay back their loans. "You kept your nose to the grindstone," she said—but now the size of the increasingly unpayable debt burdens brought the freedom of nothing left to lose.

The wheel had nearly come full circle. The college experience had once created a New Left in America—merging traditional liberal issues such as racial justice and opposing foreign imperialism with an affluence-fueled emphasis on personal freedom that seemed to reject Industrial Revolution class concerns. The student loan crisis was the most tangible sign that their desires for self-actualization had been exploited and that middle-class affluence was disappearing. What has emerged today is the New New Left—highly educated, just like the New Left before it, but with a newfound understanding of how traditional concerns over racism and sexism are bound up with a brand of extractive capitalism. The New New Left is not afraid to embrace both the word "socialism" as well as modern iterations of that ideology—which plays out in newfound support for unions, in workplace walkouts in Silicon Valley, or in broad support for a higher minimum wage.

But for the New New Left of the 2020s, the place where the rubber really hits the road is student debt.

THE RIGID LAWS OF ECONOMICS HAD STOPPED APPLYING TO THE American Dream of college, since millions were willing to pay whatever it took to get the credential of a college diploma—whether that need was social status or clinging economically to a seemingly ever-shrinking middle and upper middle class. Capitalism abhors a vacuum, so into this void developed a new venture to profit off young people's need for education: the student loan industry. And this would eventually attract new parasites from way further down the economic food chain: the worst of the for-profit colleges, which set tuition for dubious academic programs at the maximum of whatever a student could legally borrow that year.

Take a step back, and it's striking how much U.S. higher education resembles that other great American crisis of spiraling costs that has bankrupted so many citizens: health care. Just like higher education, America has flubbed multiple chances to make the wellness of its citizens a public good, by establishing the kind of single-payer health system that exists in most industrialized nations. And in both health care and higher ed, the balkanized system of for-profit and not-for-profit (but still with obscenely high-paid executives) entities left no one truly responsible for cost containment. Instead, unrestrained costs are funneled through insurance premiums—just like rising college loans—with families that fall through the cracks getting crushed financially. Ironically, while the media reported extensively for decades on America's runaway medical expenses, few people seem to know that college costs actually rose by a greater percentage nearly every year, beginning in the Reagan era.

The idealism of the so-called Liberal Hour in the mid-1960s that a grab-bag of government-backed loans and small grants could level the playing field and make it possible for lower-income youth to still attend college, while not making taxpayers pay for children of the wealthy, was steamrolled by the spiral of rising tuition that began in the late 1970s. Washington's scheme to guarantee student loans was modeled after federal mortgage programs that had revitalized the housing market during the Great Depression; private lenders were protected by the knowledge the government would take over a student loan that fell into default, paying about 97 percent of the outstanding principle. But in launching this new enterprise—the student loan industry—the government was creating a monster. In fact, one of the drafters of LBJ's 1965 Higher Education Act later would describe the Guaranteed Student Loan Program as a "fund-eating dragon." And of course, the problem with modeling student loans after mortgages is that the two have little in common. Homebuyers are trading one way for putting a roof over their head—rent—for a more productive one, tied to the tangible asset of a structure. College loans are essentially paying for the dream of a career and a certain lifestyle—a dream that doesn't always come true.

With the normal rules of supply and demand shattered by universities' high-tuition model on one end of the negotiation and families' insatiable demand for a diploma as the American Dream on the other side of the table, this new usurious industry grew exponentially in the latter twentieth century, as did the loan amounts. And once Washington had made the fateful decision to fund individuals rather than fund universities and thus eliminate the need for tuition, it was locked into a downward spiral of decisions that continually made it not only possible but certain that more students would be borrowing greater and greater amounts.

Elizabeth Tandy Shermer—an associate professor of history at Loyola University Chicago who authored a 2021 book on the history of student loans titled *Indentured Students: How Government-Guaranteed Loans Left Generations Drowning in College Debt*—has noted that even during an era of increasing partisan division, increasing the ability of students to borrow money was one thing that Democrats and Republicans seemed to agree on during the 1990s and beyond. She wrote in a *Washington Post* op-ed, "[t]hey made for-profit schools eligible for federal student assistance programs, enabled parents to borrow, made discharging student debt during bankruptcy proceedings almost impossible and launched Sallie Mae, a government-sponsored enterprise that made buying, selling and profiting off student debt easier." Evidence that the popular Pell Grants program was falling far short of meeting real college costs, which would necessitate even more loans, was met with a collective shrug from lawmakers intoxicated by keeping taxes low.

Other experts argue that the federal government's role in causing the student loan crisis is even more insidious. That's because as its own portfolio of student debt began to accumulate beginning in the 1990s, the government began to realize that college loans could become, in the infamous words of Steve Martin's character in *The Jerk*, "a profit deal." Not in real life, where the growing gap between the rising amount that young adults owed and what many of them could reasonably expect to pay back meant that billions of dollars on loans on the books would never be paid back. But the government's college debt was priceless on paper—because Congress could use the make-believe future repayments to balance the budget. To the Congressional Budget Office, the phantom revenue of skyrocketing loans that could never possibly be repaid became an asset and thus a form of "deficit control."

IN MANY WAYS, THE RISE OF THE INVESTOR-DRIVEN FOR-PROFIT UNIversity—a modern industry constructed around finding the limits of the federally backed loan infrastructure and the growing desperation of middle-class kids for a credential in a ridiculous job market—is the epitome of how the postwar American Dream of college turned into a nightmare for millions of preyed-upon young people.

For-profit colleges were not new; as you recall from this book's introduction, my grandparents and some of their heirs turned a small secretarial school into one called Midstate College in Peoria, Illinois, offering first associate and then bachelor's degrees—often to older, working-class students. Trust me, no one got fabulously rich—even before Midstate declared bankruptcy in 2019. But the new breed of large, Wall Street–funded for-profit universities were a very different animal. Their aggressive marketing tactics took the relatively genteel branding tactics of elite private universities into the realm of a highpressure, *Glengarry Glen Ross*–style boiler room. In many cases, their aggressive pitch vastly oversold the value of their diplomas in the job market, and elided the fact that courses were typically taught by harried, underpaid adjuncts. Enrollment was set up so students paid little or often no money out of pocket, even as their loan balances skyrocketed.

In March 2011—as a reporter for the *Philadelphia Daily News,* I was covering the various ways in which the Great Recession and the events leading up to it had crushed the American middle class—I first learned about the problems that students and recent for-profit college graduates were having in finding jobs and paying back their sizable debts. I focused on the Art Institute of Philadelphia, both because it had a strong presence in my home city and also because its parent company—Education Management Corp., or EDMC—was becoming the poster child for everything wrong with the industry. EDMC was very much a creation of Wall Street and its fascination with the earnings potential of for-profit colleges paid for by guaranteed government loans. The firm held a public stock offering in 1996, grew by leaps and bounds, and eventually saw a 40 percent ownership stake taken by Goldman Sachs, which just two years later would be at the epicenter of the global financial collapse, driven by a not-dissimilar fascination with subprime mortgages.

Arguably, EDMC was using hard-sell tactics to peddle subprime educations. In August 2010, Bloomberg News had published an article about the corporation with the unforgettable headline: STRIPPER RE-GRETS ART DEGREE PROFITABLE FOR GOLDMAN. The adult-entertainment worker in question had paid $70,000 toward earning her diploma at the Art Institute of Fort Lauderdale, but only found a short-lived twelve-dollar-an-hour gig recruiting video-game-industry workers before she ended up performing at the Lido Cabaret in Cocoa Beach. "I didn't know what else to do," the then-twenty-six-year-old woman said. "I've got a worthless degree. It's like I didn't attend school at all."

I spoke in 2011 with a South Jersey woman named Marianne Hicks who—bored with her jobs working in a firm's accounts receivable department and as a part-time cook—was enticed by the Art Institute of

Philadelphia's recruiters with promises of an exciting career in industrial design. After Hicks graduated the school in 2007, she struggled to pay back her $90,000 debt and was continually under the gun from collection agencies, while squabbling with a sister who'd co-signed her loans. The Art Institute had assured her she'd receive job placement help as she earned her diploma, but she told me it was mainly forwarding some ads from Craigslist. Hicks, who was forty-four when we spoke, told me wistfully, "I expected to be doing better by now."

These egregious examples would eventually turn the tide against the worst bottom-feeders in the for-profit college industry, but only after years of struggle against an army of highly paid and well-connected lobbyists. By 2014, under growing pressure—particularly from civil rights groups like the NAACP and La Raza who said these schools disproportionately preyed upon Black and Brown students—the Obama administration imposed a "gainful employment rule" that withheld financial aid dollars from institutions whose graduates weren't finding jobs that paid enough to make good on their loans. Stock in EDMC lost more than 99 percent of its value, and the firm declared bankruptcy before the Art Institute of Philadelphia closed in 2018—more bad news for scores of its then-current students left in the lurch by the move. A Wall Street–backed competitor of EDMC called Corinthian College would be fined $30 million by the U.S. Department of Education for its unmet career promises, as a judge later ruled that alums could stop paying their outstanding debt.

In going after the worst of the for-profit colleges, Washington was attacking the lowest-hanging fruit, when much of the tree—including well-known state colleges and elite universities—was going rotten from the same disease. As has so often been the case during America's move into mass university education, the students who tended to suffer the most from bad public policy were the ones who had been making small, tentative gains: women, and people of color.

Given that it's been a couple of generations now since female enrollment on campus surpassed that of men, it's not surprising that women also hold a greater proportion of America's $1.7 trillion college debt burden. But when the American Association of University Women dug deeper into the issue in 2019, the organization found that while women comprised 56 percent of college enrollment at that time, they held nearly two-thirds of the overall debt—then some $929 billion. (Given the way that 2020's COVID-19–related job losses also fell more heavily on women, that number surely exceeds $1 trillion today.) One reason for the disparity is, quite simply, the stubborn reality of discrimination. Even today, a woman who has received a bachelor's degree earns only 81 percent, on average, of their male counterpart's salary—even though they still face the exact same sky-high rents and other living expenses when living in urban areas where most good jobs are located.

Of course, another factor is that large numbers of women holding student debt are Black or Latina, and thus face the double whammy of racial discrimination. The AAUW, in its research, noted that 57 percent of Black women with a college degree report financial difficulties in repaying their debt, which often causes their loan balances to move in the wrong direction. Generations of racial bias in the labor market means that more college-bound Black students borrow larger amounts of money than their white counterparts. The obscene wealth gap in America—by the end of the Great Recession, the average white household had a net worth 20 times larger than a typical Black family—means that African American young people didn't have a ready source of cash to cover the growing gap between college tuition and available loans or scholarships.

Over the course of the 2010s—a decade in which a series of incidents around police brutality, accelerating with the 2014 unrest over the killing of a college-bound Black youth named Michael Brown in Ferguson, Missouri, would spark a national racial reckoning—these financial pressures on Black households began to take a toll. African American students as a percentage of college enrollment actually decreased by 10.7 percent from 2010 to 2018, according to the EducationData.org database. It was about more than just the money. College admissions policies that favored groups like "legacy" children of alumni squeezed the number of slots for nonwhite applicants, lower-income kids fell behind wealthier families who were paying for SAT prep or essay help, and HBCUs that had traditionally offered an alternative pathway were now struggling. The bottom line, though, was that a movement for racial equity that had begun with a gaggle of North Carolina A&T students sitting in at a Greensboro lunch counter sixty years earlier was now moving backward.

It's little wonder that the term "intersectionality"—first coined by college professor Kimberlé Crenshaw at the end of the 1980s—gained common currency. That theory—emerging from the same school of thought as so-called critical race theory, which has become such a bugaboo for the far right—challenges people to look at vast systems of racism, sexism, and oppression, rather than seeing prejudice as an individual problem, and to see the ways these systems are interconnected. In many ways, the college debt crisis—and the ways that student loans both perpetuated job and social opportunities for the privileged upper classes, but also fell hardest on women and people of color—was a gateway drug for educated people to adopt a more radical worldview. Increasingly from the dawn of the 2010s through today, young people who encountered "the college problem" in America now saw connections between seemingly disparate issues like the high cost of university tuition, police brutality and sexual harassment in the workplace. This is part of why Occupy Wall Street looks more and more important in hindsight—a surprise coming-out party for a major social movement.

Astra Taylor, a then-thirty-one-year-old progressive filmmaker and writer who'd been part of the New York activism community since the fraught Iraq War years, recalled that her good friend David Graeber, a left-wing strategist, had been after her for weeks to attend the protest that was being organized for Lower Manhattan that September. Taylor had been energized watching a recent worldwide, internet-enabled wave of protests that included the Arab Spring, the Indignados movement in Spain, and even union activists who'd occupied the state capital in Wisconsin. "There was a sense of, who knows, maybe there's something in the air?," Taylor said, although having watched the brutality of the New York Police Department in "kettling" and arresting anti-war protesters in the 2000s still left her doubtful.

So Taylor kept her word to Graeber and showed up just as the sun was rising on Saturday, September 17, 2011, with the NYPD already guarding key landmarks of American capitalism—even the statue of a charging bull a few blocks south of Wall Street. The activist hadn't brought a sleeping bag—certain the day would end in arrests and not the planned lengthy occupation—and hadn't expected either the planners' cleverness in pinpointing Zuccotti Park as a place where cops couldn't legally evict them, or the energy of the crowd that long day. "I immediately knew something was different," said Taylor, by then a slightly jaded veteran of the city's protest scene, "because I didn't know everybody there."

She went back to Zuccotti Park the next day, and the day after that, and the day after that. So did hundreds of others. "We were like moths to the flame," Taylor said. One of the oddities of Occupy Wall Street—it looked to many like a bug, but it turned out to be a feature—was its protest-in-the-form-of-a-question, "What is our one demand?" Spending the warm early autumn afternoons in assemblies and with working groups in corners of the Manhattan park, Taylor kept hearing one refrain from the protest newcomers over and over again: debt.

"People kept bringing up the issue of debt—that I will never be able to own my own home, or that my parents' house is underwater, or their student debt," she said. The protesters, after all, had targeted Wall Street for a reason. They thought that in Barack Obama they had elected someone different—only to see him call on the usual suspects from the world of finance to run the U.S. economy, as he flubbed dealing with a mortgage foreclosure crisis and watched student debt climb toward the $1 trillion mark. It was clear to Taylor and her cohorts that the system was to blame, and lower Manhattan was its capital. For Taylor, the stories of the occupiers helped illuminate her own connection to this web.

"On the second or third day, this guy had a piece of paper and he was yelling like a carnival barker, 'Step right up and write down what you are worth to the 1 Percent—not what you owe, but what you are worth,'" Taylor remembered. "And everybody in the park lined up and took the marker and wrote down how much they owed and what it was for." College and their coming-of-age adventures were now defined not by the knowledge they'd accumulated, but by their outstanding loans.

Taylor, it turned out, had $42,000 in outstanding student debt, even though she didn't have a degree, since her experiences after transferring to Brown as a sophomore had so soured her on the American way of college that she'd become an advocate of unschooling, or learning outside a classroom. She'd defaulted on the loan, watched it balloon, and felt demoralized. She would finally retire it a few years later through one of the few seeming avenues for doing so: she married a rock star. Her new husband—lead singer of the indie rock band Neutral Milk Hotel—paid it for her. She knows most folks don't have that option. The debt conversation in Zuccotti Park "was a moment when I realized that, 'Ooh this is why we're all here, actually,' because actually this is really personal for us."

Back in places like Kutztown, with Sean Kitchen's Facebook plea for a similar protest closer to home, and in Philadelphia, young would-be activists felt that same emotional response to Occupy Wall Street, and by early October 2011 Kitchen and scores of others were erecting tents on the concrete apron right next to City Hall, mimicking dozens of other new Occupy encampments from coast to coast.

I visited Zuccotti Park on October 3, 2011. It was moments after hundreds of the protesters had returned from a "corporate zombie" march past the boxy, soulless high-rises of the Financial District, faces covered in white paint, mock blood oozing from their lips. Over the course of a long day, I met a smorgasbord of dissatisfied Americans, from Iraq War vets who'd turned against the war to struggling organic farmers to guitar-toting sixtysomethings trying to find the spirit of '69, to college students outraged by videos of police violence. As a drum circle throbbed incessantly in the background, each told me a different variation on a similar story, of how they had awakened from their un-realized American Dream.

There was almost an irrational exuberance during those October Days, because Occupy Wall Street and all the other vibrant offshoots like Occupy Philly simply couldn't last forever. The physical occupation of key public spaces—the very thing that made Occupy so thrilling to many hardcore activists—also planted the seeds for the movement's doom, since the encampments also attracted so many people needing social services—in areas like drug treatment or mental health—that the protesters couldn't provide. There were also predictable squabbles—in Philadelphia, the campus idealist Kitchen found himself feuding over direction with long-time anarchists—which made it easy for big-city mayors who'd tired of Occupy to send in cops to close the camps.

That New Year's Eve—just over a month after police retook the hard ground next to City Hall to close down Occupy Philly and then chased a gaggle of protesters up and down city streets, making a bunch of arrests later found to be unlawful—Sean Kitchen and some friends traveled up to Manhattan and joined a group that pushed through police barricades and again flooded Zuccotti Park, if just for one night. He keeps a group picture of that night, in which he is holding a champagne bottle aloft. He says now, "It did—it radicalized me." He never returned to Kutztown to finish his degree—instead, he moved to Harrisburg to muckrake in state politics and support himself with gigs like bartending, even as his outstanding debt ballooned past $30,000.

THE BLACK PANTHER LEADER FRED HAMPTON, SHORTLY BEFORE HE was assassinated by the government in 1969, said famously that "you can jail the revolutionary but you can't jail the revolution." Arguably, a similar phenomenon took place after civic leaders from New York City to Seattle and in between moved to shut down the various Occupy encampments before winter arrived in 2011. While naysayers celebrated the rapid disappearance of the Occupy movement as proof the protests were a shallow fad, its key leaders found compelling outlets for the new brand of leftist politics that had been created.

Some activists never stopped trying to build on the conversations that had started in the shady corners of Zuccotti Park. That included, of course, Astra Taylor, who watched two Occupy working groups around student loan issues merge into one and then stage a nationwide protest on the date that experts said the overall debt had passed $1 trillion. Prodded again by her guru, David Graeber—the beloved anthropologist who would die, suddenly, in 2020—Taylor worked with others to form the Debt Collective, a kind of debtors' union. The group pioneered a "Rolling Jubilee" that's worked to retire $2 billion in various obligations—from medical debt to students cheated by that scammy for-profit university company, Corinthian Colleges—and has become the leading advocate for wiping out all college loans. "What we are trying to do," Taylor says today, "is engineer equality through student debt cancellation."

After Obama—who smartly picked up on the growing awareness of income inequality, traveling to Kansas in December 2011 to assail the "breathtaking greed" of the nation's top earners—won reelection in 2012, a handful of key organizers from the original Occupy Wall Street encampment at Zuccotti Park decided to apply what they'd learned about movement building to the 2016 race for the White House. Too many of the Occupiers "didn't want to build power," Charles Lenchner, an Israeli conscientious objector and expatriate who'd run the technical operation for Occupy Wall Street, told me in the fall of 2015 when I met him in his East Williamsburg apartment. But "that's what I wanted to do."

When a popular online campaign launched by Lenchner and his allies called Ready for Warren that aimed to draft Massachusetts senator Elizabeth Warren—a withering critic of Wall Street, from the left—failed to convince the first-term senator to run, the group rebranded itself: The People for Bernie Sanders.

Vermont senator Bernie Sanders would have been the most unlikely presidential candidate in modern American history had he not launched the same spring as Donald Trump. For months the mainstream media treated him as such. He was very much of the same era that had created the likes of Mario Savio, Tom Hayden, or Jibreel Khazan—the first-generation child of Jewish immigrants in central Brooklyn, first in his family to attend college. Leaving home in 1960 for the University of Chicago, Sanders discovered the civil rights movement—being famously arrested while protesting to integrate Chicago schools—and then socialism. While others on the left moved in a different direction—away from a harsh economic critique and toward the "identity politics" of what Todd Gitlin had called "marching on the English department instead of the White House"—Sanders never wavered in his postwar nurtured belief in middle-class opportunity. Now the student debt crisis had caused educated, or education-seeking, young people to see themselves less as a rising elite—the conceit of the yuppie era and the Atari Democrats—but instead finding common cause with others economically oppressed by late-stage capitalism. Suddenly, this democratic socialist with the wild gray hair was making a lot of sense.

I first saw Sanders speak in the late summer of 2015 on the unlikely battlefield of Manassas, Virginia, where an if-you-build-it-they-will-come line of cars streamed onto a dusty county fairground to see this longshot contender for the Democratic presidential nomination. The crowd ran the gamut from unreconstructed hippies to high school kids clutching Starbucks cups, but the absolute loudest cheer was when Sanders declared that tuition at public colleges and universities should be free—paid for by the 1 Percent. "We will put a tax on Wall Street speculation!" he thundered that night. "The middle class of this country bailed out Wall Street! It's Wall Street's time to bail out the middle class!"

Attending several Sanders rallies that fall, I met a number of people who'd been battered by the paper chase of a college diploma. At a rally in Boston, where a concrete box of a convention center was transformed into an endless sea of standing-room-only people flowing back from a small stage with a massive American flag, about twenty thousand spontaneously chanted, "Tell the truth!" while waiting for the Vermont senator to emerge.

A twenty-three-year-old man named Ben Schierer told me he'd come as a curiosity seeker but was sold by Sanders's message, especially on college affordability. After graduating from high school, Schierer said he'd taken what he described as "a dead-end landscaping job" even as he dreamed of doing more. "I can't afford it," he said, describing the state of higher ed by the mid-2010s. "I don't want to be under a mountain of debt."

Standing a few feet away, a fifty-five-year-old woman named Kathy—she didn't want to give me her full name—had seen the college problem from the other side, that of her son who worked at the convention center and helped her cut the long line to see Sanders speak. "My son could actually be a self-sufficient human being if not for college loans," she told me. "He's going to live at home because he's got to bang out those loans as much as he can—try to get that down to a small payment so he can move out of the house and begin to pay rent and afford food—and that's a shame."

In 2016, Sanders's talk of "free college"—modeled on legislation he'd introduced in the Senate the previous year—electrified the more than 13 million people who voted for him in Democratic primaries. His plan would have come closer to again making college a "public good" than anything since the original G.I. Bill. Pundits wondered about the plausibility of either Republicans on Capitol Hill approving the tax on Wall Street transactions that Sanders wanted to pay for it or GOP governors agreeing to finance one-third of the $75 billion annual cost of ending tuition, as the plan called for. The naysayers missed the much greater significance of the Vermonter's plan, which is that for the first time since arguably the 1960s, universal higher education—and who might pay for it—was again being debated. That was driven home that July when Sanders's Democratic rival, Hillary Clinton, proposed a modified version of his plan, which would have made public college free for the 80 percent of families earning less than $125,000, with new options for reducing the burdens for existing debt holders.

By then, Clinton had all but clinched the Democratic nomination over Sanders. While 2016 was the year that really accelerated the broader college/noncollege divide in U.S. politics—Clinton won in the fall with degree holders by 57 to 36 percent—it also highlighted a new generation gap. In Clinton's effort to break a glass ceiling and become America's first woman president, a lot of educated Democrats saw reflected their own efforts to overcome sexism or discrimination in the 1970s, '80s and '90s—an era ruled by an economically conservative flavor of Reaganism. Older Democrats who powered Clinton to the nomination had predated the era of student debt and job-market mismatches that caused so many young people to question capitalism. These voters were left bewildered—or perplexed, in their words—by the Sanders surge.

But the Left Broke generation fashioned its own politics—very much shaped by their campus experiences—into a truly intersectional blend, part updated-for-the-twenty-first-century identity politics and part European-style socialism economics. The impact was profound. In 2019, a Harris Poll found that among Millennials and Gen Z—the cohorts that began attending college in the late 1990s on up through the present—some 67 percent believe that government should provide free college tuition, which is 11 points higher than the overall population. The same survey found that nearly 50 percent of the younger adults from these two generations would prefer living in a socialist country over the capitalist beacon that was their American birthright.

In 2020, the Democrats' dilemma—increasingly the party of the college-educated, and yet deeply divided between pragmatic boomers and radicalized Millennials and Gen Zers—appeared at first blush to be even more pronounced, as Sanders saw his early primary wins fade while a coalition of older Black voters and white suburban women rallied behind Obama's former vice president, Joe Biden. Yet Biden, a seventy-eight-year-old career politician with a lifetime record of adapting, both ran and then governed after his election as 46th president closer to Sanders's vision than to Clinton's tepid 2016 agenda.

The leftward drift that ended the 2010s and moved into the 2020s went beyond Democratic Party internal politics, however. After all, the engines that drive the American establishment—from large corporations to the military-industrial complex—require smart college grads to run them, and so the cultural obsessions of their New New Left gradually seeped into the traditional Establishment. Thus, the phenomenon known as "woke capitalism" in which workers at companies from Google to Delta Airlines and Coca-Cola successfully lobbied, or pressured, their bosses to take progressive stands on everything from transgender rights to fighting voter suppression. The apotheosis of this trend came in 2021 when ultra-conservative politicians like Senator Ted Cruz even turned against the U.S. military or the CIA for stressing diversity in their recruitment videos or on Twitter. After watching an ad in which a female Army corporal speaks of marching for LGBTQ+ rights, Cruz tweeted that America doesn't need "a woke, emasculated military."

Of course, by the time of the Biden presidency, corporations, the Pentagon and other large institutions had also been shaken by the powerful protest movement that bracketed a decade that began with Occupy Wall Street: the massive marches held in the late spring of 2020 over the police murder in Minneapolis of the unarmed Black man, George Floyd. At their peak, the rallies that were held in all fifty states (as well as around the world) calling for racial justice and radical police reform—with estimates of anywhere from 15 million to 26 million people participating—dwarfed the civil rights protests of the 1960s to become the largest movement for change in U.S. history.

The largest protest, and arguably the most misunderstood.

The George Floyd uprising was, at its peak, a revolution of the college educated. Indeed, the movement—clear to anyone who participated or witnessed the larger marches, and confirmed by academic research—looked nothing like the urban uprisings that took place across America from the mid-1960s through the early 1970s, especially after the first spasms of unrest that saw random looting and some incidents of violence. Within a week or so of Floyd's May 25, 2020, murder as he suffocated under the knee of police officer Derek Chauvin, the protests didn't subside as one might expect. Instead, the movement grew larger, more diverse—which in this context meant more white—and, interestingly, more highly educated.

"The percentage of people in the crowds who had a B.A. degree or higher was extremely large," Dana Fisher, a University of Maryland sociologist who closely studies protest movements, especially during the Trump era, told me. How large? At a series of big city protests that she and a colleague, the University of Michigan's Michael Heaney, and eleven assistants surveyed that June in New York, Washington, D.C., and Los Angeles, Fisher's team found that 82 percent of protesters had a four-year college degree or higher. Interestingly, the high rate of educational attainment held for Black protesters as well, with some 66 percent boasting four-year diplomas. That's a rate three times higher than the average for African Americans. Equally surprising, a majority of the crowd at every march the team surveyed was white—some 65 percent at a D.C. rally held five days after Trump had ordered an attack on peaceful protesters at Lafayette Square.

"I was shocked to see so many white kids out here," Walter Wiggins—a sixty-seven-year-old Black man who'd been attending protest marches in his native D.C. since his parents took him to hear the Reverend Martin Luther King Jr. at the 1963 March on Washington—told the New York Times. "Back then, it was just black folks."

"We were waiting for this to happen," a thirty-two-year-old white principal in the Philadelphia school district named Meredith Lowe told me when I ventured out of my COVID-19 quarantine for the first time in ten weeks to cover the protests in the city, still going strong nine days after Floyd's murder. Snapping pictures of National Guard troops who'd been deployed around City Hall, Lowe and her wife, Karen Specht, had been to marches for five days in a row. "We think it's a great first step, and there's a lot more to do. We believe white supremacy is real, we believe [there is] systematic oppression."

The march that day was remarkably diverse—idled retail workers, students and their teachers, young Black men from working-class neighborhoods—and undoubtedly boosted by the coronavirus situation that had closed many schools, restaurants and stores, coinciding with enhanced unemployment benefits. Fisher's research showed the protests—at least initially—were much younger in average age than the so-called "resistance" events that had been more based around opposition to Trump, like the 2017 Women's March. But by mid-June, most of the anti-Trump groups like Indivisible had endorsed Black Lives Matter; millions of older, college-educated, liberal-leaning folks, and especially the women of "the Resistance," marched that month, sometimes with their children. Politically, the nation was seeing the alliance that would elect Joe Biden that autumn, out in the streets of America.

Surely the George Floyd protests were a long-overdue racial reckoning, but it was also a cultural one. The Black Lives Matter marches felt like the detonation of a fuse that was lit in Zuccotti Park nine years earlier, as debt-drenched young Americans gained awareness about wider systems of oppression around unfettered capitalism or white supremacy, and the ways those systems were connected.

On the street level, more and more people—Black, Brown, and white, and with a wide range of economic prospects—were seeing the links. I thought about Ewan Johnson, the Black man from South Jersey whose $180,000 family debt and struggles in the job market had put him at the center of the George Floyd protests, then saw him fighting for a community of the unhoused, and finally made him a leader of a debt strike. But there was also Sean Kitchen, who was still fighting for left-wing causes when I caught up with him not long before the tenth anniversary of Occupy Wall Street. After a decade on the fringes, Kitchen had landed a job at a project called PA Spotlight where he worked to expose right-wing extremism as it hardened around their issues like voter suppression and gun rights.

The political movement of young people like Kitchen and Johnson—arguably a successful one, culminating with a coalition led by more highly educated voters restoring Biden and his brand of liberal democracy to the White House—was forged in the cultural laboratory of America's college campuses. Its electoral success showed that the conservative backlash against liberal learning led by Ronald Reagan, and later epitomized by college-loan sharks, may have denied university access to millions—but that didn't stop higher education from expanding the minds of those who still managed to attend. In many ways, 2020's revolution of the college-educated—the racial reckoning and the demands for "free college" and total debt forgiveness, capped by the election of a president who might make those things happen—was the Gipper's worst nightmare.

Except it was no longer Reagan's Republican Party. It was now Donald Trump's, because the blow-up of America's postwar college experiment had created an equal and opposite reaction on the political right.

CHAPTER 7

FROM RESENTMENT OF COLLEGE TO AMERICA'S REJECTION OF KNOWLEDGE

Having Scott Walker in class, recalled one of the future Wisconsin governor's political science professors at Marquette University, "was a little like teaching Alex P. Keaton"—the teenager on the popular 1980s sitcom *Family Ties* who baffled his ex-hippie parents with his love of free-market economics and especially the then-president of the United States, Ronald Reagan.

In the style of TV's Keaton, the young Scott Walker—son of a Baptist minister—wore three-piece suits on a campus where most kids dressed in flannel shirts and baggy jeans. But to totally nail the stereotype, Walker's dorm-room desk was adorned with his prize photograph—a picture of the teenager with the Gipper himself, taken at a Boy Scouts event in D.C.

During his time at Marquette, Walker was already hopelessly devoted to Reagan and his rugged brand of conservatism, and like many disciples he would take the movement to places its founder could not have imagined. The California-governor-turned-40th-president—whose path to radio and then Hollywood fame was launched by earning a diploma at Illinois's small Eureka College—built his career on fighting campus radicalism, but he'd only pushed his war on higher education so far. Walker and his generation of right-wing crusaders seemed determined to finish the job.

After becoming governor of the Badger State at the start of 2011, Walker was the archetype of the modern GOP leader who went to war with his state's public universities. He and a Republican legislature slashed public college funding, of course. But Walker would also meddle in other, unprecedented ways. He pushed to weaken tenure protections for professors, who were assumed to be uniformly liberal. He even tried—unsuccessfully—to change the flagship University of Wisconsin's mission statement away from lofty words about the human condition and "the search for truth" to instead merely "meet the state's workforce needs."

In the years following his election to the statehouse in Madison and preparing for what would be a short-lived 2016 presidential run, Walker told reporters where he came down on the question of whether college is for improving the soul or building a résumé. "The reason I went to college, in large part, was not just to get an education for an education's sake, but to get a job," he said in 2013. Walker was trying to explain his surprising decision in 1990—when he was roughly three-quarters of the way toward earning enough credits for his Marquette diploma—to leave school, and take a job offer to begin working with the American Red Cross. That made Walker just one of a tiny handful of modern governors—by 2021, just two—who lacked a bachelor's degree.

Walker's story is complicated. His roughly four years on the Milwaukee campus were actually consumed with the culture of politics— both student government and the outside world. Elected to the student senate as a freshman, Walker helped uncover a scandal involving the leaders of the student government misusing money to throw a lavish hotel party, and in pushing for an impeachment he made a name for himself and also some enemies who called him "Neidermeyer" after the right-wing ROTC kid in *Animal House*. Walker's subsequent runs for higher student office met disaster, including a scandal of his own when the copies of the student newspaper that endorsed his opponent for school president mysteriously vanished. (Walker denies any involvement.) The conservative, anti-abortion Walker ran for school president but lost badly to a liberal student from Chicago whose main issue was wanting the university to divest from apartheid South Africa. Eventually, Walker vamoosed to forge his career in Republican politics, where he rose not only by tapping resentments against Madison, including those pointy-headed professors at UW, but by acting on them with harsh policies that punished state universities and the young folks who attended them.

The climax of Walker's twenty-year rise from college dropout to the governor's mansion coincided with the research of UW political scientist Katherine J. Cramer, who'd spent several years in the late 2000s trying to understand what she came to call "rural consciousness"—a culture and set of values that distrusts cities and feels disrespected by bureaucrats and intellectuals like college professors—and how that bred what she called, in the title of her book *The Politics of Resentment*.

In traveling the rural woodlands of northern Wisconsin and infiltrating dice games and lodges where farmers and fishermen opened up about their views on life and today's politics, Cramer sought to learn what rural folks thought not just about the government but also about her employer, UW, and the state university system. They described a taxpayer-funded ivory tower that wasn't for them—both in cost and in attitude. College professors were book smart but dumb when they left campus—and Madison was full of condescending, unreconstructed hippies. Echoing the common rural refrain that college-educated workers are lazy, one rural man told Cramer: "They shower before work, not after work." That wasn't a compliment.

Walker—whatever one thinks about his ideas or his ethics—proved brilliant on the campaign trail in channeling these resentments of rural voters toward college educators and state bureaucrats, despite his background as chief executive of Wisconsin's most urban county. "We can no longer have a society where the public sector employees are the 'haves,'" he averred at a debate on his way to winning the 2010 gubernatorial race, "and the people who foot the bill, the taxpayers, are the 'have-nots.'" Despite efforts to shift the revenue burden onto out-of-state students, the cost of attending UW for Wisconsin kids still rose 18 percent during Walker's two terms, even as the bitter politics drove some popular professors away.

Walker's Wisconsin, more than any other state, captured the zeitgeist of the 2010s in red America, as the simmering discontents of voters from rural areas and small towns that had started with talk radio gripes about "political correctness" run amok finally boiled over the top. This anger among white working-class voters wasn't new, but it accelerated rapidly during the decade, egged on by newer media outlets like the Fox News Channel and politicians like Walker who hadn't been around for the American Dream heyday of college ambition in the 1950s, '60s, and '70s. Things spiraled downward as the mostly Republican budget cuts for higher education got deeper and deeper after 2010, while the anti-intellectual rhetoric grew nastier.

Midway through the decade came a tipping point that would have once seemed all but impossible: The dominant perception of college that has been cemented in the post–World War II era—as a desirable, ambition-fulfilling machine, the punched ticket toward the goal of a better life than one's parents—began to change, and change rapidly. But the rapid decline of trust in college as an institution, and as a necessary and desirable life goal, was not uniform across the board.

The Pew Research Center's annual survey of U.S. attitudes about higher education found that, among Republicans, support for the very idea of college practically dropped off a cliff starting in 2015. That year, 54 percent of GOP voters still believed that colleges had a positive impact on the country's direction—despite a half century of political attacks against the academy—while a minority of 37 percent held a negative opinion. By 2017—just twenty-four short months later—the Republican numbers had flipped. A whopping 58 percent said institutions of higher education played a negative role, with just 36 percent holding the positive view. By 2019, Republicans were 59 to 33 percent negative on higher ed.

It's important to note that this drop occurred at a moment when trust in virtually all American institutions—from the news media to Congress to Silicon Valley—was declining in a bitterly divided nation. And support for higher education among Democrats, which was quite high in the mid-2010s, did also show a dip in Pew's 2019 survey—a reminder that "the college problem" isn't just Fox News demagoguery but a reflection of real-world problems like runaway tuition that affect everyone. (Among all Americans, 50 percent had a positive view of college's impact on the nation in 2019—a record low.)

It's impossible not to notice that the reversal in Republican voters' perceptions of university learning took place in the two years between that day Donald Trump descended the gilded escalator of Trump Tower as a longshot presidential candidate, and his installation as 45th president of the United States. This was not an overt process—Trump did not make direct attacks on college a centerpiece of his politics, as Scott Walker and others would do—but rather a complicated dance. Rural and small-town voters flocked to the GOP's 2016 nominee because his words, his style, and his policy drove those arrogant, diploma-wielding elites crazy. And the enemy of their enemy was their friend.

The 2016 election changed the delicate balance between the American way of college, our politics, and the policies that flow from that, in a couple of profound ways. Most obviously, the so-called college/noncollege divide (a term that political scientists rarely used before the late 2010s) that had in some ways been brewing since the campus protest era of the 1960s finally exploded, electorally. It's already hard to remember today, but until very recently GOP candidates—when traditional conservatives were advocating low taxes and toughness on crime—still usually won a majority of white college graduates. Trump's laserlike focus on the "forgotten Americans" of the white working class—on everything from protectionism around trade to his more rank xenophobic and racist appeals—brought out thousands of new voters, but also alienated many educated suburbanites who suddenly felt more comfortable voting for a Democrat. The college/noncollege divide had grown slowly at first, driven by social issues like abortion or LGBTQ+ rights, but after Trump it became tribal. Increasingly, to be a college grad is to be a Democrat, and to be "a deplorable" member of the working class that resents them is to be a Republican.

But the Trump years also accelerated some societal problems that went well beyond electoral politics. By planting their flag firmly as the anti-college party, modern Republicans inevitably came to grow suspicious of, if not openly despise, the deeper values that higher education stood for, and this would soon transcend political correctness or identity politics around race and gender. A conservative movement that once laughed at journalists as "nattering nabobs of negativism" now shunned fact-based reporting altogether, preferring to share conspiracy theories on Facebook or YouTube. Republicans didn't just dislike microbiologists but became the anti-science party—casting doubt on the research around climate change (to the delight of the GOP's Big Oil millionaire donor class) and then the health information needed to survive COVID-19. In a high-tech world where knowledge is both economic power and the only path toward solving humankind's most intractable problems, America was increasingly governed in angry statehouses and on gridlocked Capitol Hill by a movement of knowledge haters and deniers.

This counterrevolution's defining moment came during Trump's impeachment—the first one, that is—at the end of 2019. The House Judiciary Committee had called upon four of the nation's best, most accomplished Constitutional law scholars—professors from Harvard, Stanford, George Washington, and North Carolina—for some expertise on the thorny issues at hand. Maybe it was because three of the four argued that the president's actions in the Ukraine matter surely did warrant his impeachment, but their words and citations from centuries of British and American law didn't carry much weight with the panel's Republican members. After the hearing, several argued that what they heard was not the wisdom of legal knowledge but the arrogant contempt that campus elites hold for the real America.

"All I've got to say is, if you love America," the right-wing Texas congressman Louie Gohmert told a gaggle of reporters, summoning the time-worn lyrics of Waylon Jennings, "Mamas don't let your babies grow up to go to Harvard or Stanford Law School." The other Republican lawmakers who stood behind Gohmert giggled. For today's conservatives, Gohmert was, in the popular parlance, saying the quiet part out loud: Going to college was an un-American activity.

SCOTT WALKER'S WISCONSIN WOULD BECOME THE FRONTLINE BATtle in the college war. To be sure, the Badger State over the last century was always kind of a testing ground for the divide between "red America" and "blue America." How else to explain how the same state could send both Joe McCarthy, the midcentury architect of flag-waving right-wing demagoguery, and Robert "Fighting Bob" La Follette, the godfather of the twentieth-century progressive movement, to the U.S. Senate? La Follette was also a governor, and champion of the state's industrial working class that, for a time, made Milwaukee the center of a practical left-wing philosophy known as "sewer socialism." More than one hundred years earlier, he had a very different idea than his eventual successor Scott Walker about a role for science and education in Wisconsin's future.

Progressives like La Follette—who served as governor from 1901–05 before leaving for the Senate—believed that an activist government could serve as the antidote to the political and business corruption of the Gilded Age and the abuse of labor during the zenith of the Industrial Revolution. The special brainstorm of Wisconsin's progressives was that the state's flagship land-grant university in Madison could serve as a laboratory to develop and test innovative social policies such as worker's comp, tax reform, and utility regulation. This radical notion—which became a key milestone in forging a link between liberal education and civic betterment—was called "The Wisconsin Idea" by the time that a La Follette ally, then–University of Wisconsin president Charles R. Van Hise, described it in a 1904 speech.

But it wouldn't be until 1971—at the peak of the post–World War II expansion of public universities—that the Wisconsin Idea would be refashioned as a mission statement for a rapidly expanding system that now included not just the flagship in Madison but a network of satellite campuses across the state. That mission, it stated, was:

> to develop human resources, to discover and disseminate knowledge, to extend knowledge and its application beyond the boundaries of its campuses and to serve and stimulate society by developing in students heightened intellectual, cultural and humane sensitivities, scientific, professional and technological expertise and a sense of purpose. Inherent in this broad mission are methods of instruction, research, extended training and public service designed to educate people and improve the human condition. Basic to every purpose of the system is the search for truth.

This statement wasn't controversial, even though it came at a highly fraught time. Over the course of the twentieth century, UW—thanks to strong support from its state government—punched above its weight as one of America's top research universities, serving a mid-sized state that would become an epicenter of the Rust Belt when the Industrial Revolution petered out. Madison attracted some of the nation's top students and some of the most liberal, which had made the campus a center of protest against the Vietnam War by the late 1960s. The angst that followed the 1970 Army Mathematics Research Center bombing by anti-war radicals that killed a grad student didn't prevent the university from proclaiming an unabashedly liberal mission—but the winds of change were beginning to blow.

By 2015, the story in Madison was a familiar one. The cost of attending UW with in-state tuition had doubled over the previous thirty years, outstripping inflation, and the percentage of out-of-state students willing to pay higher tuition to attend the prestigious university spiked. The percentage of its students who were receiving federal Pell Grants was lower, at just 15 percent, than any of its Midwestern public-university rivals in the Big 10 conference. It's little wonder that Cramer found in her travels across Wisconsin near the end of this era that—beyond rooting for UW's successful football and basketball programs and their omnipresent mascot, Bucky Badger—rural Wisconsinites felt utterly disconnected.

Despite the lofty principles of the Wisconsin Idea, most of the voters that Cramer interviewed for *The Politics of Resentment* saw college useful only as a conduit to a job—especially after deindustrialization and outsourcing jobs to Mexico or Asia had decimated the small-appliance factors and other plants in regions like the Paper Valley where there'd once been a source of good-paying blue-collar work. Most rural parents said their kids couldn't compete with the expensive SAT prep of suburban kids, and fretted about the affluent international and out-of-state kids who increasingly populated the university. One man said his son was smart enough to pilot a helicopter for the military but on the home front was steered toward community college when he couldn't get into UW. He told the professor, sarcastically: "Makes sense that they are bringing kids from India, but then they are telling Chris that you can't go to Madison."

Bitterness over access and ever-escalating cost often gave way, Cramer found, to complaints about liberal professors brainwashing the local kids who did make their way to the flagship campus. Then there were elaborate tales about the arrogance and lack of street smarts exhibited by the UW professors who trekked through their towns to research wildlife in the state's expansive forests and lush lakes. According to Cramer, their dim views about academics—lazy, lacking common sense—tended to merge with feelings toward other state employees and bureaucrats they dealt with, who also had salaries and gold-plated health insurance that locals stuck in private sector jobs lacked.

Scott Walker may not have stayed at Marquette long enough to complete his political science degree, but he learned enough to masterfully exploit this resentment for electoral purposes. The 2010 midterm elections, driven by the white voter backlash against Barack Obama that also created the brief Tea Party movement, were perfectly teed up for Walker's gubernatorial ambitions, and he scored extra points by opposing a Milwaukee-to-Madison high-speed rail project that would have whipped past Wisconsin's forgotten small towns. Taking office in 2011, he made national headlines by attacking those public-employee unions— denigrated by his rural supporters—and their benefits, which triggered left-wing protests at the statehouse and a failed recall election, all of which only strengthened Walker in the eyes of his working-class base.

Walker's attacks on higher education drew less attention, yet they were central to his political philosophy. Much like a bevy of other Republican governors in states with compatible right-wing legislatures, the Wisconsin chief executive demanded steep budget cuts and got most of what he asked for. The university lost $362 million in once-expected state revenue over five years, which administrators were forced to make up largely by raising tuition and other fees.

In 2015, after Walker had both beaten back the recall and won a second term, the governor and some GOP allies amped up their attacks on the core of university governance. A new law seriously weakened tenure protections for University of Wisconsin and gave broad power over both tenured positions and the ability to eliminate academic centers and programs to the university's Board of Trustees—an eighteen-member panel that was packed with Walker's allies and political supporters. Some of the top professors in Madison—like education-reform leader Sara Goldrick-Rab, who made headlines by criticizing Walker and the changes on Twitter—drifted away to other schools.

The new, amped-up Republican war on higher education was driven home in one dramatic move that, in the end, didn't happen. Some Wisconsinites were stunned when, amid the flurry of Walker moves against the university in 2015, it was reported that the administration was re-writing UW's 1971 mission statement—the essence of the more-than-a-century-old Wisconsin Idea and its progressive legacy. In one draft, the high-minded language about promoting public service, bettering the human condition, and searching for the truth were wiped out with a strikethrough line. Instead, the mission statement would make clear the purpose of UW was "meeting the state's workforce development needs."

The proposed change would have been a declaration of victory of a fifty-year-long project that had begun when Walker's hero and role model, Reagan, had asserted that taxpayers shouldn't be funding the intellectual curiosity of California's young people. Walker's mission statement would have sounded a death knell for any lingering notions of liberal education and ratified that college—at least in formerly progressive Wisconsin—was to produce adults who'd be cogs in a capitalist system, but not necessarily deep thinkers. In the end, this was a bridge too far for too many citizens, even in an era where overall approval of the American way of college was dropping. Walker went on to falsely claim the change was "a drafting error," an assertion that was rendered ridiculous when activists forced the public release of his administration's emails.

But while Walker's Wisconsin Idea debacle proved there is a reservoir of faith in the most moral vision of what college can be, it was also, arguably, a pyrrhic victory. For Walker's playbook in taking on UW was copied by other Republican governors from coast to coast.

As the American right wing became both more powerful and more extreme, dominating a number of statehouses after a GOP "wave" election in 2010 and a skillful-if-devious campaign of legislative gerrymandering, its leaders were emboldened to take an aggressive approach against universities that they viewed as hostile pockets of unreconstructed leftism. Republican governors increasingly stacked university trustee boards with their wealthy allies or even lobbyists—often with little background in higher education, and occasionally even lacking a bachelor's degree—and worked with their legislative allies to limit tenure protections or shut down academic centers that seemed to serve a liberal agenda—often thinly disguised moves against critics of their conservative counterrevolution.

Aside from Walker's Wisconsin, one epicenter of the new Republican war on higher education was North Carolina. It was an ironic locale for a higher ed skirmish; not only is the University of North Carolina's flagship campus in Chapel Hill the oldest public university in America, but the Tar Heel State's reputation for academic excellence had made the state and its so-called Research Triangle into an economic powerhouse. To the Republicans who rode both the Tea Party upheaval and a flood of dark money from free-market billionaires, the reputation of UNC and its sister schools mattered less than their potential to indoctrinate North Carolina's youth with leftist ideas about capitalism or race relations.

"The main problem has to do with the ideas that are being discussed and promoted," Jay Schalin, the policy director of what is now North Carolina's John William Pope Center for Higher Education, told *The Nation* magazine in 2016. He specifically identified those problems as "multiculturalism, collectivism, [and] left-wing post-modernism." The chief financial backer of that center—which urged funding cuts for public universities in tandem with attacks on liberal ideology—is billionaire discount-store magnate Art Pope, who has also invested millions in electing Republicans in North Carolina. During the years that Pope was mounting his attack on UNC, GOP lawmakers took control of the process for naming trustees—thus bypassing Democratic governor Roy Cooper, elected in 2016—and by 2021 a *Daily Tar Heel* student newspaper probe found that sixteen of twenty-four trustees identified as Republican, and just one as a Democrat. One of those GOP trustee was Art Pope himself, whose 2020 appointment was the grand finale of a decade-long far-right takeover. His nomination was approved over the objection of Democrats who traced how Pope's millions filtered down to projects like Divest U., which has sought to redirect $1 billion away from the nation's already underfunded public universities because they are "indoctrination factories for leftist, anti-American sentiment."

The GOP takeover at UNC wasn't just about rhetoric, but results. In 2015, the university's Board of Governors undertook an extensive review of academic centers throughout the system, then ordered three of them to close. The targeted programs dealt with biodiversity, civic engagement and social change, and poverty—selections that only fueled criticism that the cuts were politically motivated, to shut down research and other efforts that might undermine Raleigh's right turn on climate change, voting rights, and the welfare safety net. The closure of the Center on Poverty, Work and Opportunity at the UNC School of Law drew special attention, because its firebrand leader, Gene Nichol, was also a vocal critic of the GOP then-governor, Pat McCrory, and state lawmakers in a column he wrote for a local newspaper. Whether the trustees didn't like Nichol's politics, or worried that his center might call attention to the fact that North Carolina had the nation's twelfth-highest rate of poverty, the closure was a sad day for liberal education. The dean of the law school at Chapel Hill said the move "contravenes core principles of academic free speech and inquiry"—a gross understatement.

The growing Republican attacks against the academy served the day-to-day agenda of the conservative movement—getting rid of their fiercest left-wing critics by killing their programs or cowing them into silence with the threat of losing tenure, or using the budget cuts to instead pay for tax cuts for the rich or for corporations, thus delighting their big money donors like Art Pope. But there is something else that might explain why anti-college politics became louder and more aggressive in the mid-2010s. As Barack Obama's eight years in the White House wound to an end, politicians like Walker were starting to grasp the ways that resentment of educated elites had more loudly become the core rallying cry for an increasingly blue-collar base. As the wide-open 2016 presidential election drew closer and the field of would-be GOP candidates grew larger, starting a war with pointy-headed intellectuals on campus could be a way for a dark horse to emerge.

How else to explain the harsh, regressive policies of Bobby Jindal, the ambitious Republican governor of Louisiana during that era? An alumnus of Brown University and the son of two highly educated engineers who'd emigrated from their native India, it's possible to imagine an alternative universe where Jindal might have invested in Louisiana State University, and education generally, as a long-term solution to the worsening prospects for his state's bedrock industry, oil and gas. To the contrary, Jindal—perhaps worried about how his elite schooling might play with GOP primary voters in the heyday of the Tea Party—slashed taxpayer support for public universities from 55 percent of their budget to just 20 percent. Tuition soared, and enrollment dropped. In 2015, as the governor prepared to leave office and launch a White House bid, another round of proposed higher-ed cuts was stopped by lawmakers in Baton Rouge who thought Jindal had gone too far and instead dipped into a rainy day fund to finance the campuses. Pundits speculated that Jindal was reluctant to raise new revenue to fund universities out of fear it would violate an anti-tax pledge he'd signed with the influential GOP group Americans for Tax Reform.

As it turned out, Jindal's brief run for the GOP presidential nod was a disaster, ending in November 2015, or even before the first tallies of the Iowa caucus. Scott Walker—the face of Republican opposition to union workers and college professors—performed just as badly, and exited the race in September. Governors like Jindal and Walker had staked their political careers on tapping into the rising rural anti-elite resentment, without seeing the obvious flaw that they themselves were career politicians—the very government employees that many of their constituents despised. In opting for a true outsider, the American Heartland would stick it to the cosmopolitan college crowd with a multimillionaire Ivy League graduate: Donald John Trump.

The politician who chiseled the college/noncollege wedge in American politics into a vast chasm didn't say much about college on the campaign trail, other than to remind voters that because he was (under dubious circumstances, we'd later learn) admitted to the University of Pennsylvania, he must be "very, very smart." As Trump's campaign to become 45th president went down to the wire in the fall of 2016, writers on the higher-education beat conceded the GOP nominee had offered few clues about his policies, even though the rising cost of college was a top concern for middle-class voters. Other than some Republican boilerplate about the outrageousness of soaring student debt—linking it to bloated administration salaries and large endowments—any Trump higher-ed policy "remains a mystery," wrote *Inside Higher Ed*. Maybe Trump understood that actual policies toward college in America were for boring pols like Bobby Jindal and Scott Walker.

The voters who packed hockey rinks across Middle America to cheer for Trump and random moments of thuggery against liberal protesters didn't want a new tenure law as much as they wanted a man (and only a man) who could drive those pointy-headed professors crazy, along with their friends in Hollywood and the newsrooms of New York and D.C. The new politics of resentment was very much an id-driven affair, and whatever Trump didn't learn as a mediocre-or-worse student at Penn's Wharton School, he instinctively understood with a God-given talent for low-brow marketing. Trump had become Trump in the 1980s, after all, by selling a noncollege low-rent version of the American Dream at his zirconium-plated Atlantic City casinos, and he'd learned how to ridicule political correctness with the help of his media friends like Howard Stern.

He'd find that marketing Trump 2016 wasn't that different from marketing the faux glamour of Trump Vodka or the faux knowledge of Trump University, which hadn't been a university at all but the essence of how Trump perceived the education racket, as another get-rich-quick scheme. The germaphobe didn't much like the lower common denominator among his new supporters, but he was able to bond with them from his elevated podium because they hated the same people—know-it-all reporters, do-gooder liberals—even if Trump's contempt stemmed from personal knowledge and not a "rural consciousness." Most important, he welcomed—at a social distance—their affection. After winning the Nevada caucus in February 2016, Trump, in a typical moment of self-love, led the crowd through all the demographic groups he'd won—young and old, evangelicals, and (by a whopping 37 percent margin) "the poorly educated." At this, Trump looked up over the arena and proclaimed, "I love the poorly educated!" A few reporters probably smirked, but the crowd roared.

But why did the poorly educated love Trump back? As Joan C. Williams dissects in her book *White Working Class: Overcoming Class Cluelessness in America*, the Heartland middle class might loathe the professional and managerial elites, yet they retained strong affection for the very rich—especially when that very rich individual is a self-made entrepreneur who functions as his own boss and who seems to share their values, just with a ton more money. She quotes one man who'd moved economically from working-class origins, or a "class migrant": "There's an almost mystical desire among the working class to see a rich person from the upper class reach out to them." Yet these same folks resent the arrogance and condescension from managers and professionals.

If working-class folks truly wanted to have a rich person reach out to them and embrace their rural consciousness, then Trump's chaotic rallies—where violent fights in the crowd were cheered from the podium as if for the World Wrestling Entertainment (WWE) play-actor Trump had occasionally been, and where the candidate urged the crowd to turn toward and boo the elite journalists trapped inside a press pen, like the rage release of Orwell's Two Minutes Hate from *1984*—must have felt truly cathartic. Perhaps there was no more powerful symbol of what Williams calls "class cluelessness" than the inability of those cosmopolitan Beltway pundits to understand Trump's popularity. From the moment Trump descended the elevator at Trump Tower with his ex-model wife, Melania, pundits predicted the meltdown of his campaign. The meltdown never came.

Indeed, Trump's march to the Republican nomination at that summer's Republican convention in Cleveland agitated not only the Democrats' growing base of college-educated voters but also the campaign of their nominee, Hillary Clinton. She and her aides thought Trump's crudeness, his business scandals and history of sexual misconduct made him easy prey in November—which caused them to commit a series of unforced errors. In one awkward moment in Ohio, Clinton tried to explain her commitment to finding clean-energy jobs for displaced workers, adding "[b]ecause we're going to put a lot of coal miners and coal companies out of business"—touching the rural nerve that bureaucrats and professor types are coming for their jobs. That fall, the would-be first female president sought to shore up her support among educated suburbanites by famously charging that the more racist or hateful half of Trump supporters were "a basket of deplorables."

Trump's stunning November 8, 2016, victory wasn't just a defining day for America's path in the twenty-first century. It also marked, arguably, what political scientists called a "realigning election," but not like epic ones of the past like FDR's New Deal in 1932 or Richard Nixon's "law and order" coalition in 1968. Indeed, this was a realignment that couldn't have been possible in Franklin Roosevelt's time—a realignment constructed around college education. Although exit polls—a most inexact science—varied, the most extensive postelection survey by Pew Research Center found a huge educational disparity. White voters with college diplomas said they voted for Clinton by 55 to 38 percent, while Trump won the much larger pool of noncollege white working-class voters by 64 to 28 percent, powering him to his narrow wins in the Rust Belt that proved decisive in the Electoral College. America was now split down the middle between voters who felt they were enlightened, and those who resented that other half.

Of the unexpected states that put the Republican over the top, the biggest shock was his 22,748 vote win in Scott Walker's Wisconsin. A huge Trump turnout from those ice-fishing lodges and card games in the thick northern forests that UW's Cramer had visited years earlier barely offset the Democrats' traditional edge in Milwaukee and Madison. Clinton's college-educated data gurus, from their office in the hipster heart of Brooklyn, had advised their candidate that she wouldn't even need to campaign in Wisconsin, and so she hadn't.

WHAT HAD CLINTON'S POLITICAL BRAINS MISSED? ONE OF THE MOST in-depth surveys of white working-class voters, particularly in the Rust Belt, during the fall of 2016 showed that the greatest motivators for Trump voters were not so much factors connected to "economic anxiety," despite the closed factories and boarded-up homes across much of the Heartland, but dread over cultural change in America. The study that was conducted by the Public Religion Research Institute in conjunction with *The Atlantic* magazine showed that key drivers were fears over America's losing status as a world power and, even more strongly, immigration.

But the No. 1 cultural fear was over lack of access to higher education. Their survey found that 54 percent of working-class Americans, and 61 percent of the men, felt that college education today is "a risky gamble"—and two-thirds of those voters went for Trump. The institute's director, Robert P. Jones, told the magazine this decisive factor in Trump's shock victory wasn't economic hardship but something he called "economic fatalism." He explained: "The enduring narrative of the American dream is that if you study and get a college education and work hard, you can get ahead. The survey shows that many white working-class Americans, especially men, no longer see that path available to them."

This was a tough concept for the pundit class to wrap their minds around. They had been trained to look for economics-driven elections, not the culture-driven ones. Nate Silver, the polling-data guru, did his own deep dive after Trump's 2016 win to show that educational attainment, not income, had determined the outcome. Indeed, the data was striking. In the fifty large- or medium-sized counties with the highest level of four-year-college degree holders, Hillary Clinton performed better than two-time winner Barack Obama in forty-eight of them, while she underperformed Obama in all fifty counties with the lowest rate of university diplomas. The pattern held in unique counties with either high educational attainment and lower incomes—often home to large colleges—or a handful of places with high incomes but fewer degrees, like Suffolk County, New York, or Staten Island, home to many well-paid NYPD cops and FDNY firefighters. In both Suffolk and Staten Island, narrow Obama wins in 2012 flipped to healthy Trump victories in 2016. On the flip side, Clinton held her own in Ingham County, Michigan, home to Michigan State University and government jobs in Lansing.

Perhaps the highest form of Trump men—and they were mostly men—showing off both their shower-at-the-end-of-the-day material success and their in-your-face affection for a president that college eggheads loved to hate emerged four years later in a spectacle called the Trump boat parade. On wide lakes, crowded rivers, or intercoastal waterways through the heart of Trump Country, owners of recreational boats—some of them large, or garish, or both—hoisted massive blue TRUMP 2020 flags and cruised slowly and defiantly across one anothers' wake. In the fall of 2020, the *Washington Post*'s Jenna Johnson attended such a demonstration on Lake Erie in Sandusky, Ohio, where "[m]any have done well for themselves without a college diploma, and they're living a version of the American Dream that involves owning a boat and a truck to haul it."

Of course, the culture war between elitists and anti-intellectuals—important as it was—wasn't the only thing happening in American politics in 2016 and beyond. Much attention was deservedly cast toward Trump's unrelenting appeals around xenophobia (suggesting Mexican migrants were criminals and rapists), racism, and misogyny (the endless chants of "Lock her up!" directed at Clinton)—a focus that grew more intense with the 2020 police murder of George Floyd and the racial reckoning that followed. But it's important to understand the intersectionality of the far right's racial resentments and its animus toward the college-educated. It's clear that declining support among both GOP voters and budget-cutting Republican governors has always dovetailed with evidence that college was empowering Black Americans—from the Greensboro sit-ins and Mississippi Summer to rising nonwhite enrollments in the affirmative action heyday of the 1970s to campus support for Black Lives Matter. The threat that higher education poses to white supremacy has always been hiding in plain sight.

But America's political realignment around race has been well-documented. It's now taken as gospel—even though historians say it's probably apocryphal—that LBJ grumbled to an aide after signing the Civil Rights Act of 1964 that "we've lost the South for a generation," since that's exactly what happened. Conversely, it's unfathomable to imagine FDR signing the G.I. Bill in 1944 and saying, "This is going to kill us with the white working class someday." College then looked like an opportunity for the New Deal coalition, not a future source of frustration and resentment.

It didn't have to be this way. Higher education could have flourished as a public good—instead of a fake meritocracy rigged to make half of America hate it. It took only a couple generations of bad decisions, exploitive politics, and Wall Street greed to take college from making the American Dream to breaking it. Donald Trump was only the apostle delivering the bad news.

TRUMP PROVED A POLARIZING FIGURE IN THE TRUEST SENSE OF THE word. In making low-rent appeals to white working-class populism the public face of a Republican Party whose elites had preferred coded "dog whistles" around subjects like race or immigration, Trump didn't only fire up a previously untapped pool of disaffected rural voters. His appearance on the American stage became a time for choosing, forcing voters who'd once held more nuanced political views instead come home to their natural tribes. The slow but steady trickle of college-educated whites into the Democratic Party that had begun with Reagan in the 1980s, especially among women eager to protect their gains on campus and in the workplace, became a tidal wave in the Trump years, drawing in men who in the past might have voted their wallet over their culture. In many suburban or more affluent urban zip codes, Trump's victory brought a sprouting of rainbow-colored yard signs declaring HATE HAS NO HOME HERE—a declaration to neighbors that the owner wasn't one of *those* people.

The 2016 election brought the end of an era in which the college-educated—holding not just the economic power but the cultural power to shape the national narrative from Hollywood to Silicon Valley to newsrooms in New York and D.C.—could dismissively ignore the Rust Belt working class as people who live in "flyover country." Trump had allowed the people that he, echoing Nixon from an earlier time, called "the forgotten Americans" to beat the elites in the only way they could win—with their raw numbers, at the ballot box. To the class-clueless, Trump's election was almost a 9/11-level event—both, after all, prompted a spate of essays asking "Why do they hate us?"— signaling that Middle America was no longer to be flown over, but an existential threat to their status and their morals.

It was telling that among the wide variety of groups threatened by the ascension of Trump, white college-degree-holding suburban and urban women were perhaps the most aggressive in forming what they quickly called "The Resistance" to the uncouth new president. This led most prominently to the Women's March, organized in just ten short weeks, but also scores of groups like Indivisible chapters or homemade offshoots like Pennsylvania's Tuesdays with Toomey, the vast majority of these ad-hoc outfits led by women. While more marginalized groups, such as people of color, saw an extremist riff on old familiar themes in Trump's rise, white suburban women seemed suddenly shocked into action. Of course, the new turn toward activism among these educated types only made working-class voters distrust if not despise them even more—as America's fault lines grew even wider.

Yet even as the educational divide drove Trump's victory, higher-education policy—either punishing colleges for their liberal heresies or, heaven forbid, making universities more accessible for the working class—was a low priority during the four years of his presidency. His controversial pick as education secretary, billionaire Betsy DeVos, had made her name pushing charter schools on the K-12 level. Her few moves pertaining to higher ed—making it easier for the much-maligned for-profit universities or for male students accused of sexual misconduct to get off the hook—reflected boilerplate free-market conservatism. The real significance of Trump's governing years was the anti-intellectualism that drenched almost every move the administration made—not so much a rejection of college as a rejection of knowledge itself.

AS TRUMP CLOSED IN ON THE PRESIDENCY IN 2016, HE'D BRAGGED TO the *Washington Post* that as a (debatably) successful businessman he'd always had little use for experts, that he generally saw them "as people who can't see the forest for the trees." He insisted that he'd always made sound business or political decisions "with very little knowledge other than the knowledge I [already] had, plus the words 'common sense.'" The future president's almost magical thinking about his own decision-making powers may have been a function to some degree of his extreme narcissism, but rejecting expertise also put Trump on the same wavelength as millions of voters. Anti-intellectualism in American life was nothing new—indeed, that was the title of the 1963 essay by renowned historian Richard Hofstader, which traced anti-elite populism back to the nation's early days, and just a few years later Richard Nixon and Spiro Agnew weaponized those tendencies against the media and campus radicals. But basic science seemed safe from the culture war—until it wasn't.

Years before Trump arrived on the scene, the test range for the new Republican war on science was the issue of climate change. Arguably, the world's wealthiest corporations that controlled the fossil fuel industry conducted their own scientific experiment—to see if spending millions on malevolent spin like purposefully biased think tanks could convince the masses that the consensus view of the world's top climatologists was actually bunk. This project backed by the likes of Exxon-Mobil and Chevron succeeded beyond Big Oil's wildest dreams. Even by 2016, with weather emergencies like droughts or deadly flooding on the rise, only 41 percent of Americans believed climate change was an immediate problem, a lower rate than the world average, and U.S. climate deniers were heavily tilted toward the Republican Party. Trump promised Appalachia's shrinking number of coal miners that he would bring their industry back, and—while that pledge proved impossible to keep—he ensured that on federal policy America would be moving backward right at the moment when scientists said the planet's future hinged on immediate cuts in fossil-fuel pollution.

Some of Trump's war on science was simply to take traditional Republican kowtowing to Big Oil and Gas to new but predictable depths—withdrawing from the global Paris Climate Accords (for nearly four years the United States was literally the only nonsignatory nation in the world), undoing anti-pollution rules passed under Obama, and naming a pro-industry critic of the U.S. Environmental Protection Agency, Scott Pruitt, to run his EPA. But the Trump administration also shut down a number of lower-profile scientific studies about pollution or perceived health hazards across an array of federal agencies, driving scores of experts to leave the government in dismay. Scientists had never been viewed as especially political—but Team Trump's hostility toward their very existence would radicalize them.

Just three months after Trump took office, hundreds of thousands of researchers and academics and their liberal allies took to the streets for a first-ever event called the March for Science. "The march is allowing the public to know that this is what science is, and it's letting our legislators know that science is vitally important," Ashlea Morgan, a doctoral student in neurobiology at Columbia University, told the *New York Times* that day. Behind her, demonstrators chanted, "Who runs the world? Nerds!"

But politically, that was kind of the problem, wasn't it? Not the presence of nerds, but the millions of everyday Americans who thought college types like these anti-Trump marchers either ruled the world, or at least insisted on telling folks that they did. Scientists were now feeding the same cycle that was driving the bigger college/noncollege divide in America. The more that far-right extremism in the unappealing person of Trump egged on the scientific community to defend itself in the political arena, the more it confirmed a conservative worldview that the academy was stacked against them.

This rejection of basic science by one half of the American political divide would soon have deadly consequences with the arrival of the coronavirus on U.S. soil in the winter of 2019–20. Scientists had long warned that America might not be ready for a global pandemic on the scale of COVID-19. But not only had Team Trump shown zero interest on the topic, it even disbanded a Global Health Security and Biodefense unit that had been created by Obama three years earlier and also disregarded a pandemic "playbook" that had been left behind by the prior administration. Not that it's likely access to information would have mattered to the 45th president, focused only on the looming election, and fearful that too much virus talk would tank a stock market that had soared in the first three years of his presidency. "I wanted to always play it down," Trump famously told Bob Woodward in an interview that wasn't released until 190,000 Americans had already died. By then, a former head of the National Intelligence Council was calling the federal response—with confusion over mandating masks and a lack of tests and needed hospital supplies—"a real blow to the sense that America was competent."

But while the mounting death toll likely turned off some voters—especially some white college-educated suburban men who'd backed Trump in 2016—it didn't damage the president's standing with his base, which turned any anger not toward the White House or even the virus but those pointy-headed scientists whom they believed wanted to take down their hero before the election. In pro-Trump social media, misinformation thrived—about quack cures like hydroxychloroquine or even ivermectin, also used as a horse dewormer, or with falsehoods trashing the new COVID-19 vaccines—and anger toward health authorities grew. "I would also like to know where do you get the authority to reduce my oxygen," one woman in a white TRUMP GIRL shirt demanded of the Palm Beach County, Florida, commissioners as they met to issue a mandatory-mask-in-public order to fight a surge in COVID-19 cases in the Sunshine State.

Both the COVID-19 crisis—which saw American deaths pass the 1918–19 "Spanish flu" tally, with more than 700,000 by September 2021—and the Trump years generally will remain permanent stains on U.S. history, but they also marked something else: The final defeat of the post–World War II dream of an America where citizens would be widely inoculated against dangerous propaganda and the kind of political demagoguery that had nearly destroyed Europe, and the dream that this intellectual vaccine would be liberal education. In 1947, the Truman Commission had laid out the case that, "In a real sense the future of our civilization depends on the direction education takes," and that a U.S. commitment to work could bring "a stronger, freer social order" that recognized the dignity of all work. Instead, after an initial burst of promise, America has spent seventy-five years creating a worldview that disrespects those high-minded ideals in almost every way.

We missed the moment to make higher education a public trust that would benefit all American society through economic invention, civic engagement and general enlightenment. Instead, we privatized college and called it a meritocracy so that it could be rigged for the winners while the perceived losers are mocked and ridiculed. Liberal education was mostly overrun by the business majors who invented the financial instruments to saddle the generation that came after them with bottomless debt. The social order grew weaker, and also less free. The deep democracy thinkers of 1947 feared these outcomes if the United States didn't make higher education accessible to all—but only in vague, general terms. It took three generations and finally the annus horribilis of 2020 to see exactly what the American nightmare these postwar visionaries feared would look like—the world's formerly most powerful nation paralyzed by climate inaction, lacking the news literacy to separate fact from fiction, refusing to trust the science as a virus devoured the countryside, and coming within 55,000 votes in three states of handing a second term to a president who lied 30,573 times during the first one, for the sole purpose of owning the college libs.

In the end, those diploma-wielding voters did buy America a four-year reprieve from the downward spiral of Trumpism. After Joe Biden was elected 46th president in November 2020, political analysts from sites like FiveThirtyEight.com found the college/noncollege divide was even greater in 2020 than it had been in 2016. Pretty much the sole reason that Biden flipped five states that Trump had won four years earlier was his expanded margin among white, college-educated voters in densely populated suburbs like Oakland County, Michigan, or Chester County, Pennsylvania. But while a narrow win by the self-appointed enlightened ones of the Democratic Party over resentful Republicans would bring policy results on vaccines, climate, and other key issues, it did nothing to heal America's social and political divides. And there were signs in the 2020 results that some working-class Blacks and Latinos are peeling away from the Democrats as the party rebrands around college degrees. A political party engineered for 37 percent of the nation is a tenuous one, at best.

Biden's victory did little to reduce the fever of misinformation on the still-simmering far right, where anti-science distrust of the COVID-19 vaccines fueled by ratings-driven conspiracy on Fox News and by Trump's political allies threatened to further drive a national wedge between a blue America that was inoculated and open for business and a red America where needlessly high rates of hospitalization and death would linger. Meanwhile, on the nation's college campuses, the harsh impact of the coronavirus—which meant billions in lost revenue while the necessary changeover to remote learning raised new questions about what a diploma is really worth—offered the greatest opportunity since the return of millions of young people from Europe and Asia in 1945 to reinvent the American way of college.

CHAPTER 8

THE SOUL OF A NEW TRUMAN COMMISSION

When the *New York Times* sends its teams of reporters out to find riled-up Trump voters in faded Formica diners, they usually send them to places like Tower City, Pennsylvania—the sleepy burg where a twenty-year-old named Aaron Tallman grew up.

Tower City, a Reading Railroad town in the rural east-central part of Pennsylvania, saw its population peak in 1930 and then decline every decade since then, to its current 1,277. "In the 1950s and '60s, 70 percent of the people in the county I live in were employed in coal mines, or something that supported the industry," Tallman told me. Close to 70 percent of the older folks who stayed behind in Schuylkill County went for Donald Trump in 2020. The younger people that Tallman knows from high school consider themselves lucky when they get a job at one of the region's new warehouses, paying eighteen dollars an hour, or less, in return for often backbreaking physical labor.

Their future is not Tallman's future, and the arc of this young man's story fits few of the grease-splattered clichés about growing up in Trump Country. At an age where the best and the brightest of his friends face two more years of college, a rising debt load, and an uncertain job market, Tallman attended a recent job fair where grade-A employers were tugging at his arm and practically tripping over each other to meet him, even though his associate's degree was still a year away.

"I have a job interview tomorrow, but I'm afraid because it's not necessarily the job I want," Tallman told me in May 2021, as we sat inside an empty classroom. "Coming from a school like this, it's almost that your biggest fear now is having to say no to somebody."

The "school like this" where Tallman was wrapping up his junior year is called the Williamson College of the Trades, located in Media, Pennsylvania, a suburb southwest of Philadelphia. Williamson—all-male, military-strict, completely free to attend—is one of the most unique institutions of higher learning in America, and arguably impossible to replicate, not least because of the sizable endowment that supports its roughly 250 students. But just because there are few—if any—schools quite like Williamson in America doesn't mean we shouldn't be thinking about how to clone it. It blends a concept that's popular with progressive Democrats—a free trade school—with classes that adhere to an arguably conservative worldview on morality, and that's a recipe that's working for both a small sliver of the millions of young Americans who don't want a conventional college—let alone the debt—but desire a demanding career, and for employers who insist it's hard to find applicants like these.

When I met Tallman, he and his friend and classmate Jimmy McChesney—vice president and president of their junior class, respectively—had been sweeping the floors and thoroughly cleaning up Williamson's machine shop. It's a large cluttered shed with rows of blue and gray pieces of equipment for cutting and making tools, which feels to an outsider like stepping back into the 1950s even if most of the devices are state-of-the-art, often donated by Williamson alums who've become CEOs of small and obscure yet thriving industrial or construction firms.

The two friends weren't getting paid a dime to spend their last two weeks of the school year wiping down every piece of equipment or mopping the floors. The annual year-end cleanup—along with the rest of the regimen of chores, like slinging breakfast in the cafeteria one morning a week, or (at least pre-COVID) cleaning the bathrooms in the dorms—is just acknowledged as a payback for getting a free education. As we walked back to the classroom where we could get away from the noise, Tallman and McChesney instinctively sprinted ahead to hold the door open for me, just like a half-dozen other Williamson students I would meet that morning.

If the yin of the modern college is a place like the University of Arizona or LSU, with their lazy rivers and rich out-of-staters shopping for the coolest "beer and circuses" experience, then the Williamson College of Trades is part of a very tiny yang—with its 6 a.m. military-style wake-ups and inspections, its sports-coat-and-tie dress code for academic classes, and a "zero tolerance" drug and alcohol policy that forces the expulsion of a couple of dozen young men each and every school year. "My roommate said, at the beginning of the year, 'Why do we have to shave every day?,' Tallman said. "I said, 'It's not necessarily the shaving. It's having the discipline to do it.'"

McChesney came to Williamson from an equally Trump-y hometown, a small, shrinking community called Enon Valley on the border of Pennsylvania and Ohio, not far from the rusted-out industrial city of Beaver Falls. The guidance counselors at McChesney's high school told kids there was only one way out—work hard to get into a traditional college. But McChesney, like a lot of the other young men I met at Williamson, wanted to work with his hands rather than sit in a classroom for four years. And then there were the increasing number of horror stories he heard around debt.

"But everyone is focused on the four-year degree—and then they have problems finding a job when they graduate," McChesney said. "I know a lot of people who went to college and then when they graduate they're working in a grocery store." Tallman nodded his head. He'd been thinking about entering the military, when he found out about Williamson. Most of the students I interviewed heard about the all-expenses-paid trade school in different ways—from a family member, or a knowledgeable high-school shop teacher—but had the same general thought, that it sounded too good to be true.

Until some unknown, doubtful day when America decides that educating its young adults is a public good, Williamson *is* too good to be true.

ISAIAH WILLIAMSON WAS A PRODUCT OF THE NATION'S ORIGINAL Gilded Age even as in some ways he was repulsed by it. A modest Quaker born in 1803 and raised on a farm north of Philadelphia, Williamson made so much money in the dry-goods business and as a wholesaler as the city thrived in the years before the Civil War, he retired at age thirty-five and—in the fashion of a modern internet billionaire—resolved to give his money away.

Dubbed "the threadbare philanthropist," Williamson was given to walking in his rumpled clothes around Philadelphia as the city became the center of an Industrial Revolution. He was troubled by the sight of so many of what he called "corner boys" who loitered without a regular source of income, so he hatched an idea to construct a school where idle young men could learn a trade. His multimillion-dollar gift in 1888 to buy 220 acres of land in what was then rural Delaware County, build a grand campus, and leave $1 million to fund its yearly operations was said to leave his trade school with a larger endowment than Harvard or Yale at that time.

Williamson approved the Media site on the day before he died of heart disease in 1889, two years before the Williamson Free School of Mechanical Trades opened its doors. Some 130 years later, herds of deer still forage on its 220 acres less than a mile and yet 100 years removed from the traffic-clogged commercial strip of U.S. 1, as students sleep in Victorian-style dorms and attend class in grand brick and masonry buildings designed by Frank Furness, Philadelphia's great architect of the nineteenth century. It seems like the perfect setting for a school that carries on as if the great upheavals of postwar America and its extended adolescence—coeducation and the sexual revolution, the drug scene and the party culture, or campus activism—had never happened.

"The days can be kind of rough—there's a lot of oversight, I would say." This from one of the eight or so students that Williamson's administrators had handpicked for me to interview, a twenty-year-old horticulture major named Marcello Shayeghi. "You always have people checking up on you." That included the random drug tests that had caused some of their peers to get the boot, but it was more than that.

This wasn't a complaint. Shayeghi, like all the other young men I spoke with, just wanted to make the point that Williamson wasn't for everyone—but it was fine for them. The hand-picked interviewees all seemed to share a hard-work ethic, as well as an ability to see a future past the next Saturday night. Several told me that growing up in the working class, sometimes with difficult family situations, had matured them even before they arrived on campus at age eighteen or nineteen. David McCann, a twenty-one-year-old horticulture major, started working in a Bucks County, Pennsylvania, bagel shop when he was fifteen and became a baker, worked for a general contractor, and—because of his love for working outside—co-founded a small tree-pruning and landscaping business that he still runs on the weekend. He also tried taking some classes at Bucks County Community College when he was a senior in high school, but decided that school wasn't worth the nearly thousand dollars he was shelling out for each course.

"I decided I was done with college—that it wasn't worth the time or money," McCann said, but then his older brother told him about Williamson, and the ability to learn a trade more quickly and possibly get on a management track, without taking on any debt. Now he was about to intern for a second straight summer at a major tree-care company in Philadelphia's affluent western suburbs. "It gives you that extra stepping-stone." Even with the coronavirus slowdown, more than a hundred firms had come to Williamson's three-day job fair that spring—more companies than the sixty-five or so graduates.

Not all Williamson students are as entrepreneurial as McCann, but the employers also like things like their ability to show up for work on time—and pass a drug test. Something else unique about the student body is that it skews conservative in its politics, apparently. "There's definitely a lot of Republicans here," McCann told me. "The student body tends to lean more on the conservative side."

That's inevitable in the 2020s, where all college is political, and all politics is influenced by college. It's hard to write about a place like Williamson without making it a political story, and—indeed—even though I live less than twenty minutes away in Delaware County, I knew nothing about the cloistered campus or its unique niche in American higher education until I read about it in late 2019 in a conservative, politics-oriented publication called *City Journal*. In her piece, writer Kay S. Hymowitz plays up the elements of Williamson that would appeal most strongly to her readers from the "traditional values" crowd—classes that instill classical moral values, the daily nondenominational chapel where students might hear a lecture from a successful capitalist, drenched in patriotism and testosterone. Her critique of traditional college—as dens of amoral decay, where the students who don't miss class because they are hungover get indoctrinated by their woke, leftist professors—falls mostly between the lines.

But the facts of the Williamson story—that the school has been a lifeline for hundreds of middle-class kids who lack either the interest or the aptitude for four years of university lectures, and that its job fairs prove there's a mostly untapped market for skilled, dedicated trades workers—are undeniable. What's more, while I—a progressive writer who views authority-defying rebel students like Mario Savio and Tom Hayden as heroes—and Kay Hymowitz probably see eye to eye on next to nothing when it comes to ideology, her diagnosis of what's wrong with the modern American way of college—the high tuition, the unfathomable debt, the middle-class obsessions with test scores and admissions, and a system that "has demoralized a significant portion of the population with little talent for, or interest in, academic work, and thus contributed to the angry state of our politics"—is the exact same critique that's been presented in these pages.

In pivoting to a conversation about how we might fix the sorry state of higher education in twenty-first-century America, I choose to spotlight Williamson—an institution of higher education that's not like any other today, and with a culture and philosophy that might strike some readers as too authoritarian—because I want people to think about the conversations that we're not having when we talk about the U.S. "college problem." This one trade college in suburban Pennsylvania is addressing one of the biggest problems facing our nation in the 2020s—young middle-class kids falling through the cracks of a higher-ed system that mostly works for the few and the privileged—and yet it feels like a grain of sand on a large beach. Through the fluke of one millionaire's generosity and his long-term vision back in 1888, Williamson offers a frustratingly tiny glimpse of what a different, and better, way of American higher education could look like: a mix of practical career training and classes around becoming a better citizen, provided for free, with no debt burden.

But how much could Williamson scale up? Would the college's model work if the program was funded by the U.S. taxpayers instead of the discipline-minded executors of a millionaire's trust—and would it work without the 6 a.m. inspections? And once the nation met its clear yet finite need for skilled trades workers, what would public higher education look like for the millions of others also not bound for a traditional college campus?

THESE ARE TOUGH QUESTIONS, BUT ONES WE NEED TO GRAPPLE with. The most active debate about "the college problem" takes place among people—most of them liberal or progressive Democrats—who've been to college and who are, or plan to, send their own kids to a school like theirs, albeit increasingly needing to borrow money to do that. Their proposed solutions around canceling a lot, if not all, of the nation's $1.7 trillion student debt and providing free public universities may be in the spirit of making education a public good—yet they can also feel self-interested.

On the day that the major networks called the 2020 presidential election for Joe Biden—November 7, 2020—the Senate Democratic leader Chuck Schumer boldly (and wrongly, it turned out) declared that the incoming 46th president was going to eliminate the first $50,000 of every debt holder's college loans by executive fiat, and he would do so in the first one hundred days of his term. Progressives, already thrilled by Trump's defeat, were ecstatic at Schumer's statement, but some political watchers threw a caution flag. "I think Dems are wildly underestimating the intensity of anger college loan cancellation is going to provoke," Damon Linker, a writer for the political journal *This Week*, posted on Twitter. "Those with college debt will be thrilled, of course. But lots and lots of people who didn't go to college or who worked to pay off their debts? Gonna be bad."

If liberals are approaching the college problem with tunnel vision, far too many conservatives are going after higher education in bad faith, seeing college campuses as a place to score cheap political points—to "own the libs," as the popular saying goes—rather than offering serious ideas on how to make America's young people better prepared to enter the job market and a voting booth. While progressive Democrats were debating when and how to cancel student debt, right-wing Republicans were largely focused in the early months of Biden's presidency on how to keep conversations about structural racism in America, including the legacy of slavery, out of America's classrooms—not just in universities but in high schools and middle schools. Rarely did national Republicans discuss ideas for ending "deaths of despair"—despite findings that the highest rates of suicide and drug overdoses among those lacking a college education are in counties that voted for Donald Trump.

Still, in embarking on this project, I looked for that serious Republican policymaker who not only acknowledged the nature of the problem for their constituents—that too many middle-class kids lack access to opportunities for college or career training, a breeding ground for resentment and social-class divisions—but had constructive ideas for fixing it. In 2019, I thought I'd found such a conservative in the Stanford-educated right-wing populist GOP senator Josh Hawley of Missouri.

In July 2019, during his first year in office, Hawley introduced two pieces of higher-ed legislation that summed up his worldview that colleges held too much hegemony over career training in America and were also the primary villains in the college debt crisis. His first measure, which would expand the federal Pell Grant program to cover initiatives like short-term job training, digital boot camps, and employer-based apprenticeships, was similar to ideas supported by a number of Democrats. His second scheme—which would require a university to pay half the cost when a student defaults on his loan, theoretically giving colleges more of a stake in making sure grads are trained for viable careers—was attacked as both unworkable and more geared toward scoring cheap political points. Indeed, Hawley couched his proposals—which made a flurry of headlines when announced in June 2019, then vanished in the haze of D.C. gridlock—in the rhetoric of right-wing talk radio, saying "You shouldn't have to take on a mountain of debt and get a four-year degree you don't want in order to get a good job in our state and in our country."

Less than two years later, Hawley's once rising political star was badly tarnished. Whatever dreams the junior Missouri senator might have harbored about a kind of blue-collar populism that would actually do things for the middle class, in January 2021 he opted instead for what he hoped would be a shortcut to political prominence. He voted with a minority to deny certification of Biden's election victory in key states, and was caught on camera giving a raised-fist salute to January 6 insurrectionists about to overrun the U.S. Capitol. (In two subsequent polls of the 2024 presidential race, Hawley netted 0 percent—and then they stopped listing him as a candidate.) ·

On one hand, the issue of college access and affordability is now arguably higher on the nation's political agenda than it has been any time since the 1960s. But—in arguably a mirror of the debate over a true federal commitment to universal higher education after World War II, which foundered over narrow interests ranging from elite Ivies to small religious colleges to Southern segregation—the most talked-about fixes are not just halfway measures but partisan solutions that aid each party's core supporters and punish enemies. In an era of the worst partisan divide since the Civil War—divisions that have been fueled by economic and social anxiety around college—there was real danger that bad policy fixes around higher education could only exacerbate a climate of resentment and misunderstanding, instead of promoting national unity.

In 1944, the massive upheaval of a global conflict—which sent millions of young citizens halfway around the world and back—became the accidental trigger for a complete reinvention of how Americans entered adulthood, better educated than any generation that had come before them. More than seventy-five years after this spectacular launch, the mission has flown way off course, and our nation's top minds will have to repair the aircraft while it is already aloft, at its unsteady cruising altitude. And yet, anything short of a massive, second reinvention will leave in place the guts of today's system that crushes American Dreams for millions of young women and men by forcing them to choose between debt or despair, still nurturing resentments that could take down our entire democracy.

It's long past time for another Truman Commission–style look at the state of higher education. Any true fix for "the college problem" needs a set of strong moral governing principles, or a strategy, to be carried out before we embark down the roadmap of policies, or tactics. America owes its young citizens these foundational principles.

Universality

In essence, the massive societal change that occurred from 1944 to 1970 was a shift from what experts call an elite system of higher education—targeting the top 5 percent of families—to mass higher education, in which both college enrollment grew exponentially with the help of affordable options for anyone who wanted to attend. Idealists saw this as a transitional step toward universal higher education—or, in today's political jargon, "college-for-all." But the reality has been that enrollment growth slowed, with an American system that lacks the capacity and, now, the funding, to accept everyone on our current network of campuses—nor does a "college-for-all" scheme match either the aptitudes of all young people or, frankly, the needs of the U.S. economy.

Today, the principle of universal higher education demands thinking outside the confining box of our current web of institutions and programs. Instead, the U.S. body politic should agree that government has an obligation to help young Americans navigate the perilous straits that run between high school and entering adulthood, with an ambitious "new deal" that offers a tuition- and debt-free traditional university education to those who desire one, but different kinds of opportunities—vocational or trade training, shorter bursts of online or targeted learning, apprenticeships, internships, civilian or military opportunities—for those seeking a different path. Because critics will stress—and understandably so—that these different types of education typically come with wildly different price tags, with a bachelor's degree the most expensive, the challenge for policymakers will be to design a new higher-ed regime with substantial benefits for everyone, while also selling taxpayers on the notion all of society would reap economic and social benefits through helping out young people.

Matt Bruenig, a progressive writer and lawyer, wrote a 2017 essay attacking the notion that "college is the new high school and we should want everyone to attend it because that is the only way to get a good middle-class job these days. This kind of rhetoric seems to rally the crowds, but is as dumb as it is stirring." Bruenig argues instead for what he calls "attachment benefits" for America's eighteen-to-twenty-four-year-olds—government subsidies that would fund the development of young adults which would, of course, include tuition- and debt-free public college but also offer dollars for "free vocational training, subsidized apprenticeships, in-work subsidies, public jobs, and whatever else it takes to ensure a lasting labor force attachment." It's a rough idea that, like any solutions, would need to tiptoe through the political minefields of the 2020s—but it's also a good faith strategy to straddle the political and practical obstacles of today's college/noncollege divide.

A "Public Good"

The original sin of the G.I. Bill/Truman Commission years—which laid out the myriad ways that the American people would gain through civic engagement, the enrichment of liberal learning, and as an inventive economic powerhouse—was in failing to capitalize on widespread support for expanded access to higher education when public interest was high and the issue was popular. Many note that the G.I. Bill—which proved that middle- and working-class students could benefit and even thrive with advanced education—was only possible in the wake of World War II. Today's young men and women are coming off the biggest life disruption of the twenty-first century—a pandemic that kept many off campus for a year. COVID-19 was tragic for many families and also rattled the foundations of the American way of college, as shutdowns and online learning raised new questions about what a modern university education is really worth. Higher ed is facing its greatest crisis, but a crisis is also an opportunity for complete reinvention.

Today, the gap in job opportunities and earnings potential—not to mention happiness and self-esteem—between Americans with just a high-school diploma and those with a four-year college degree is wide and growing wider by the day. For example, today's Millennials who've only completed high school are earning just 62 percent as much as college grads, and their unemployment rate during the Great Recession was more than twice as high. Under these circumstances, higher education—and again, I'm using an expanded definition that includes job training and internships—is no longer an add-on for society's elite, but a basic human right for all citizens.

Throughout American history, ideas and norms around whether public education should be mandatory and funded by taxpayers have constantly evolved to incorporate more of a person's formative years—adapting to both social and economic norms. It wasn't until 1852, or seventy-six years after the Declaration of Independence, that Massachusetts made school attendance mandatory; by 1930—spurred on by the Industrial Revolution, which both placed a higher premium on skills and led to child labor laws—most American children were required to attend school until at least age fourteen. Today, with sixteen- and seventeen-year-old dropout rates on the decline, the vast majority of American youth attend school fully at taxpayer expense through age eighteen—yet in a world where most experts say anyone who stops acquiring knowledge and new skills beyond age eighteen is doomed to fail in our economy.

In that context, the eighteen-year-old cutoff for free public education seems not only arbitrary but cruel. In a world where Republicans and Democrats agree on virtually nothing, support for taxpayer-funded elementary, middle, and high schools as a "public good" is close to unanimous—with the exception of a handful of Ayn Randian–libertarian cranks ranting about "government schools." What's more, today's American public—at least when not being fed angry partisan political cues—already broadly supports higher education as a public good. Remember, a growing number of Americans, but especially Republicans—now believe that college is "a risky gamble," but that's because the current system wants them to wager their own hard-earned dollars. In a 2018 Teachers College poll, however, 76 percent of Americans said taxpayer spending on higher education is an "excellent" or "good" investment, with healthy support for the role that college plays in fostering scientific advances, boosting the overall economy, and promoting citizenship.

Even lacking the wide social net of European and other developed nations, America has embraced a large vision of the public good that includes not only public education through high school but also a vast, if rusty, network of infrastructure that includes everything from interstate highways to sewers, not to mention the world's largest military, by far, and a vast archipelago of prisons. Given that, America's failure to invest properly in its most valuable, and most fragile, human infrastructure—its young people awkwardly entering adulthood—can only be seen as a gobsmacking failure. The deliberate decision to instead make higher education a personal good—with a stiff financial burden on those who pursue college dreams—under the banner of a rigged meritocracy has caused bitterness, resentment, and despair among the millions either cast aside or bankrupted.

And that's only the psychological toll. Consider the dollar cost of everything else—the drug overdoses and suicides among those left out by this system (an estimated $1 trillion on the opioid crisis by 2017), the states that spent billions ($71 billion from 1980 to 2013) on a "school-to-prison" pipeline while they cut aid to their university systems, the rising costs of fighting climate change ($2 trillion, give or take) or pandemics like COVID-19 because of (sometimes willful) scientific ignorance, and the cultural chasm between college and noncollege voters that has reached the point of threatening U.S. democracy. Yes, shifting the burden to make higher education a public good would look very expensive on paper. But how can we afford not to?

Forbearance

Then, consider this: If a true solution to "the college problem" in America involves not just making college accessible and affordable to today's rising generation but also offering tangible benefits like career training for the millions who aren't college-inclined, then what about the older generations that are currently paying the price for forty years of failed and sometimes dishonest higher education policy? Critics of proposals for massive student loan forgiveness—up to and including wiping clean the bulk of the $1.7 trillion debt now managed by the federal government—say that such an arrangement would be grossly unfair to families that somehow saved enough to pay rising tuition bills or to adults who did borrow for college and diligently paid the money back. Beyond fairness, some numbers-crunching economists say the power of student loan forgiveness to boost the U.S. economy—in freeing up young adults in their twenties or thirties to buy new homes or cars—is vastly overrated.

Ultimately, ending the college-debt crisis in America isn't only a matter of economics but a question of morality, and justice. We will remain an unfair and grossly unequal nation if we find a way to provide mostly free education to today's college-age youth yet continue to saddle adults—but especially people of color and women—with hundreds of dollars in monthly payments that will weigh them down, possibly for the rest of their lives. That's especially true when one remembers that the college debt crisis was launched in a sea of bad faith—the Wall Street investment banks and other money changers who found a way to monetize young people's hopes even while crushing them, the government bureaucrats who loosened loan standards with faulty assumptions about families' ability to ever pay the money back, the college administrators who did little to warn admitted students about the financial risk. What we call a crisis is actually a national scandal.

Astra Taylor of the Debt Collective, appearing on the *New York Times*'s *The Argument* podcast in 2021, said "this isn't tens of millions of people making bad personal choices. This is a structural issue. This is about the way our economy is organized." She also noted that debt cancellation would mark "a return to this egalitarian tradition of providing education for everyone on equitable terms, because it's good for society as a whole. So there's a way in which what we're saying that sounds so out of the box now is a restoration of these foundational principles."

But let's be honest: That altruistic stance is a hard sell in the nitty-gritty world of politics, Indeed, fear of the potential fallout from the 63 percent of Americans without a bachelor's degree, in addition to grads who've already paid back their loans, is likely a key factor in Biden holding off the pleas from Warren and Senate majority leader Chuck Schumer in the early days of his presidency. To succeed, in my opinion, a president would need to (a) sell college debt forgiveness as benefiting all Americans, by boosting the economy (new home construction for younger people, for example), as well as racial equity in reducing the huge wealth gap for Black and Brown families; (b) make blue-collar benefits such as trade school or lifelong learning opportunities front and center; and (c) perhaps offer a package overtly paired with a political perk for noncollege grads, like the $15 minimum wage.

Liberal Education

The great thinkers of post–World War II who believed that general, or liberal, education—that is, a curriculum with a focus on broad knowledge rather than a narrow career outlook, that aim to develop moral values and civic engagement—was essential for world peace and democracy in an era of rising totalitarianism and nuclear bombs were clearly onto something. Since the tumultuous 1960s and '70s, the move away from liberal education in favor of campus careerism—both in course offerings but also in student preference—has rivaled rising tuition as the defining college trend of our time. Between 1971 and 2009, the number of freshmen entering UCLA—according to its annual survey—who placed importance on "developing a meaningful philosophy of life" plunged from 73 to 48 percent, while the number who stressed becoming "well-off financially" soared from 37 to 78 percent. Given that California's public universities were tuition-free in 1971 while many of 2009's freshmen were facing thousands of dollars in debt that would need to be paid back with a high-paying job, that shift is not shocking.

But it's not exactly clear whom the career-focused American university of the twenty-first century is helping. The résumé-reading employers for whom the careerist diploma is targeted say they're actually looking for more applicants with better communication skills as well as a knack for solving new and unexpected problems—the kind of abilities better honed by a general education. A 2019 survey commissioned by the Association of American Colleges & Universities found the qualities that job recruiters most desired were "oral communication, critical thinking, ethical judgment, working effectively in teams, written communication, and the real-world application of skills and knowledge"—not surprising after an era in which new technologies like the internet and social media has rendered outdated training in yesterday's technical abilities as obsolete.

But more important, the surge in careerism—and the turn away from the civic-oriented values of a liberal education—coincided with some of the worst fears of mid-twentieth-century education planners coming to pass. True, it's difficult to parcel out blame for increasing scientific ignorance and worsening news illiteracy amid the complex calculus of not only what's taught on college campuses but who has access to higher ed—especially when civic education in high schools and middle schools has also declined. But the simple fact that America's rapid decline toward populist authoritarianism under Trump, and the civil-war-grade political division that accompanied it, coincided with a sharp decline in liberal education is also a powerful argument for its return.

IN 2012, AN AMBITIOUS YOUNG ALASKAN NAMED JONATHAN KREISS-Tomkins was just one credit away from a coveted Yale University diploma. Kreiss-Tomkins had had a whirlwind college career that ranged from the Yale Symphony Orchestra to exploring mountaintops in South America—yet he'd always had one foot each in two very different worlds. When he saw an opportunity to run—successfully—for the Alaska legislature and represent his remote hometown of Sitka, nestled along the frontier state's coastline in the shadows of three towering mountains—he pulled up stakes from New Haven.

Kreiss-Tomkins, now a key leader in his isolated community, has some thoughts about the Ivy League education he'd nearly completed. In many ways, he found it lacking. "I felt like college was great for the community and social reasons," he said in an interview, but he was disappointed by the academics, particularly the classroom teaching. In the opinion of this young Democratic lawmaker, top professors at top universities tend to focus on their research skills and not on pedagogy.

Those thoughts stayed with Kreiss-Tomkins as he pondered a more specific problem in his Sitka hometown: the shutdown several years earlier of a small religious school called Sheldon Jackson College. The legislator and several of his allies thought about bringing a new kind of college to the Alaska port town. In particular Kreiss-Tomkins kept thinking about a California program he'd heard about called Deep Springs College. Deep Springs was founded in 1917 as an endowed experiment where a handful of students would get a tuition-free two-year education heavy on liberal and classical learning, blended with hands-on farming and other manual labor in desert isolation. The Alaskans' idea was to adapt the Deep Springs model—except that the physical work would be community service inside a real town with a large Indigenous population that could use some help. Their concept called Outer Coast College started to become a reality in 2015 through summer and then one-year programs, although the school has so far faced a slog in attaining accreditation to offer two-year degrees—not helped, obviously, by the pandemic.

Today, students who do make the trek to western Alaska absorb a range of readings from Plato to the bard of 1960s' revolutionaries, Herbert Marcuse, while spending their nonclassroom hours either fixing up the campus or running its food services, or out in the Sitka community rebuilding homes or tutoring younger students. The program may be small but its 2010s launch wasn't unique, either. The Arete Project in the Blue Ridge Mountains of North Carolina is also closely modeled after the all-male, century-old Deep Springs, but exclusively for women. There are a handful of others—each promising to instill a blend of self-reliance and moral values, with an emphasis on critical thinking over targeted career skills. Most, like Outer Coast or the Arete Project, seek philanthropic money and ask students to pay what they can, with free tuition for lower-income students.

Kreiss-Tomkins told me that the ability to perform hands-on work in a small, close-knit community is central to his concept for Outer Coast, one of the small set of miniature schools that the *New York Times* dubbed "the anti-college." Said the young lawmaker: "People are looking for outlets—as we become more digitized, we become more isolated from tactile experiences, yet a lot of people want and need that." More broadly, these anti-colleges are experiments in returning to the core values of the G.I. Bill era: general education, promoting civic engagement—and at a low cost.

The fascinating thing about both Outer Coast's Plato-reading outdoors enthusiasts and Williamson, with its flag-waving, chapel-going, beloved-by-conservatives hands-on trade education, is that they are essentially saying the same thing: There are different, better ways to prepare young people for the world, in a time when the vast American college-industrial complex clearly is not working for so many. Though one is laser-focused on job training and the other centers more around philosophy and learning self-governance, both Williamson and Outer Coast nonetheless offer a vision centered around moral values.

Such experiments are a cry in the literal wilderness for a radical rethinking of the U.S. system of higher education; the problem so far is not a lack of boldness but a lack of scale. Schools like Outer Coast, Deep Springs, Arete, and Williamson only have the wherewithal to train, combined, about three hundred young Americans at any given time, and even when you consider schools with somewhat similar visions you only get up to the low thousands, at best. Meanwhile, nearly 3.5 million eighteen-year-olds knock on the door of American adulthood every year, from the sizzling sidewalks of Bed-Stuy to the big sky of Montana reservations, all demanding both wisdom and opportunity. How, realistically, could America bring universal higher ed, loan forbearance, and liberal learning to such a large cohort, given the power of an elite status quo that likes the college regime just the way that it is?

Another of the many similarities between America's higher-ed crisis and the nation's long-running health care debacle is the question of why so many developed nations, especially across Europe, are able to offer either tuition-free or low-cost college education—just as most of those same nations provide single-payer health insurance. To many outside of the United States, the matter of the $1.7 trillion college debt seems just as absurd as the medical bankruptcies. But in the United States it's too late to start from scratch, and we must figure out how to address the vast political influence of powerful incumbents, whether that is the private insurance giants and hospital chains, or universities with huge endowments and their alumni scattered throughout Congress, the government, and the billionaire donor class.

"I used to joke that I could just take all my papers and statistical programs and globally replace *hospitals* with *schools*, *doctors* with *teachers* and *patients* with *students*," Dartmouth economist Douglas Staiger—who studies both worlds—told *The Atlantic*'s Amanda Ripley in 2018. Both systems lack any kind of cost control and because of their privatized, free-market nature present their consumers—be they patients or students—with a confusing array of choices that don't always lead to the most cost-savvy decisions. The per-student cost of attending college in America is about double that of the average developed nation—partly because of those lazy-river-style perks but mainly because of fixed costs like the salaries needed to attract all those highly educated professors and administrators.

But is college really free in Europe and other forward-thinking places? The answer is, as you'd expect, complicated. Overall, though, surveys have found that tuition is indeed free in about a third of developed nations and relatively modest (at least by U.S. standards) in another third (in 2018, that meant less than $2,400 a year). When German universities decided to impose tuition for the first time in 2006, the outcry was so loud that public college again became free eight years later—leading to a 22 percent jump in enrollment. Other countries, like in Scandinavia, report that free-tuition college doesn't only boost attendance but also provides hopes to lower-middle-class families that their children can move up the ladder—quite a contrast to the "economic fatalism" of the American Rust Belt.

It's important to note—and this might be obvious to anyone who's watched the rise of right-wing populism and class resentments in Europe, with similar root causes as America during the Trump years—that free college isn't a panacea. For one thing, tuition-free college doesn't eliminate the other costs associated with surviving as a young adult such as food and housing—those same expensive factors that animate the #RealCollege movement in the United States. That means students in some nations hailed for "free college" still graduate with some debt from loan programs to cover those other costs—although Norway forgives the loans by reclassifying them as stipends if the recipients successfully graduate.

What's more, free tuition, and the attendant higher enrollment, can lead to overcrowded classrooms, or cutbacks on other areas such as research. A number of nations with free or low tuition end up testing kids to see who gets into the most sought-after universities—or who can get in, period—which just like in America can lock in advantages for affluent kids better prepared for the test. Students from more affluent families might also see their parents pay their housing—instead of loans or having to work a demanding job while attending classes. Class inequity is a broad global problem that may be exacerbated by expensive U.S. universities but doesn't vanish in nations with free college.

And then there's the primary conservative critique of "free college," which is that higher education should not be considered free when the cost is distributed through higher taxes on all citizens, including—to use the Reagan administration's go-to example from the 1980s—that taxi driver who has neither the need nor the inclination to sit inside a university classroom. Countries like Norway and Finland where universities are 96 percent publicly funded (compared to less than 35 percent in the United States) also have a substantially higher income tax. Critics note that despite free tuition Europeans are less likely to attend college, but again that might not mean what it would on American soil. Nations in Europe such as Germany continue to offer apprenticeship programs (covering a whopping 60 percent of its workforce, according to some estimates) on a scale seen only in a tiny number of trades here in the U.S., and surveys show much stronger interest in and support for vocational training across the continent. Of course, once those workers are trained and enter blue-collar professions in Europe, they also get generous vacation or child-care policies—meaning that going to college, or not, feels like less of a life lottery than it does in the United States.

Here at home, the rise of the New New Left over the course of the 2010s, culminating with the 2020 election of a president in Joe Biden who's been willing to work with their movement, has breathed new life into ideas about tuition-free college as well as debt forgiveness that would have been unthinkable in the decades after Reagan. But even with Biden entering the White House and with the nation's leading advocates of "free college" politics like Senators Bernie Sanders and Elizabeth Warren whispering in his ear, the massive hurdles for the United States toward adopting a European model are both political and structural, in ways that are sometimes intertwined.

The latest iteration of Sanders's "free college" plans, long a centerpiece of his rising political influence, was introduced in the spring of 2021, cosponsored by the leader of the Progressive Caucus in the House, Representative Pramila Jayapal of Washington State. It called for free community college as well as trade schools with a curriculum similar to Williamson to be free for all students. Public four-year colleges and universities would also be free for all families making less than $125,000 a year, as would all historically Black colleges and universities. In addition, the Pell Grant—the cornerstone for federal financial aid for a half century—would be doubled to $12,990, from its then-level of $6,495, which would give lower- and middle-income kids more options to attend private campuses as well.

Significantly, the Sanders and Jayapal bill contained a number of measures that seemed influenced both by the growing success of the #RealCollege movement in raising awareness about the role of food and housing costs in both hampering today's students and in driving future debt, and also around the racial reckoning that began in 2020. For the first time, under the proposal, Pell Grant money could be used for college costs outside of tuition, including living expenses. Also, the Pell program would be expanded to include the so-called Dreamers—students who've thrived after coming to America as undocumented immigrants. Additionally, the program would include additional dollars both to support students at HBCUs and also for programs that help first-generation students, people with disabilities, or those from underprivileged families adjust to campus life.

The price tag for such an ambitious program, which would make college in America as close to universal as possible, was set at $2.4 trillion over a ten-year period. Like other past proposals by Sanders, Warren, and others, the chief way to pay for it would be a tax on the wealthy classes who've thrived under the "knowledge economy" that emerged in tandem with rising college attendance. The Sanders/Jayapal plan would tax Wall Street transactions, while Warren—during her ultimately sputtering 2020 presidential bid—backed a wealth tax that would tackle the assets, rather than just the income, of 1 Percenters like Jeff Bezos or Warren Buffett. Neither has been tried before in the United States, and both ideas have critics—beyond those libertarians who think success shouldn't be penalized by taxes—who fret about either unanticipated economic harms or the abilities of the superrich to find new shelters to evade such schemes.

The recent history of Republican Party lawmakers—who in 2021 fiercely united in opposition to a modest plan to return income taxes on the wealthy back to what they were in 2017 to deal with the nation's universally acknowledged infrastructure crisis—suggests that gaining political approval for this type of funding plan in the near term is all but impossible, even with polling that shows most Americans support higher taxes on the rich. But an even bigger poison pill in the Democratic plans to fund free college is our complicated blend of state-run public, not-for-profit, religious, and for-profit universities. In particular, any scheme to make public universities free would require buy-in from the states that control them—including financial buy-in. In the Sanders/Jayapal plan, the federal government would provide 75 percent of what it took to eliminate tuition, but the states would need to make up the other 25 percent (going down to only 10 percent in the event of an economic recession).

Little of the recent history in the so-called red states run by Republican governors and lawmakers—as well as more purple states like Wisconsin and ex-governor Scott Walker—suggest widespread enthusiasm for this plan. Arguably, the philosophy of anti-college resentment might prove a greater obstacle than raising the billions of dollars involved; many of these states had long rejected free dollars dangled by Washington to expand Medicaid to poorer residents after 2010's Affordable Care Act. In addition to recalcitrant conservatives, "free college" would also face the same problem as other sweeping reform proposals dating back to the Truman Commission—fears by incumbent institutions, from the Ivy League down to small religious colleges, that such schemes would hurt their enrollment and wreck their pricing models.

The toughest thorn, though, might be the fairness issue. Many economists argue, not without evidence, that most of the "free college" models currently floated are regressive, because too many benefits would flow to upper-middle-class families that now pay the most under the current system, while far less gain would flow to the middle-class or lower—especially for young people who might not attend college, even if it were free to attend. This same fairness issue dogs the debate over forgiving some, much, or even all of the nation's $1.7 trillion college debt bomb. Total debt forgiveness, critics argue, would reward those who borrowed a lot to attend professional schools like law school and who are on track to earn the money to pay their loans back. Adults who worked overtime or more than one job to pay off their debt on time get nothing—not to mention our apocryphal cabdriver who didn't attend college at all and won't see a dime from this bailout.

Consider this: The fundamental unfairness that was baked into the American way of college from the moment it was determined that higher education wasn't a public good but a private benefit means that any meaningful solution is also fated to contain elements of unfairness. Arguably, the main reason that student loan forgiveness became a front-burner issue in the early days of the Biden presidency was the success of advocates in proving that the burden of college debt fell so disproportionately on Black and Brown youth, intertwining the issue with that of racial equity.

Given the many roadblocks to radical college reform, it's not surprising that attention has finally turned to the education infrastructure that was already in place, if too often neglected: America's coast-to-coast network of nearly one thousand community colleges. The idea was not exactly new. Obama, you may recall, made expanding and revitalizing community college a cornerstone of his higher education agenda, but even his relatively modest $12 billion proposal failed to see action from a GOP-led Congress that stymied most of his agenda. His vice president, Biden—whose wife, Jill, is a longtime community college professor—went much bigger in his 2020 campaign with a pitch for free two-year programs, which he backed up with a formal $109 billion proposal after taking office. The ever-pragmatic Biden saw this as a way to satisfy some of the aggressive demands of the Sanders-led New New Left but with a less expensive program that was more targeted to the needs of working-class students.

Centering reform efforts on community college is a throwback to the Truman Commission, which in 1947 urged America to make the first two years of higher education free "for all youth who can profit from such education." The report is indeed credited for the boom in community college construction that occurred across America in the 1950s and '60s, with many of these programs at that time tuition-free. Today, the average annual tuition—excluding the other costs of going to school—at community colleges in my home state of Pennsylvania is $5,330, making it hard for middle-class kids to fill the gap with financial aid. Not surprisingly, enrollment at these no-longer-free community colleges fell sharply during the 2010s, and took another hit in the pandemic.

And yet many education experts say community colleges could build on their existing strengths to truly become the foundation of American higher education they were intended to be. On one hand, more funding and more attention could help these highly localized institutions do an even better job of working with nearby industries—like the ones that line up for the employment fair at the Williamson College of the Trades—to target curriculum for students to get jobs close to home that don't require a bachelor's degree. And yet community colleges— perhaps because they train so many children of immigrant families, or kids from underwhelming high schools—are also already doing a better job than many realize in teaching kids about writing, literature, and other touchstones of a liberal education.

In 2021, a study by a project under the American Academy of Arts & Sciences found that degrees in the liberal arts and the humanities from U.S. community colleges have been rising at a steady rate and reached their all-time high in 2018, the final year of the survey. This stood in sharp contrast to the trend at four-year colleges and universities where students majoring in the humanities reached an all-time low—just half the number of business-related majors and just one-third of graduates with science- or health-related degrees. The survey suggested that— three quarters of a century later—America's two-year campuses were best hitting the Truman Commission's lofty goals for melding liberal education with career prep.

The Biden administration plans for free community college also proposed funds that would address the systems' biggest problems in the twenty-first century—#RealCollege economic hardships, like food insecurity, for lower- and middle-class students that prompted young people to either drop out or take a longer time to achieve degrees. If the federal government could work with the states to not only make community college free but elevate their standing in the complicated world of higher education, more students and parents would take advantage of two-year schools as a ladder to an eventual bachelor's degree.

Despite the seeming win-win aspects of an amped-up community college system, the political obstacles are still daunting. If anything, the logistics of the federal government trying to implement free community college across the fifty states is even more complicated than the convoluted Sanders/Jayapal plan for free four-year colleges and universities. Over time, states have developed wildly different systems with varying costs and levels of accessibility. A *New York Times* analysis of the Biden plan noted that students in Vermont were then paying community college tuition at a rate six times higher than students in California. An influx of federal money aimed at making community college free might either unduly reward states that have scrimped on their systems, or else require states to come up with extra dollars—with no guarantee they would do that.

Beyond the significant financial hurdles, centering the solution to America's higher-ed problems around community college also has to deal with the branding issue. In an era in which so many families believe that where their kids attend college says something about their social status, how many would still shun two additional years of free education to float down the lazy rivers of presumably still-expensive four-year colleges, thus adding billions of dollars of new college debt? After two decades of selling America's youth that they'd need a bachelor's degree to get anywhere in our modern economy, rerouting their pathway through two-year schools could be a tough sell.

AMERICA WILL STRUGGLE TO MOVE FORWARD UNTIL IT ASKS ITSELF some hard questions about how to reasonably apportion the cost of higher education. That includes the role of those who reap capitalist benefits from a pool of highly trained workers: corporations. Remember, America's businesses have played a key role in raising demand and thus the cost of a college diploma, by slowly and steadily increasing the need for credentials from their job applicants. At the dawn of the 2020s, some of those corporations—seeing college costs increasingly out of reach for middle-class families—are beginning to rethink the monsters of credentialism and careerist college they arguably helped to create.

"There's no need even to have a college degree at all, or even high school," tech guru Elon Musk said of his automotive company, Tesla, at a 2020 forum, explaining that when interviewing job candidates he presses for people with "evidence of exceptional ability," regardless of whether they attended an elite university or, indeed, any university. In addition to Tesla, technology stalwarts such as Apple, IBM, and Google have increasingly made known their willingness to hire applicants from the 63 percent of Americans without a bachelor's degree. Google—noting that during the depths of the pandemic its search engine registered an 800 percent increase in searches for "jobs with no college degree"—launched a new program called Google Career Certificates that seeks to offer focused, low-cost online training, usually over a period of just three to six months. The program targets relatively high-paying jobs in fields such as project management or data analytics.

Silicon Valley—whose record profits only grew during the COVID-19 crisis—surely should take more responsibility for job training, and we're likely to see more innovative private-sector solutions if four-year colleges continue to become both more expensive and more unpopular. But most employers aren't Google or Tesla, and are still likely to look to the university system for both credentials and to train their prospective hires.

Only the public—through our elected officials in the various state houses, on Capitol Hill, and in the White House—can un-privatize college in America. The goal of universal higher education proved elusive back in 1947, when the nation's masses were in general agreement about the virtue of a college education. In the near future, most of the nation's public colleges and universities won't change for the better as long as one of our two major political parties sees campuses as places for liberal indoctrination and "critical race theory," rather than a ladder to uplift the children of its own voters. If the divisions that were exacerbated—if not caused outright—by unequal educational and job opportunities in the United States have broken us in two, how can we expect our bankrupt politics to fix things?

There is one small but significant way forward that would involve your country doing something for you, as long as you did something for your country. A way that would be one small step for entering American adulthood, but one giant leap for civic engagement—breaking down some of the siloes that now sort us into struggling city neighborhoods, forgotten rural towns, and leafy suburbs, and restoring a sense of a national purpose that normally only comes with the human tragedy of war. A way that a few smart people have been talking about, and yet too few people have been listening. It's time to start talking about universal national service.

CHAPTER 9

A BLOODLESS WAR TO SAVE AMERICA'S YOUTH

Pedro Soto wasn't happy in college. Coming of age in the gritty, working-class Philadelphia neighborhood of Juniata, Soto went about fifteen miles west of the city to the lush green campus of Cabrini College (now University) in the uber-affluent Main Line suburbs. It might have been the dark side of the moon as far as he was concerned.

"I felt like such an outsider," he recalled, after he was paired with a roommate from Princeton, New Jersey. "They would be telling their stories, or ask, 'What are you doing this summer? . . . I'm going to my beach house in Stone Harbor.'" Soto would respond with a shrug, "Well, I'm going home for the summer and working." Actually, he went home to Juniata after one semester and never looked back.

Now twenty-seven, Soto feels so much more at home at the place where I met him—a postage stamp–sized park and community garden wedged between a crooked alley of rowhouses and the busy thorough-fare of Vine Street in West Philadelphia, on a sweat-drenched June morning when it was already 90 degrees and the sun had several more hours to rise. This is Conestoga/Pearl Gardens—"Home of the Veggie Kids!" its sign proclaims in clean blue script—where about twenty young men and women in their late teens or early twenties are getting some work in before the worst of the heat, spreading mulch around thriving trees, hauling away dead branches or weeding an herb garden before seeking the last pockets of shade for an ice pop break. The workers' day had been mapped out ahead of time by Soto, who is now a project coordinator for PowerCorpsPHL, a service and apprenticeship program under the national umbrella of AmeriCorps. It employs and trains Philadelphia youth aged eighteen to twenty-eight who need a boost out of joblessness or underemployment, involvement with the criminal-justice system, or the other woes found in one of America's poorest big cities.

Soto believes in PowerCorpsPHL because it helped him get on the right track after his college stint didn't work out. Twice a year, the city-affiliated program enrolls a cohort of sixty young people, puts them to work on environmental projects like fixing up parks or clearing Philadelphia's chronically clogged stormwater drains for at least four months but as long as two years, while—despite chronic underfunding—paying a stipend, currently eleven or twelve dollars an hour. To hear Soto tell the story as a pair of long metal shears dangles from a belt loop of his blue jeans, it's a miracle that he stuck with PowerCorpsPHL any longer than his first arduous day.

"My first work day we were at the Please Touch Museum"—a popular Philly attraction—"and we were clearing something called the Devil's walking stick, which is an invasive plant that has spikes growing out of the side of it—really huge spikes! It was a very delicate task. I was like, 'This is what trees can do?' It was scary. It was very intimidating. Like, this is the stick of the devil!" Yet there was something that Soto found surprisingly uplifting about working with this team of people in his age bracket. "It was hot, it was humid—but this was like, 'Wow, I'm enjoying myself! I'm not just here to kick up my feet, or collect a check.'"

Soto said he got a vibe from his first, spiky day at PowerCorps that he never got inside the soft ivory tower of college. "I started to feel the energy—it's weird that so many people were checking in on me . . . 'Hey, Pedro!' In a room full of people, my name was remembered. That really makes a difference." It certainly has. Soto plans to return to college down the line to earn a degree, perhaps in urban forestry.

I CAME TO THIS POWERCORPSPHL WORKSITE IN WEST PHILLY FOR two reasons. One was to illustrate how America's lawmakers and deep thinkers aren't really solving the crisis for our young adults when they only focus on issues like college debt or runaway tuition. In that case, they are doing nothing not only for the Pedro Sotos of this country but the others who emerge from their high school years on the fringes— maybe with a diploma but maybe not, and often with some involvement with the criminal justice system, in a land where more than 2 million youths under eighteen are arrested every year. The prime target of a program like PowerCorps PHL is what experts now call "disconnected youth"—part of the cohort I've described here as the Left Out—which social scientists have identified as 4.6 million Americans between the age of eighteen and twenty-four who aren't attending school or working a full-time job.

But even more important, PowerCorpsPHL is just one small yet powerful example of what can happen when society stages an intervention to help its young people—even, in this case, some of its most troubled ones—transition toward adulthood with a mix of career skills and personal growth, and even a dollop of civic responsibility. The numbers for PowerCorps PHL, established in 2013, are striking: Roughly nine of every ten young people who enlist end up in a job, while less than one in ten who'd been previously incarcerated will return behind bars. But the numbers are also small, not just for the Philadelphia program but for youth service programs nationally, which today can handle just a small fraction of the eighteen-to-twenty-eight-year-olds who apply. Given the public harm caused by everything from massive debts to rising "deaths of despair" that result from our current sink-or-swim edict to youth coming out of high school, the time has come for a massive national service program. But do we Americans have the will to make it happen?

One benefit of service programs like PowerCorpsPHL, of course, is that they improve the local communities where they operate. I was reminded of that when I spoke to Kea Greene, the support services coordinator for the program. She'd grown up just a few blocks away from this park, and when she was a kid—she's forty-eight now, with three grown children—they used to cut through this slice of land on the way to the local shopping center, even though their parents begged them not to. "Those weeds were so high that no one could see you if you were in distress," Greene recalled—a sharp contrast with today's open park with its art-decorated planters and boxes full of fresh vegetables and herbs.

In her job, Greene cultivates not plants but people—people who often need significant off-the-job help, from dealing with the criminal justice system or other complicated bureaucracies to accessing therapy services. "Many of their needs . . . all I can do is get it started—get the ball rolling, identify the resource, connect them with people, create a game plan," she told me. It sounds basic, but millions of disconnected youth aren't getting this help.

For PowerCorpsPHL, the incredibly thin line between giving a young adult that final boost over the wall that's keeping them from finding a decent job or maybe returning to school or losing them forever was driven home during the COVID-19 pandemic, which put a giant crimp in the program. Although its leaders scrambled to find donors to replace a $1 million cut in city funding, the mandatory lockdown kept the young participants out of the parks and storm drains, forced instead to conduct workshops on Zoom—assuming they had good wi-fi service, which many did not. Meanwhile, right at the moment when PowerCorps couldn't provide the structure and shelter of daily work, a second epidemic—one of gun violence—erupted in Philadelphia. During 2020, six participants in PowerCorpsPHL were fatally gunned down—equal to the number killed in the entire first six years of the program. That's a stunning number when one recalls only 120 new young adults enroll each year. Today, no project means more to PowerCorps members than a sliver of the city's large Fairmount Park called PowerCorps Memorial Grove, a refuge to remember these fallen.

In focusing on Philadelphians in that eighteen-to-twenty-eight age cohort, Greene said, the service program is tackling "the hardest decade of people's lives—it really is . . . One of the greatest disservices you can do to someone who is eighteen is throw your hands up and say, 'They're grown,' and let them figure it out. That is the most confusing and scariest time that I find, working with young people."

JACON SNIPE IS TYPICAL OF POWERCORPSPHL ALUMNI WHO NEARLY didn't make that leap into adulthood. He'd graduated from North Philadelphia's Simon Gratz High School—a landmark city school that was taken over by a charter operation—but after a fractured tibia crushed his dreams of playing football, he didn't have much of a backup plan. "I was going from job to job trying to figure it out," he told me—a common refrain among the young people working in the park that morning. Any plan was further hindered by several entanglements with the law in his overpoliced, low-income neighborhood, a pattern that he says began when cops arrested him when he was still in middle school.

Another thing that Snipe shares with a lot of PowerCorps participants is that he likes to work—just not in a classroom or an office. Indeed, he applied to the program after his younger brother had joined, and Snipe saw how exhausted his sibling was when he came home. "He used to come home sweating every day like he was working hard," he recalled. "I'm like, 'I like working hard . . . that's a good look for me.'"

Now twenty-five, Snipe—like his colleague Soto—got so much from the program that he's been hired on as a site supervisor. He's also become an activist around criminal justice issues, working with the National League of Cities. When he joined his PowerCorps cohort a couple of years ago, he said, "I wasn't in a right state of mind, going through personal issues. I knew I needed help so I took therapy, stuff like that. It did help me—now I'm more humble and I'm growing."

And in cleaning up neglected, disadvantaged neighborhoods, Snipe has learned one other thing—what it's like to be appreciated for giving something back to the community. Today, as he travels around Philadelphia in a van with a crew cleaning out clogged storm drains, he sometimes marvels at the reaction he gets. "We were working and somebody came out clapping," he said. "They don't see people in their neighborhood. That was a good feeling when she came out."

APPLAUSE AND CIVIC GOODWILL SEEMED IN SUCH SHORT SUPPLY AT the dawn of the 2020s. Rock bottom—or what one hopes is rock bottom—came on January 6, 2021, when hundreds of riled-up Trump supporters stormed and infiltrated the U.S. Capitol in order to disrupt the counting of the Electoral College votes that would end Donald Trump's presidency and anoint Joe Biden as his successor. The Capitol Hill insurrection failed to prevent the transfer of power to the Democrats, but it did serve as a wake-up call to any Americans who had still been in denial that national disunity was now a public disease, not just a symptom of something else. Suddenly, the fate of U.S. democracy soared to the top of the issue charts—rivaling economic prosperity and ending the COVID-19 pandemic. The difference was there didn't seem to be a tangible fix—like a carbon tax or the $15 minimum wage—for America's tribal factionalism and growing hatreds. To the contrary, social resentment and governmental gridlock felt like an impenetrable downward cycle. How could politics play any constructive role in breaking it?

In these pages, and in tracing the rise and fall of college as the postwar American Dream, I've tried to make a case that—despite the mistakes of privatization and misguided meritocracy that divided the nation—a renewed commitment to a true higher education can help to heal us. That means universal schooling or training benefits for all young adults, funded as a public good and not as a high-stakes pass/fail test of individual self-worth, centering critical thinking and civic engagement over rote workforce development. But the fault lines we face today will never get us there. A Democratic Party of college-educated elites that only pitches trillion-dollar plans to send their own kids to free universities, and offers nothing for the other half, is doomed to failure. But a Republican Party that only responds with a McCarthyism-inspired witch hunt to find liberal indoctrination on campus is badly failing its own education-starved kids. Somehow, from the ashes and flaming embers of January 6 and everything that led up to it, America will need to summon a shared sense of national purpose buried deeply within our souls.

The last such moment may have been the American victory in World War II—which came barely a decade after the depredations of the Great Depression had alarmed the nation's political pundits that we might devolve into fascism or communist totalitarianism as was happening across Europe. It was, of course, also a flawed time (featuring Senator Joe McCarthy and the abuses of the Cold War), and its economic prosperity and social benefits were not shared equally by

Blacks, women, a closeted LGBTQ+ community, and others. But faith in democracy as the vanquisher of Nazism was high, as was the belief amid unprecedented middle-class prosperity that the next generation would surely do even better. The G.I. Bill—which proved that young people from working-class backgrounds could thrive on a college campus when given the opportunity—would not have happened without the unity of victory, nor without the enthusiasm uncharacteristically shared by liberals and conservatives of doing something for returning veterans.

Today, it must be asked: Could America somehow rekindle the spirit of that immediate postwar era—that fleeting moment of unity, when the battle-tested sons of factory workers thrived in college classrooms alongside Boston brahmins and Main Line bluebloods? Could the United States somehow draft its young people—morally, if not with an actual induction board—for a national crusade that would offer the benefits of winning a war, without all the carnage?

IN 2012, ONE OF THE HOTTEST TICKETS AT THE ASPEN IDEAS FESTIVAL was a talk by General Stanley McChrystal, the just-retired U.S. Army general who was not only a national hero for his exploits in Iraq and Afghanistan but also an outspoken lightning rod for controversy, which had caused his commander-in-chief Obama to order him home early. Now a private citizen, McChrystal—with a buzz cut and sharp facial features—appeared in a baggy polo shirt that hung over his fit fifty-seven-year-old body. In the spirit of an ideas festival, the ex-general fired off his contrarian thoughts like they were Hellfire missiles. These included his belief that the military draft should be brought back.

His interviewer, CBS News anchor Bob Schieffer, began reflecting on his own youth during World War II, when everybody had close family members fighting in the global conflict. "There seems to be no real common experience anymore," he mused, and he asked McChrystal about expanding national service.

"I think we need national service and I think we need it either at the conclusion of high school or university," the ex-general said. "I don't think young people would really fight it—if it was fair, and everybody did it. You could only take a small part of that in the military, so I'm not talking military, I'm talking all kinds of things. But I also think the payoff is not what they do—it's not whether they go off and build roads or parks or that sort of thing. It's what you put inside them"; McChrystal gestured at his heart as he spoke. "Because once you have contributed to something, you have a slightly different view of it. And I think it's good if everybody had a shared experience. If every person aged twenty-five or older meets, and the question is, 'Hey, where did you serve? . . . What did you do? . . .' if that's the start of the conversation, I think it would be powerful."

The roomful of Aspen idea seekers erupted in applause. Within the small and closely connected community of advocates for the concept that McChrystal was talking about that day—universal national service for young Americans—the speech is still talked about, a decade later. Understandably so, since McChrystal's Heartland plain talk and his reputation as public servant made him a perfect pitchman for a Big Idea that has languished on the back burner of American politics. In fact, the Aspen Institute launched a program with McChrystal at the head, called the Franklin Project, and in 2016 it merged with several like-minded outfits to form the Service Year Alliance, now the loudest voice on the issue.

And yet for all the hubbub over the former general's pitch, McChrystal wasn't really saying anything particularly new. At least since the Civil War and the upward rise of the Industrial Revolution—which radically changed both when and how young people came of age in America—public intellectuals have fantasized about a corps of teen or twentysomething enlistees (or draftees) who could tackle the country's myriad social and infrastructure problems in a spirit of national unity and moral purpose. And at various key moments, from Franklin Roosevelt's New Deal to JFK's New Frontier, U.S. citizens have actually seen a brief glimpse of what a youthful army can conquer in peacetime.

For America, the idea was born in a moment when income inequality between a new breed of superwealthy capitalists and millions of workers toiling for low wages in brutal conditions had caused such a wide rift that some wondered if we could keep the republic. The year was 1888, and the writer was journalist Edward Bellamy, whose pioneering utopian novel *Looking Backward*—while little remembered today—was the runaway publishing sensation of the late nineteenth century. Bellamy's tome described America in the year 2100, when the social problems of his time had been resolved through a welfare state that bordered on socialism, but also a sense of shared purpose that manifested in a civilian force he called the Industrial Army.

By the turn of the twentieth century, it was another great American writer and thinker, the philosopher William James, who would refine and advance Bellamy's concept. James was the first of many advocates to argue that civilian service could instill many of the positive virtues that soldiers gain during wartime—minus the war. He also voiced the soon-to-be-common complaint that the new prolonging of adolescence was dragging down the nation's youth. "Our gilded youths would be drafted off to get the childishness knocked out of them, and to come back into society with healthier sympathies and soberer ideas," James argued.

Instead, America's youths—even a few of the gilded ones—were drafted to fight in World War I. Indeed, the chaos of the first two-thirds of the twentieth century, as cycles of war and economic despair gave rise to great dictators and the radical, competing visions of fascism and Communism, put such importance on the military draft that it was

hard for utopian visions of civilian service to get a word in edgewise—
except during the Great Depression.

The crisis of 25 percent unemployment—and fears that a struggling
America could follow some of its former European allies into fascism—
gave Roosevelt and a heavily Democratic Congress the political capital
shortly after taking office in 1933 to overcome Americans' traditional
resistance to large-scale public works programs (which flourished after
the Russian Revolution of 1917 and its alarm bells that worker-led collectivism could pose a threat to U.S.-style free enterprise). Now, programs in which the government put the unemployed to work for the
public good tackled problems like infrastructure (the Works Progress
Administration) and even aided starving writers (the Federal Writers Project). But the one that truly inspired today's national service
schemes—and which was also the most popular in its day—was the
Civilian Conservation Corps, or CCC.

The CCC targeted the large numbers of jobless young men, initially
in the eighteen-to-twenty-five age bracket, and put them to work in
America's national and local parks and its wilderness areas on an array
of projects that included building new trails and fire lookout towers,
tree planting, flood control, stocking ponds, or spraying for mosqui-
toes. If you've visited a national park today, you've almost certainly
seen the CCC's handiwork. Over its nearly ten-year run, the agency
employed a total of 3 million men—nearly 90 percent of whom hadn't
graduated high school—and peaked in size at 500,000 in the mid-1930s.

By all accounts, the conservation program was mostly beloved.
Families welcomed the money these young and formerly unemployed
workers sent home, and rural communities were mostly grateful for
the outside help, and pleasantly surprised that the CCC enlistees were
so well-behaved as they pumped dollars into the local economy. One
woman sent a testimonial to an agency official that "the boys are safe
there. They are young and inexperienced and need someone reliable

to teach them and I think the discipline and strictness are what they need now in their teen age." Leaders in cities like Chicago and New York left behind by these young men reported a drop in crime. In their hastily constructed camps across the U.S. countryside, young men also received civics education, job training, or schooling.

Were there complaints, and actual problems with the CCC? Of course. Critics on the far-right and far-left seemed to share the idea that the corps was a form of creeping, pro-FDR fascism. Like most New Deal programs, the CCC was largely a raw deal for Black Americans, who were denied opportunities to move up the ranks and who were forced to live and work in segregated camps, even in the North after a brief period of integration at the start. Likewise, women were barred from the CCC until a small, almost token program near the end (that some called the "She-She-She"). By 1942, the program fell victim to the need to funnel its pool of healthy young men into World War II. But its gesture, at least, toward a broader sense of shared purpose lingered as a positive memory for many.

After the New Deal, the cycles of wartime mobilization and economic prosperity dampened interest in national service efforts—until the White House arrival of young Democrats who were eager to capture the spirit of FDR, but with programs adapted to both changing times and America's different priorities. After John F. Kennedy famously challenged citizens to ask "what you can do for your country," his signature Peace Corps took on his administration's biggest concern—the Cold War, and boosting the international image of the United States—but also serviced a different constituency than the CCC: college graduates in their early twenties, flush with the liberal-education idealism of the early 1960s. The Peace Corps and its later domestic counterpart, VISTA—which aimed to tackle U.S. poverty in regions like Appalachia—established a template for decades to come. Republicans like Ronald Reagan who saw such programs as needless government social engineering slashed the Peace Corps or VISTA to the bone, while JFK-inspired Democrats like Bill Clinton pushed expanded volunteerism among young people, rebranding VISTA as AmeriCorps and boosting opportunities. That same era—so dominated by privatization—also saw the rise of non-governmental service programs like Teach for America.

Despite Clinton's commitment to AmeriCorps, which he touted extensively throughout his 1990s' presidency, the problems that advocates say could be most helped by an even bigger national service program only got worse. Clinton's push to find shared national purpose, after all, came during a 1990s marked by Rush Limbaugh and the ascent of angry talk radio, by the partisan impeachment that almost took down his presidency, and by the recognition of "red states" and "blue states." The opportunities to get scholarship money or pay down a college loan by joining AmeriCorps resulted in $2.7 billion paid out over the first 20 years of the program—the same era when the nation's overall student debt rose by nearly $1 trillion. A program that progressive dreamers hoped would engage 1 million young people a year maxed at about 75,000, with many applicants turned away.

It's little wonder that these well-intentioned but modest national service programs have failed to rekindle the spirit of 1946. Back then, it wasn't only the moral rectitude of defeating the Nazis and ending genocide that brought people together. For men, World War II military service was all but mandatory (in a way that subsequent wars like Vietnam, with its college deferments and elite string-pulling, were not). The war-movie trope of an American unit with its Alabama farm boy, wise-cracking Brooklyn Jewish kid and Princeton-bound WASP exists because that's pretty much what happened in World War II, and for one critical moment Americans saw only the things they had in common. (Except, immorally, and as must be noted every time, with Black troops, who served in segregated units until 1948.) The decline of American comity as the nation stumbled into the twenty-first century indeed gave new life to the argument for national service, but—if the program aimed to bring a postwar unity divide, and break down the silos of the Big Sort—wouldn't it need to be mandatory, like a wartime draft?

It took a near-perfect storm of factors to restart the conversation about universal or mandatory public service, and perhaps making it more of a "gap year" that would come after high school as opposed to the postcollege focus of Peace Corps or Teach for America. The first one: the increasing evidence that making age eighteen the focal point of an all-or-nothing lottery to decide who will sink or swim in a faux American meritocracy has been a failure. Few young people— even the upscale suburban or urban kids hovered over by "helicopter parents"—make good decisions at that age. Too many college-bound youth were not only choosing a campus for superficial amenities, or declaring academic majors without the maturity of knowing what they wanted to do, but also making terrible bets with student loans. And the 18-year-olds who didn't go to college seemed to be dropping off the map, until they started showing up in the death notices. A "gap year" would take some of that pressure off harried teenagers, giving them at least 12 months to develop new skills and new ideas about themselves.

The other factor—the one that aroused a growing circle of public intellectuals—was a rising clamor for national service as an antidote for the country's deep disunity. "The American electorate is losing a common sense of what it means to be American," Lilliana Mason, the University of Maryland political scientist who focuses on the growing political divide, wrote. "That won't be solved by finding the most popular policy or more civil language. We need to be reintroduced to each other in a place where we are all on the same team." She cited academic research from the Korean War—when the U.S. armed forces finally were desegregated—that showed that white troops who served in racially mixed units returned home more tolerant than those who didn't fight alongside Black comrades.

The arguments for universal national service are compelling, but at the start of the 2020s any radical new program that could make an impact faces the same obstacle as other more conventional fixes to the higher education mess in America: We're too politically divided and angry to come to a consensus on any plan to tackle our political division and anger. Beginning with the Reagan era and intensifying in the decades since, Republicans are increasingly wary not just of using taxpayer dollars on a large government program but today see a liberal agenda in the kinds of things these young enlistees would do, like tackling climate change. That's on top of the increasingly libertarian bent of the Republican Party—but shared by a fair number of boomers weaned on the 1960s' New Left—that objects to the federal government telling a young citizen what to do and where to go, even for just a year.

The Cato Institute, the leading libertarian think tank, published what grew to practically a laundry list of reasons why mandatory national service, in its opinion, is a horrible idea. Many participants would be unwilling to participate and thus uncooperative; make-work jobs wouldn't be worth the cost to taxpayers; it would hurt recruitment for the military; it might be involuntary servitude barred by the 13th Amendment; generally it would represent government taking over tasks now done by the private sector. Some of these arguments also resonate with activists on the left, which has been wary of any "draft" concept ever since the Vietnam era.

With high-minded support from intellectuals but facing massive roadblocks on the ground, Congress did what it does best: it appointed a blue-ribbon panel. The National Commission on Military, National, and Public Service (which also looked at issues around the Selective Service) was created in 2016—the same year as the leading advocacy groups for national service launched the Service Year Alliance. These two initiatives moved toward a new consensus on a scheme to greatly expand opportunities—universal national service, they call it, even though one can debate what "universal" means in this context.

Backing away from ideals of "mandatory" or "compulsory" framing still popular with newspaper op-ed writers, these more-grounded advocates say "universal" programs would mean funding to meet the huge unmet current demand for slots in programs like the Peace Corps and aim to increase benefits to make service even more appealing than it is now. The Service Year Alliance goal of an annual service cohort of 1 million is a whopping fourteenfold expansion from today's level, but it's less than a third of the number of Americans turning eighteen every year. In addition, advocates are pushing a stronger focus on "gap years" for teens leaving high school as opposed to the post-college focus of late-twentieth-century programs—an acknowledgment of new problems facing today's youth.

Kristen Bennett, the chief strategy officer for Service Year Alliance, told me the expansion to 1 million "would make service a part of growing up in America"—and that it's increasingly clear the roughly eighteen-year-old cohort is the best age to target. "It's a good opportunity—one receives financial support to have a skill-building process that exposes you to sectors you might not be aware of—and (personal) strengths you might not be aware of." For the college-bound, she added, a gap year "could help you figure out your path before committing to finance a four-year degree."

A 2019 report from the Service Year Alliance and the Brookings Institution countered many of the arguments against universal national service, noting that—while a mandatory program is clearly not feasible politically—expanded opportunities for a service year are not only highly popular but can be shown empirically to offer a huge cost-benefit upside. But their argument leans most heavily on the national unity argument. "When trends in social fragmentation, cultural narcissism, political polarization, and economic inequality are examined together since the beginning of the twentieth century, those trends have moved in virtual lockstep," the report notes. It traces the start of the downward slide to the 1960s—the era of backlash against liberal education and campus protest.

Steven Barney—a retired Navy captain who went on to serve as a top aide to the late senator John McCain on the Senate Armed Services Committee, and then as a key member of the commission that reported to Congress on national service—said the testimonials he heard from young people begging for new opportunities made him a powerful advocate. "Young people need to experiment, and we need to support it when it does work out," he told me. Like others with a military background, the lessons America learned—and then somehow unlearned—from the G.I. Bill loom large for Barney. "We have seen that when you have a service experience—like these folks in World War II—then they bring something different to the college experience," he said.

On January 20, 2021, the push for a more universal national service received a huge ally with the inauguration of President Joe Biden. Three months into his presidency, Biden endorsed the eventual goal of 1 million annual national service positions with a call for an immediate expansion to 250,000 AmeriCorps slots and 10,000 more in the Peace Corps. That would be accompanied by a panoply of efforts to raise the profile of national service—a marketing push, grants to help localized service programs like PowerCorpsPHL, a White House–level coordinator, and more. Less than a month later, the 46th president signed an executive order creating a Civilian Climate Corps that he hoped to fund with $10 billion from his ambitious national infrastructure proposal. The move inspired a string of glowing articles remembering the success and popularity of FDR's original CCC, but some noted that

Biden's twenty thousand initial slots fell far short of the hundreds of thousands of men put to work during the Great Depression.

WE CAN DO BETTER THAN THAT. WE MUST. A MASSIVE WARTIME MO-bilization commitment to national service would be a powerful acknowledgment that the path America has traveled down since the 1970s of simply throwing our young people to the harsh whims of a privatized society—from the loan sharks of college debt to an aimless future of McJobs and YouTube radicalization—has turned out to be a catastrophic failure.

In other words, while the immediate tangible benefits of universal national service—the win-win of making it easier for millions of young Americans to transition into adulthood through projects that would improve our faltering schools or help us cope with worsening climate change—are a policy slam dunk, the even greater import would be to signal a national do-over on what we mean by higher education, equal in impact to the cataclysmic changes wrought by World War II and its aftermath. The naysayers poking around the 13th Amendment or looking for other excuses not to try a bold new social experiment like a universal gap year are really fighting to maintain a hopelessly broken status quo.

To be sure, there are a lot of moving parts when proposals for national service are added to the mix of remedies around college, job training, and other help for our young adults. On one hand, the most ambitious proposals for sweeping debt relief or free public universities by the likes of Senators Bernie Sanders or Elizabeth Warren would arguably undercut the need for 1 million national service slots, since scholarship aid in return for service would become redundant. On the other hand—given the long odds in an era of political gridlock for those proposals—universal national service could be the way to get

AFTER THE IVORY TOWER FALLS

conservative buy-in to get a foot in the door. That could start turning the tide on America recognizing the public good of aiding its citizens on the road to adulthood. It would certainly harken back to the spirit of 1944, when Republican support for veterans provided the spark for government college aid.

How could America afford these bold ideas—whether it's wiping clean the $1.7 trillion student debt, or tuition-free public universities and related aid at another $240 billion a year or more, plus the tens if not hundreds of billions of dollars more for a universal "gap year" or the expanded job training or apprenticeship programs needed to aid the young people who won't be attending college? Maybe that's not the right question. How much is America losing—in lost economic opportunity and, increasingly, in lost lives—in a society where our young people can't afford to buy a home or even start a family, where too many turn to drugs, or suicide, and where the fallout threatens our very democracy?

The truth is that the United States of America has always had the money. The real problem has been our increasingly warped priorities. We've proved this since 1990 when, according to a 2016 study released by the U.S. Department of Education, state spending for colleges and universities remained flat while outlays for prisons doubled, to the point that eighteen states—including my own, Pennsylvania—spent more money on incarceration than on higher education. That's the inevitable outcome when a resentful society would rather lock away its young people, like the ones I met sweating and spreading mulch in a West Philadelphia park, than make the effort to give them a second chance.

In fact, America could easily afford to offer its young people unlimited tuition-free college or advanced training in the trades—as so many other developed nations do—if we only brought our Pentagon budget in line with our rivals, instead of today spending more than the next ten largest militaries combined. That would require the recognition that the real threats to our national security no longer come from offshore but from within—that the danger this time is not a new Pearl Harbor but another January 6.

Of course, we'll also need to acknowledge that America is too far gone to simply cure all of its problems by ending college tuition or debt, even if we can summon the political will to do that. Today, we'll need to address the societal inequality caused by our past mistakes in failing to provide growth opportunities to all of our young people. That would mean taking seriously Warren's proposal for a wealth tax—on those who won the most in the rigged lottery billed as a meritocracy—to make higher education truly universal, but also imposing a livable minimum wage for those wanting to enter the workforce more quickly. One pleasant side effect of curbing the worst abuses of late-stage capitalism would give Americans the economic freedom to again view higher education not merely as a do-or-die career path, but as a vehicle for becoming a better citizen—well-informed, valuing diversity, and feeling the need to ask what they can do for their country.

Ultimately, changing America for good will start with changing our mindset, the one that arbitrarily—and foolishly, we can now see—picked the age of eighteen for flipping the switch that turns education and growth from a public responsibility into a private one, with so many added hurdles to jump. Every stakeholder in this country has paid a price since we dismantled the American Dream to create a virtual debtors' prison for those desperate enough to still chase it, and insult those we've forced to drop out of this rat race as "lacking merit." In botching the American way of college so badly, the price we pay in terms of debt, death, despair, and ignorance that prolonged a pandemic and threatens a climate disaster, and a San Andreas–sized national fault line around educational attainment has been incalculable. The real U.S. "student debt crisis" is what all of us owe to our young people to do better.

We owe this to the legacy of past Americans like my Grandma Arline and so many others in the twentieth century who dreamed of education not just as an escape from small-town life but a pathway out of small-mindedness. We owe this to today's college students and recent graduates like Ewan Johnson, after handing them a hard-earned diploma in one hand but a Miami-nightclub-4 a.m. insane bar tab of a bill in the other. We owe it to all the high school classmates of Aaron Tallman back in the rust-bitten railroad town of Tower City, Pennsylvania, who didn't win a full-freight scholarship to trade school and are wondering what to do next. And we owe it to those kids working up a sweat in Conestoga/Pearl Gardens in West Philadelphia to lift more of their peers off the streets, before the next bullets fly. It seemed fitting that I ended my reporting—a journey I traced back to an overheated roadster on the original Route 66—just a couple of miles from Independence Hall, and just a few days ahead of the Fourth of July fireworks. It's well past time to offer America's young people what was promised them there in 1776: The pursuit of happiness.

ACKNOWLEDGMENTS

This book has been at least fifteen years in the making. Its roots go back to a special time in my life, when my two children were still in grade school and middle school back in the 2000s. On the home front, my generous bosses at the *Philadelphia Daily News* allowed me to work a split shift so I could be home for them after school in the late afternoon—which also meant spending three hours a day or more in the car. When I was back at work, I was launching a blog heavily focused on trying to understand America's political right turn.

So I started doing something wildly out of character during those extra hours behind the wheel—listening to right-wing talk radio, especially Rush Limbaugh, who was on Philadelphia's WPHT-1210 when I raced home to pick up my kids. What struck me the most was how much anger was directed toward a certain class of people—and not the people doing the most harm to Limbaugh's heavily white, heavily male, heavily working-class audience, which were the billionaires outsourcing their jobs to China. Instead, the villains were college professors, or movie actors, or especially people like me, journalists. Was the root cause of division in the twenty-first century that simple? The differing worldviews, psychology, and lifestyles of folks who went to college, and folks who didn't? The deeper I got into it—researching a book about the Tea Party at the end of that decade, and then watching the rise of Donald Trump like a slow-motion train wreck, the more serious "the college problem" looked.

And so finally, in 2022, here we are.

There are so many people who helped in the making of this book. The bulk of them are the people—from top professors and academics to some remarkable veterans of the student movements of the 1960s to today's students and debt-ridden alums and political activists from far left to far right—who were so generous with their time and their ideas. I won't repeat their names because their contributions are scattered through the text, but I want to express my profound gratitude.

Some people who aren't mentioned in the book but who helped make it happen were my patient and understanding coworkers at the *Philadelphia Inquirer*, who not just tolerated but encouraged my taking on this project. That includes my patient bosses in the Opinion section—first Sandy Shea, then Rich Jones—and my all-time favorite personal editor, Erica Palan, as well as my amazing friends and teammates including Av Gutman, Trudy Rubin, Elena Gooray, Kevin Riordan, and Dan Pearson. There's a reason that, in an homage to Chase Utley, we call each other the "WFCs" (google it).

This book definitely wouldn't have occurred without the encouragement, support, and hard work of my literary agent, Will Lippincott of Aevitas Creative Management, who's been a great friend and ally for more than a dozen years now. What's more, it was Will who connected me with this book's editor, Nick Amphlett of William Morrow, who steered this project through the shoals of a global pandemic with his good humor, patience, and ever-calm nature. Maybe one of these days, the world will reopen, and I'll get to New York again and actually meet Nick and buy him a beer! (And also thank HarperCollins executive editor Matt Harper, who edited that 2010 Tea Party book and allegedly put in a good word for me.)

And then there's the people whose support, love, and good humor got me not only through this book but through life in general: my family, including my wife, Kathy Boccella, my two amazing children, Julia and Jesse, my two canine companions, Daisy and Bella, and the wider cast that includes my parents, Bryan and Maryanne Bunch, my siblings, Sally and Jim, and also my G.I. Bill father-in-law, Fred Boccella, who helps to remind me that the past is often not even past.

NOTES ON SOURCES

I tried to build the foundation of this book on what is essentially a three-legged bar stool. Its supports were a combination of (a) in-person reporting and observation—from places like Knox County, Ohio; Kutztown University; Williamson College of the Trades; etc. (visits that were delayed by the pandemic lockdowns that existed to some extent throughout the writing of this book), (b) several dozen in-person interviews conducted either face-to-face, as in the case of the four people or families profiled for the chapter "The Quad," or over the telephone or via computer, and (c) reading many of the foundational books of the last thirty years dealing with issues around modern college, the rise of identity politics on the left and class resentments on the right, and the nation's social isolation and growing division. I've credited these authors and their research throughout the body of the book—along with many contemporaneous newspaper and magazine articles—but these notes are intended both for the reader to both better understand what's behind each chapter and also steer people to where they can explore some of these topics in greater depth.

Introduction

This essay is based heavily on my own memories and the stories passed down in my family, although I had lengthy phone conversations with my dad, Bryan Bunch, and my uncle, R. Dale Bunch, the longtime president of Midstate College, to fill in the gaps. A couple of the anecdotes are from my earlier writings: The Knob Creek Machine Gun Shoot is from a chapter in my 2010 book, *The Backlash: Right-Wing Radicals, High-Def Hucksters, and Paranoid Politics in the Age of Obama*, while I reported on Occupy Wall Street for a 2011 Amazon Kindle Single, or e-book, titled *October 1, 2011: The Battle of the Brooklyn Bridge*.

Chapter 1

The bulk of this chapter of based on a slew of interviews and personal observations visiting Knox County and the Kenyon College campus during the week of March 14, 2021, as life was sort of returning to normal (in fact, I literally got my first Pfizer COVID-19 shot with my suitcase in the trunk and immediately drove the seven hours to Mount Vernon, Ohio). Although not mentioned in the text, Evey Weisblat, the then-editor in chief of the *Kenyon Collegian*, was super helpful in convincing me that coronavirus restrictions wouldn't hamper my reporting, and giving me the lay of the land. The essay that Kenyon president Sean Decatur wrote on his observations as Black leader of a liberal college in the heart of Trump County was published by *Belt Magazine* in November 2018 (*https://beltmag.com/life-belonging -knox-county-ohio/*). Another Kenyon student journalist worthy of a shoutout is Adam Samet, who wrote about the 2001 snowball fight that created tension between undergrads and the Knox County sheriff's department (*https://kenyoncollegian .com/features/2021/02/2001-snowball-fight-dark-moment-kcso/*). I'm also grateful to photographer Graham H. Stokes for volunteering his dramatic pictures from the Signs on the Square protests, which can be found at *https://www.grahamhstokesphoto .com/covid-images*.

Chapter 2

I'm extremely grateful to Brad and Marla Balfour for sharing their memories of their dad, Don Balfour, the first American to receive college aid under the G.I. Bill. His alma mater, George Washington University, has several articles and archival material about Balfour that can be found at *https://searcharchives.library.gwu.edu/reposi tories/2/archival_objects/144839*. Thanks also to Nicholas Strohl for sharing his doctoral dissertation, *The Truman Commission and the Unfulfilled Promise of American Higher Education*. Two books were extremely valuable for this chapter. *Over Here: How the G.I. Bill Transformed the American Dream*, a 2006 tome by Edward Humes, served as a primary source for both the backstory on how this unlikely bill became a law and also captures the zeitgeist of how free education inspired "the Greatest Generation" to give something back to their communities. Another critical source for this chapter—as well as some of the more recent developments on college campuses described in Chapter 5—is *American Higher Education Since World War II: A History*, by Roger L. Geiger, a sweeping overview that describes some of the critical trends, such as the push for liberal education in the 1940s and '50s. Passages on Clark Kerr and the California model for higher education were informed by Simon Marginson's *The Dream Is Over: The Crisis of Clark Kerr's California Idea of Higher Education.*

Chapter 3

In our extremely helpful interview, Mario Savio's widow Lynne Hollander Savio steered me to the best book on her late husband, *Freedom's Orator: Mario Savio and the Radical Legacy of the 1960s,* by Robert Cohen. Jabreel Khazan's comments on the 1960 lunch counter sit-in are from a 2020 oral history in the Greensboro News & Record. I was grateful during 2020 to interview two of the nine students who were wounded in the 1970 Kent State shooting, Thomas Grace and Alan Canfora, who would pass away in 2021. The 1980 book *Fire in the Streets: America in the 1960s,* by Edward Viorst, provides an overview of some of the critical events from a decade of campus unrest not long after they happened. A critical resource on the largely forgotten role that low-tuition public universities played in the rise of youthful dissent is *Campus Wars: The Peace Movement At American State Universities in the Vietnam Era,* by Kenneth J. Heineman. *Democracy in Chains: The Deep History of the Radical Right's Stealth Plan for America,* by (my Brown '81 classmate) Nancy MacLean, reveals the importance of Nobel-winning economist James Buchanan as a critic of low—or free college tuition.

Chapter 4

Rush Limbaugh's formative years are described in the essay *The Political Socialization of an American Icon:* Rush Limbaugh III by M. Catherine Bergerson and Peter J. Bergerson for the Southeastern Missouri State University Press (at his almost alma mater). A series of books chronicle the breakdown of America's civic and industrial hierarchies following the 1960s—most notably Bill Bishop's 2008 tome, *The Big Sort: Why the Clustering of Like-Minded America Is Tearing Us Apart*; 2000's *Bowling Alone: The Collapse and Revival of American Community* by the Harvard sociologist Robert D. Putnam; Richard Florida's *The Rise of the Creative Class*, from 2002, and the very much of-the-moment (1992) *America: What Went Wrong* by the then–*Philadelphia Inquirer*'s Donald L. Barlett and James B. Steele. One of the best explainers of how this growing cultural divide played out in rural America is 2017's *White Working Class: Overcoming Class Cluelessness in America*, by Joan C. Williams, which explains in clear layman's language why voters in small-town America have steered their anger toward the professional and managerial classes. In addition to the flood of news coverage about "political correctness" at the dawn of the 1990s, the best real-time critique of identity politics on campus—from a progressive perspective— is 1995's *The Twilight of Common Dreams: Why America Is Wracked by Culture Wars* by Todd Gitlin, the academic and historian who was also the mid-1960s president of Students for a Democratic Society.

Chapter 5

In exploring the train wreck of American higher education in the twenty-first century, I was able to draw on some remarkable investigative reporting by the Pulitzer winner Daniel Golden, who broke the story of Jared Kushner and his unorthodox admission into Harvard in his 2005 book, *The Price of Admission: How America's Ruling Class Buys Its Way into Elite Colleges,* as well as Ron Lieber, who told how High Point University takes campus luxury to the ultimate extreme in his 2021 tome, *The Price You Pay for College.* (Apparently it's hard to write about college in the new millennium without mentioning "price.") The previously cited historical overview by Roger L. Geiger was particularly useful to understanding why college tuition began to skyrocket at the end of the 1970s and the "selectivity sweepstakes" that began to obsess college administrators. Ozan Jaquette's 2017 paper, "State University No More: Out-of-State Enrollment and the Growing Exclusion of High-Achieving, Low-Income Students at Public Flagship Universities," is a particularly valuable resource for tracking how these institutions have come to rely upon wealthier out-of-state kids to survive, a phenomenon that's just starting to get wider attention. Likewise, *Paying for the Party: How College Maintains Inequality* by the Michigan professors Elizabeth A. Armstrong and Laura T. Hamilton is especially helpful in using sociological methods to better track a phenomenon we all know, the impact of party culture at modern colleges. Scott Galloway, the NYU business professor, was interviewed by Michael Smerconish about the low acceptance rates at elite universities for the Sirius/XM POTUS Channel in 2021 (https://www.youtube.com /watch?v=sxm0m0fbMGM).

Chapter 6

Other than the introduction, the chapter "The Quad" is the most self-explanatory: I found four people who really told the story of their generation and their cohort in American society, and I sat down and listened to them. I'm blessed to live and work in one of the most politically, racially and economically diverse regions in the country, so it made perfect sense to find my exemplars close to home in eastern Pennsylvania and from South Jersey. The one book that's critical to understanding the interview with Jacqui Redner and the section on the Left Out generation is obviously 2020's *Deaths of Despair and the Future of Capitalism* by the married Princeton academics Angus Deaton and Anne Case. They were the first to notice how rising rates of suicide, drug overdoses, and alcoholism among the working class was lowering U.S. life expectancy, to establish a link to college attendance, and give the problem a name.

Chapter 7

Each passing year seems to bring greater awareness that America's college debt load—$1.7 trillion and counting as I write this—isn't just some fluke of the financial markets but a national emergency. Thus, 2021 saw the publication of the Loyola University Chicago professor Elizabeth Tandy Shermer's investigation *Indentured Students: How Government-Guaranteed Loans Left Generations Drowning in College Debt* as well as *Wall Street Journal* reporter Josh Mitchell's *The Debt Trap: How Student Loans Became a National Catastrophe,* which revealed that even the former CEO of the government-backed lender Sallie Mae is flummoxed by high tuition. In our interview for the book, Astra Taylor of the Debt Collective turned me on to her short but insightful (and cleverly named) 2020 documentary, *You Are Not a Loan,* with moving testimonials from the debt-burdened. (You can watch at https://theintercept .com/2021/01/25/student-debt-you-are-not-a-loan-film/) I'm also grateful for the work of University of Maryland sociologist Dana Fisher, perhaps today's leading demographer of American protest movements, who shared her groundbreaking research on the makeup of 2020's George Floyd protests.

Chapter 8

It's impossible to write about the mindset that made Scott Walker a two-term governor—and gave the Badger State to Donald Trump in 2016—without consulting the University of Wisconsin's Katharine J. Kramer's *The Politics of Resentment: Rural Consciousness in Wisconsin and the Rise of Scott Walker.* It's also worth noting that *The Atlantic* consistently offers some of the best higher-education coverage outside of the specialty magazines; its May 2017 article by Emma Green headlined "It Was Cultural Anxiety That Drove White, Working-Class Voters to Trump" introduced the theory of "economic fatalism" among non-college voters as an explanation for the 45th president's victory the year before. Likewise, Nate Silver, polling guru and founder of the website FiveThirtyEight.com, deserves enormous credit for using data to show that educational attainment, and not economic success, is the dividing line in American politics. (https://fivethirtyeight.com/features/education-not-income-predicted-who-would-vote-for-trump/)

Chapter 9

Both the president of the Williamson College of the Trades, Michael J. Rounds, as well as Arlene Snyder, the school's vice president for institutional advancement, were incredibly gracious in hosting me there for the day in May 2021, even as they seemed amazed at the interest from the *Philadelphia Inquirer*'s most left-wing columnist. Two important pieces that really break down the issues in unprivatizing American higher education are the Medium essay by lawyer and writer Matt Bruenig (https://mattbruenig.medium.com/the-college-debate-is-as-incoherent-as-ever-d8a0db0e8bd8) that makes the case for universal "attachment benefits" that would aid U.S. eighteen-to-twenty-four-year-olds, regardless of whether they have the interest or aptitude for college, and the *New York Times* 2021 episode of the *Argument* podcast in which Astra Taylor of the Debt Collective makes her best case for complete loan forgiveness. (https://www.nytimes.com/2021/03/10/opinion/biden-student-loans-cancellation.html)

Chapter 10

Amanda Gamble, the city of Philadelphia's chief service officer, didn't make it into the text of the book, but she was extremely helpful in both giving me the lay of the land regarding youth service programs and in connecting me with several groups, including PowerCorpsPHL. The director of PowerCorps, Julia Hillengas, went out of her way to show me around an outdoor job site on maybe the hottest day of 2021. The best, most succinct case for universal national service was probably made by retired general Stanley McChrystal at the 2021 Aspen Ideas Festival, which you can watch on YouTube (https://www.youtube.com/watch?v=rYdNcsE4998).

INDEX

INDEX

INDEX

INDEX

INDEX

INDEX

midterm elections: 1982, 110; 1994, 113, 124; 2010, 224, 226; 2018, 164
military: draft, 273, 281–283, 287–292; gay people in, 103
military-industrial complex, 59, 68, 82, 210
millenials, 210, 255
Miller, Jeffrey, 92
Milwaukee, Wisconsin, 221–222
Mississippi Freedom Summer, 77–80, 107, 235
Mitchko, Dave, 175–182
Morgan, Ashlea, 239
mortgages, 196, 204
Moses, Bob, 78
Mount Vernon, Ohio, 12–15, 21, 23–28, 31–36, 39
Mount Vernon Nazarene College, 24
Mount Vernon News, 28
Musk, Elon, 271
Mussolini, Benito, 73

NAACP (National Association for the Advancement of Colored People), 78, 200
NAFTA (North American Free Trade Agreement), 180
napalm, 82
NASA (National Aeronautics and Space Administration), 60, 150
Nash, Diane, 71
Nashville, Tennessee, 71
Nashville Student Movement, 71
Nation, The magazine, 147, 227
National Bureau for Economic Research, 151
National Center for Education Statistics, 88
National Commission on Military, National, and Public Service, 288
National Defense Education Act of 1958, 59–61
National Guard, 91, 92
National Institutes of Health (NIH), 56, 60
National Intelligence Council, 240
National League of Cities, 279
National Public Radio (NPR), 120
National Science Foundation, 55, 56
Nelson, Libby, 142
New Beginnings Ministries Church, Warsaw, Ohio, 25
New Deal, 8, 9, 45, 46, 65, 77, 89, 124, 232, 235, 283, 285
New Frontier, 66, 283
New Left, 74, 76, 95, 108, 111, 122, 124, 195, 288
New New Left, 159, 195, 211, 265, 269
New York Times, 7, 12, 103, 104, 106, 120, 144, 147, 171, 176, 178, 212, 239, 243, 258, 262, 270
Newfield, Christopher, 124–125
Newman, Paul, 30, 41
Nichol, Gene, 228

1984 (Orwell), 231
Nixon, Richard M., 50, 89, 90, 92, 93, 95, 97, 119, 232, 236, 238
Nixonland (Perlstein), 92
"No College Kid Needs a Water Park to Study" (Koch), 144
Nobel Prizes, 50, 93
North Carolina A&T, 70, 202
Northwestern University, 93

Obama, Barack, 24, 177, 180, 193, 228, 239, 240, 281; economy and, 194, 204; education of, 140; health care and, 168; higher education and, 139–140, 268–268; 2012 election and, 207, 234; white voter backlash and, 224
Ocasio-Cortez, Alexandria, 164
Occidental College, California, 140
Occupy Philly, 205
Occupy Wall Street movement, 7, 44, 174, 191–194, 202–207, 211, 213
Office of Naval Research, 56
Ohio State University, 15, 149
Olyphant, Pennsylvania, 175–177, 179–181
Orwell, George, 231
Other People's Money (movie), 117
Outer Coast College, Alaska, 261, 262
outsourcing, 115–116, 223
Over Here (Humes), 46
Ozark Mountains, 2, 105

Paglia, Camille, 121
Palme, Olof, 18, 29, 40, 41
Pantsuit Nation, 167
Parent PLUS loans, 171, 173
Paris Climate Accords, 238–239
participatory democracy, 76
Paying for the Party: How College Maintains Inequality (Armstrong and Hamilton), 149–151
Peace Corps, 285–287, 290
Peace Democrats, 29
Pell Grants, 13, 99, 100, 139, 170, 197, 223, 251, 266
Pelosi, Nancy, 178
Penn State University, 173
Pennsbury, Pennsylvania, 182, 186
Pennsylvania State System of Higher Education, 135–136
Pentagon, 60, 62, 82, 88, 211, 292–293
"People Are Heard, or At Least Those Who Call Talk Radio, The" (Kolbert), 103, 104
People for Bernie Sanders, 207
Peoria, Illinois, 1–3
Perlstein, Rick, 92, 97

INDEX

INDEX

INDEX